Alternative Cornwalls

Alternative Cornwalls

Literature and the Invention of Place

GEMMA GOODMAN

UNIVERSITY
of
EXETER
PRESS

First published in 2024 by
University of Exeter Press
Reed Hall, Streatham Drive
Exeter EX4 4QR
UK

www.exeterpress.co.uk

Copyright © 2024 Gemma Goodman

The right of Gemma Goodman to be identified as author of this work has been asserted by her in accordance with the Copyright, Designs and Patents Act 1988.

https://doi.org/10.47788/HATK8600

British Library Cataloguing in Publication Data
A catalogue record for this book is available from the British Library.

ISBN 978-1-80413-063-6 Hardback
ISBN 978-1-80413-064-3 ePub
ISBN 978-1-80413-065-0 PDF

Cover image: Kurt Jackson, *Washing in the Sunshine*. Littlejohns China Clay Works, Cornwall 2018, mixed media on paper 57 × 61 cm.

Every effort has been made to trace copyright holders and obtain permission to reproduce the material included in this book. Please get in touch with any enquiries or information relating to an image or the rights holder.

Typeset in Goudy Oldstyle Std by S4Carlisle Publishing Services, Chennai, India

To Mum

'This is my Cornwall and this is my home'

Contents

List of Illustrations	viii
Acknowledgements	ix
Introduction: Cornwalls	1
1 Mining Class and Gender	21
2 Beyond England	49
3 On the Edge	95
4 Urban Cornwall	132
5 Moor and Clay	162
Conclusion: Looking and Seeing	184
Notes	189
Bibliography	211
Index	227

Illustrations

Figure 1 Mevagissey poster from Sally Mitchell's *Overrated Cornwall* collection (by kind permission of the artist)

Figure 2 Balmaidens appear behind The Volunteer in Mark Jenkin's *Enys Men* (ENYS MEN—Courtesy of Bosena © Steve Tanner 2021)

Figure 3 Jesse Leroy Smith's *Bal Maiden* (by kind permission of the artist)

Figure 4 'The Wessex of the Novels' map first included with the Osgood, McIlvaine collected edition of Hardy's work (1895)

Figure 5 Engraving of Boscawen Street (c.1830) (Courtesy of Kresen Kernow)

Figure 6 An unidentified nun walks down Lower Lemon Street towards Boscawen Street (c.1911) (Courtesy of Royal Cornwall Museum)

Acknowledgements

This book has been a long time in the making, and so there are many people who deserve thanks for the support and sage advice that has enabled me to finally reach this point; apologies if I have forgotten anyone. If we're going all the way back, then thanks should first go to my English teacher at Brannel School, Rob Lane, who, through his brilliant teaching, inspired my love of the subject. Now at last a book, this all started more years ago than I like to admit when I ventured onto a Master's and then part-time PhD at the University of Warwick. The concept for this book started life as my PhD thesis, some of which has been reworked for publication here. The majority of *Alternative Cornwalls* is new writing which builds upon the ideas central to my thesis. Thanks, therefore, to my PhD supervisors, Gill Frith and Graeme Macdonald, for their ideas and fresh perspectives. I never left a supervisor meeting without feeling motivated. Thanks also to Emma Francis, who has been an academic mentor to me since I started out as an undergraduate at Warwick, and who for many years has also been a good friend. I am also very grateful to all my past colleagues in the Residential Life Team at Warwick, and in Warwick Accommodation; without those roles and their support I would not have been able to take on a PhD. Particular thanks to Emma Salmon, who was both a lovely boss and remains the most supportive of friends.

Philip Payton has been continually supportive of my work since the early days, and it is very much appreciated. The Arthur Quiller-Couch Memorial Fund provided much-needed funds to support my research on two occasions, once during the PhD and once whilst writing the book. Thank you for your support. Thanks also to Kim Cooper and Ben Stanley-Butcher at Kresen Kernow for showing me around some of the fantastic archive. It has given me plenty of ideas for future research projects once I have recovered from this one! I am also grateful to Paul Caruana who, though he did not know me, jumped into action to use his Facebook contacts to track down an image for me that I could not find. It turns out that it was available in a pretty obvious place! Thank you so much to Sally Mitchell, Denzil Monk, Steve Tanner, Jesse Leroy Smith, Kresen Kernow and the Royal Cornwall Museum, for giving permission for me to include your images in the book. Grateful thanks also to Kurt and Caroline Jackson for giving permission to use 'Washing in the Sunshine' on the front cover, and for being so generous as to donate the fee to St Austell Foodbank.

There are so many family members and friends who have had to witness me on this writing journey, over so many years. Thanks for putting up with my stresses about it and for politely not always asking 'haven't you finished it yet?'! It took a long time for me to work out how to use my thesis as a basis for the book and, in the end, it contains a lot of new writing. I wouldn't have been able to do that without my mum and dad allowing me to move back home (for much longer than anticipated!) to get the process started. They never questioned me invading their retirement and I will be forever grateful for that love and support.

The last four years has been a very difficult time. It is also when I wrote most of the book, and this would not have been possible had it not been for the unwavering support of many people. Firstly, thanks to Anna Henderson and David Hawkins, Editors at University of Exeter Press, for always being supportive, and understanding of the need for me to work at a slightly different pace and take breaks when real life came crashing in. To my fellow 'chronic sisters', I would not have got here without your understanding, friendship and advice—thank you. Last, but certainly not least: David Coates, thank you for the academic chats and for being master organizer of the much-needed social interludes. Rachel Moseley, thank you for being my academic collaborator and friend, for always being encouraging, and for always giving bang-on advice. Emma Bird and Sarah Penny, thank you for the academic support but, much more than that, for getting me through.

G.G., 2024

Introduction

Cornwalls

> *There are the cliffs, the familiar places*
> *Recognisable, recognised only by me*
> *As the ship goes by and passengers crane to see*
> *Land. 'What land is it?'—a foreigner turns to me*
> *To ask. 'What land, indeed?'*
> *Shall I deny him, as I was denied?*
> *Pride refuses to utter the word:*
> *'This is the coast of Cornwall.'*
> A.L. Rowse, 'Passing by the Coast of Cornwall' (1967)[1]

Alternative Cornwalls is concerned with the ways in which Cornwall is imagined in literature, and so the question posited in Rowse's poem—'What land is it?'—is a suitable point of departure. In this poem, the contingent factors that necessarily influence how place is seen and understood are immediately evident. The foreign traveller, looking upon the Cornish coast from the deck of a passing ship, has no frame of reference for the scene before him; the viewed landscape is empty of meaning. Beside him, however, the poem's narrator figures as the possessor of knowledge and meaning—the land is 'recognisable' to him. Yet he chooses to retain rather than impart his knowledge, leaving the foreigner isolated in his ignorance, the narrator in his world of meaning. The narrator's reaction indicates his complex relationship with the place in view before him; in what way has he been denied? His current position, passing by Cornwall on board a ship, suggests an enforced exclusion—this is no homecoming. He no longer, after all, inhabits 'the familiar places', but instead looks on momentarily, en route to other locales. His role as the knowledgeable insider is therefore destabilized, diminished even, by what he calls in the poem's opening line his 'long exile', perhaps explaining his refusal to share his knowledge. Foreigner and indigene, despite their disparate systems of meaning, in that moment occupy the same physical position, looking upon the Cornish landscape from outside. While the wording of the poem's opening—'[a]fter long exile'—suggests an end to that exile, it is only illusory; the scene of Cornwall retreats as 'the great ship leans to the land, then turns away', and the narrator 'leans with the ship, then turns away'.[2] His exile remains.

Through Rowse's poem we can begin to think about themes which are crucial to this book. He draws our attention to, as well as complicates, the position of the writer—insider and visitor—and so the perspective this affords or denies them of place. The understanding and exploration of multiple Cornwalls—some dominant, some alternative, hidden, or misunderstood—is central to the project of this book. As a Cornishman in the context of academia at Oxford, Rowse would possibly have been aware of the homogenous, stereotypical way in which Cornwall is often viewed from outside. 'Passing by the Coast of Cornwall' demonstrates his awareness of, and use of, some of the common ways in which Cornwall appears in literary form. Yet his experience of Cornwall begins with, comes from within: a Cornish world that is less well known, particularly outside Cornwall, and more rarely reconstructed in literary form—that of the china clay mining region of mid-Cornwall.

The genesis of this book is my experience of growing up in the china clay area in mid-Cornwall, and then living outside Cornwall for eighteen years, which exposed a contrast between my lived experience of place, and the romanticized versions of that same place from people who pilgrimage there on holiday. It was a jarring juxtaposition which sent me in search of literary versions of place at variance with those which dominate the collective cultural consciousness when it comes to Cornwall. This book, therefore, sets out to identify and explore alternative literary Cornwalls, created by both Cornish and visiting writers from the nineteenth century to the present day, and to understand the relationship of these versions of place to dominant Cornwalls existing during the same time period.

To paraphrase Elaine Showalter, this work is an attempt to fill in the terrain between the cultural landmarks that dominate the ways in which Cornwall is imagined and understood, thus producing a more detailed map or cultural geography of place.[3] What happens when submerged versions of Cornwall are brought to the surface? In what ways do multiple versions of place relate to each other? Such a study requires digging down to identify and explore versions of Cornwall that have been lost, hidden, subsumed, or kept in shadow by the dominant landmarks. Alternative Cornwalls can be classified as such because they are less well known or have completely disappeared from cultural consciousness. They are often the other side of the coin from that which is renowned, prominent, and taken for granted, and can be a complete departure from, or antagonistic to, the dominant narrative. Alternative Cornwalls are, by their very nature, not easily identifiable because they are either counter to, or suppressed by, the power structures in place. In this book, unfamiliar versions of place are identified by producing new readings of familiar texts (and their social, historical, and cultural contexts) and by introducing little-known, forgotten, or rarely studied texts back into the context in which the dominant versions of Cornwall exist.

The act of digging is a fitting metaphor, given the importance of mining to the historical and cultural context of this book. Mining and tourism are the two key paradigms which impact upon the period of study. All of the Cornwalls identified are influenced by the economic shift from mining to tourism which begins in the late nineteenth century. Mining's replacement by tourism as Cornwall's primary industry gives impetus to different ways of representing Cornwall in literature and other cultural mediums. Tourist-friendly Cornwalls—Celtic, exotic, or Arthurian Cornwalls, for example—become the dominant ways in which Cornwall is portrayed. These different versions of place are not necessarily new, and are not necessarily, therefore, created by the tourist industry. Tourism does, though, draw on existing cultural or historical elements, and dictate which versions of place are emphasized. Economic necessity requires that these Cornwalls are popular, and that they persist to radiate an enticing version of Cornwall to potential visitors. As will become clear in later chapters, however, there is by no means a straightforward narrative of change from mining to tourism. For Cornwall the nineteenth century was a time of acute upheaval, a period of historical and cultural turmoil, the impact of which reverberates into the twentieth century and beyond. It is within this context that the texts under study here are 'enmeshed', being influenced by and contributing to the cultural map through their version of Cornwall.[4]

This book looks at novels set in Cornwall written by both Cornish and non-Cornish writers. It looks to contribute to an existing body of work on the literature of Cornwall written in English. Alan M. Kent has classified three areas of study within Cornish literary studies: Cornish Literature (texts in the Cornish language), Anglo-Cornish Literature (texts written in English about Cornwall by Cornish and visiting writers), and Cornu-English Literature (texts in Cornish dialect).[5] Denys Val Baker's two volumes *The Timeless Land: The Creative Spirit in Cornwall* (1973) and *A View from Land's End: Writers Against a Cornish Background* (1982) provide the most comprehensive overview of writers of Cornwall at that time. Within Val Baker's texts, both visiting and indigenous writers are considered side by side, including Thomas Hardy, Jack Clemo, Charles Causley, and D.H. Lawrence. Academic work in the 1990s includes John Hurst's 'Literature in Cornwall' which looks at a small range of authors connected to Cornwall, such as Jack Clemo and Daphne du Maurier. Kent's *Wives, Mothers and Sisters: Feminism, Literature and Women Writers*, from 2000, provides a snapshot of how much unstudied literature by women and set in Cornwall is waiting to be unearthed. It is hoped that this book will contribute to that discussion through the exploration of the work of Salome Hocking in Chapter One. The 1997 collection edited by Ella Westland entitled *Cornwall: A Cultural Construction of Place* is an important precursor for the study of literary Cornish place in this book. The publication of Kent's *The Literature of Cornwall* in 2000, covering the extensive time period of 1000–2000, is the first attempt to gain an overall picture and produce a detailed literary history of the literature of Cornwall. The text provides that overview with particular focus on continuity, identity, and difference. Since its publication there have been a number of works which focus on particular authors, genres, or topics, including: Payton's *A.L. Rowse: A Paradoxical Patriot* (2005) and *John Betjeman and Cornwall* (2010), Shelley Trower's *Rocks of Nation: The Imagination of Celtic Cornwall* (2015), and Joan Passey's *Cornish Gothic, 1830–1913* (2023).

In 1993 Philip Payton identified Cornish difference as 'at root the *raison d'être* of Cornish Studies'.[6] Colin H. Williams, in reference to the field of Cornish Studies, states that, 'the big issue it must face is the relationship between Cornwall and the rest of the United Kingdom'.[7] To evolve this relationship requires academics within the field to voice counter-narratives of Cornwall, and to voice them within wider contexts—contexts where the stereotypical or over-simplistic representations of Cornwall are current. It is hoped that this book will form part of that ongoing conversation.

Multiple Cornwalls

This book is situated within a theoretical framework that begins with Bernard Deacon's notion of multiple Cornwalls and seeks to implement and develop aspects of this concept in relation to the literary construction of place. In his assessment of Cornish Studies in 2000, Deacon identifies a gap in the field's academic scope, stating that 'Cornish Studies as a discipline has produced relatively few studies of differences, for example of identity or class or gender, *within* Cornwall'. He calls for practitioners within the field to take 'greater account of the internal diversity of the geography of Cornishness', and argues that 'in order to explain aspects of historical and contemporary Cornwall, we have to be aware of processes simultaneously operating at a number of different scales'.[8]

Developing such a perspective is contextualized by the political shift towards devolution which has led to the creation of a separate parliament in Scotland and assemblies in Wales and Northern Ireland. In early 2023, a devolution agreement for Cornwall was rejected, but the deal was not offering an assembly as with other Celtic territories of the United Kingdom. However, within a positive devolutionary political climate, greater acceptance of heterogeneous nationalities and identities existing within, contributing to (and antagonistic to) Britishness is perhaps possible.

Therefore, within this context, how do we go about revealing and defining multiple Cornwalls? In his advocacy of critical discourse analysis, Deacon defines a discourse as 'a way of understanding and talking about the world that can be distinguished from other ways of understanding the world'. This definition has influenced the way in which the various novelistic worlds under discussion in this book have been understood to exist, so that they can be thought of as different worlds, as well as different ways of understanding the world. Deacon goes on to explain that

> [d]iscourses also clearly do more than just reflect the world: they actively constitute the world they describe. There is only one Cornwall, in the sense of its tangible and physical settlements, fields, roads, moors, cliffs and the like. Yet there are several, sometimes complementary and overlapping, discourses of Cornwall.

The notion that discourses of Cornwall 'actively constitute the world' is a significant point of consideration with regards to literary constructions of place. Not only does the act of reading create a world in the imagination, but with literatures of place, the imaginary world relates to an actual place (even if locations within that place are made up). Literary versions of place influence how actual places are experienced, and popular (widely read) narratives impact on how place is publicly understood. While we can think of the various Cornwalls as different worlds, though, they do not exist in isolation. Deacon's notion of 'complementary and overlapping discourses' provides a jumping-off point in this book for understanding the relationship between multiple versions of place.[9]

Don Mitchell suggests that '"culture" is never any *thing*, but is rather a struggled-over set of social relations, relations shot through with structures of power, structures of dominance and subordination'.[10] This is a particularly useful way to approach Cornish culture, a starting point for understanding the unequal power dynamic within which cultural versions of Cornwall exist. It also explains why it is important to be aware of the power structures within which cultural production is 'enmeshed'—it goes to the very core of what culture is and how culture is created. Mitchell's comments also remind us that there is a relationship, subject to change and dependent upon structures of power, between cultural versions of place.[11] While Deacon describes this relationship as 'complementary and overlapping', a useful starting point for understanding how cultural Cornwalls relate to each other, Mitchell's contention is that this relationship is 'struggled-over', suggesting a less harmonious interaction, which is fitting when talking of 'structures of dominance and subordination'.[12] Culture, then, according to Mitchell, is contested, and not simply in the abstract, but in and 'over real spaces, over landscapes, over the social relations that define the places in which we and others live'.[13]

With this in mind, this book will approach the relationship between multiple versions of place from a fresh angle by applying more emphasis to the power structures behind discourses: the power dynamics which determine which discourses dominate and which discourses are suppressed. The concern is not to identify the real, authentic, or truthful discourse, but rather which discourses are interpreted as such or are given primacy within a social and cultural context. Who gets to speak and who is heard? If we recognize a power dynamic which enables or prevents the dominance of discourses, all discourses are historically contingent and so subject to change over time. Different discourses resonate within different historical or cultural moments. Discourses are therefore never equal. They are also never static; we, through language, are able to 're-negotiate existing meanings and to attach new ones'. Discourses are therefore always in flux and open to change by those that use them, yet, crucially, access to discourses also occurs within a social power dynamic and so 'our ability as agents to change the meanings of discourses, particularly "strong" discourses, is clearly limited by a variety of social positioning'.[14] Within this framework it is possible to analyse alternative or suppressed discourses, and to understand how they relate to the dominant discourse (or discourses) as well as why they are alternative, or have been lost or forgotten. In short, we can enable discussion of alternative versions of place within a cultural context in which dominant discourses exist.

Of course, Cornwall is not the only British territory to be characterized by dominant narratives of place; such power structures exist elsewhere within the British Isles and Cornwall has most in common with other peripheral Celtic territories. For instance, like Cornwall, Scotland has also been characterized as a romantic, Celtic 'other'. The popularity of writers such as Sir Walter Scott has enabled a romanticized version of Scotland to dominate. Similarly, it is instructive that Virginia Woolf, alive to the dominance of particular narratives in Cornwall, was able to shift the setting of *To the Lighthouse* from St Ives (the scene of her childhood holidays) to the Scottish Isle of Skye. While Michael Bender argues that this was partly because St Ives 'would have been all too stifling and close-to-home', Skye also, crucially, 'mirrored aspects of the original situation in St Ives'. Skye provided Woolf with 'another colonized "Celtic periphery" inhabited by people who were also clearly "other"'.[15] While Woolf ultimately exchanged one Celtic territory for another in *To the Lighthouse*, from an English perspective, Cornwall is often the comfortable Celtic 'other' when compared with Wales, Scotland, and Ireland. It is, therefore, an intriguing case study with regards to the cultural construction of place. As will be discussed in more detail in later chapters, Cornwall occupies a paradoxical relationship with England which the other Celtic territories, as separate countries, do not.

Space and Place

Yi-Fu Tuan defines space as 'a blank sheet on which meaning may be imposed'. Place can therefore be understood as '[e]nclosed and humanized space'.[16] Whilst recognizing that there are multiple, competing ways in which to understand the relationship between space and place, in this context, Tuan's definition is a useful starting point. If we position Cornwall as bounded, by sea on three 'sides' and by its border with England on another (the construction of which will be interrogated in the chapters below), we can also look to identify multiple spaces operating within it. Therefore, these spaces can be understood as socially constructed, and as 'politicized, culturally relative, historically specific, local and multiple constructions' which can be read in the same way as we would read a text, and which we can also use to read how texts imagine space to invest it with meaning.[17]

The theorizing of place as socially constructed is, therefore, important to how the different Cornwalls identified and discussed in this book are understood, and I draw on a range of work here in order to think through the concept. Andrew Thacker's view of space is slightly different to that of Tuan's, but both are interested in how meaning is produced. Referring to the work of geographer Neil Smith, instead of beginning with a blank sheet, he instead positions space 'not [as] a neutral canvas but as "social space", produced according to social aims and objectives, and which then, in turn, shapes social life'.[18] In previous work, I have also drawn upon studies from within the field of feminist geographies, and I do so again here because that field too has ways to understand place as socially constructed, and to theorize how place and identity is created in and through bodies within those spaces.[19] Doreen Massey argues that 'what is at issue is not social phenomena in space but both social phenomena and space as constituted out of social relations, that the spatial is social relations "stretched out"'.[20] We can think about how place is created, or imagined, in and through social relations, as well as how this shapes identities. Linda McDowell states that 'bodies in space raise all sorts of questions about the space and place they occupy', but also that 'space is not inert, not merely a container for social action, but is a significant element in the constitution of identity'.[21] There is a mutually constitutive relationship here, requiring us to pay attention simultaneously to people and place, and people placed.

This way of understanding space and place needs to be extended into rural contexts, which are often overlooked in favour of studies of urban life. Specifically, it is necessary to do so with regards to Cornwall in order to identify multiple imaginations of Cornish place. Taking our cue from geographers such as McDowell, and seeing place as 'contested, fluid, and uncertain', opens up fresh ways to access alternative versions of rural, peripheral locations, which are so often fixed in the cultural imagination as unchanging and timeless.[22] With regards to Cornwall, as Rachel Moseley and others have pointed out, its status in relation to England is 'contested' and we can therefore think about how readings of literary texts open up an understanding of, and create imaginations of, place through this uncertainty.[23] McDowell goes on to argue that '[p]laces are made through power relations which construct the rules which define boundaries'.[24] It is these power relations which inform which versions of place remain on the surface and which are buried. It is necessary to understand this, and how place is created, in order to go about digging up alternative and multiple versions of Cornish place.

Cornwall's Cultural Geography: Mining and Tourism

> *Hast ever seen a mine? Hast ever been*
> *Down in its fabled grottoes, wall'd with gems,*
> *And canopied with torrid mineral-belts,*
> *That blaze within their fiery orifice?*
> *Hast ever, by the glimmer of the lamp,*
> *Or the fast-waning taper, gone down, down,*
> *Towards the earth's dread centre.*
>
> John Harris, 'Christian Heroism' (1853)[25]

As mentioned above, mining and tourism are the two main cultural contexts for this book. They influence how Cornwall is seen and understood, by insiders and outsiders, and the versions of place which are created. This section provides a brief overview as a cultural geography for the chapters which follow.

The narrator of John Harris's poem 'Christian Heroism' invites the reader to descend with him 'into the earth's black breast'.[26] It is likened in the language used to a descent into hell, yet crucially, it is within the mine that Harris also finds the beauty which other poets find in nature. Cornish scholars have recognized John Harris as one of the most important writers of industrial Cornwall. For example, Alan M. Kent sees Harris as 'the Cornish poet who most typifies Cornish experience in the nineteenth century'.[27] Harris's lifetime (1820–1884) spans the highest and lowest points of Cornish mining, of which he had first-hand experience through working in the mines from the age of twelve. Harris is important because he is able to render his personal experience of the mine in poetic form. He is a rare example of a Cornish working-class miner who produced literature about his experience (of which we are aware, and to which we have access). His self-awareness of his industrial experience, and his ability to communicate this experience, provides us with access to the miner's world from his point of view, rather than, as is more often the case, from the perspective of a passing visitor.

Wilkie Collins was one such visitor, and *Rambles Beyond Railways* (1851) is his record of his journey around Cornwall in 1850. In this travelogue he anticipates the primacy of mining in the mind of his readers. He begins the chapter on Botallack mine with the following:

> I have little doubt that the less patient among the readers of this narrative have already, while perusing it, asked themselves such questions as these: 'Is not Cornwall a celebrated mineral country? Why has the author not taken us below the surface yet? Why have we heard nothing all this time about the mines?'[28]

Although his itinerary, and accordingly the chronology of his narrative, is determined by the geographical location of places of interest in Cornwall, he is still concerned about neglecting mining until part-way through his travelogue. As a visitor providing an overview of Cornwall primarily to a non-Cornish readership, Collins felt unable to produce a complete picture of Cornwall without reference to mining. The response he anticipates from his audience in the quotation above demonstrates the centrality of mining to outsider representations of Cornwall in the mid-nineteenth century, and Collins's description of Cornwall as a 'celebrated mineral county' confirms Cornwall's industrial success as a positive, shared narrative.

Nineteenth-century Cornwall, then, is an industrial world. Mining, fishing, and agriculture were all crucially important to Cornwall's economy. It is mining, however, which predominates, and which has the biggest cultural impact and influence on Cornish identity. Mining employed thirty per cent of the Cornish population in 1861, with the landscape in West and East Cornwall, and sections of mid-Cornwall, dominated by the visual apparatus of the industry.[29] This included engine houses: stone structures that housed pumping or winding engines, the remnants of which remain very much a part of the Cornish landscape today. In this book, the image of the engine house is a touchstone via which we can grasp the cultural and economic changes precipitated by the demise of mining, and its impacts. Payton argues that '[m]ining as a central plank of the Cornish identity was firmly established by the middle of the nineteenth century, asserted by the Cornish themselves and acknowledged by external observers'.[30] Mining enabled a confident identity based on 'industrial prowess', and industrial enterprise fostered the 'redefinition of Cornish society as modern and progressive'.[31]

While there are some points of connection between Cornwall's narrative of industrialism and the experience of other industrial areas in Britain—other areas also witnessed success, collapse, emigration, and the definition of their area by one particular industry—Cornwall's industrial story was always seen, by the Cornish at least, to be unique. As Payton explains, '[t]he Cornish economy was one of the very first in the world to industrialise, […] achieving for Cornwall an envied place at the forefront of technological innovation'.[32] It was also one of the first areas to experience deindustrialization and so all of the above, coupled with Cornwall's geographical distance from other industrial centres such as the North, accentuated its sense of isolation and distance from external industrial contexts.

Payton argues that 'it is now recognised that the process of industrialisation promoted regional differentiation rather than homogeneity'.[33] Deacon takes a slightly different line and argues that there was a 'tension' between the differences created by Cornwall's 'specialisation in mining', and the 'spirit of industry [which] was erasing differences'. He argues that the result was 'the appropriation of new symbols of "peculiarity", new banners around which the "imagined Cornish community" could be proclaimed as somehow different from others'. He explains that these differences were both real and invented. Ultimately these symbols made the Cornish inhabitants feel that their situation was unique. Emphasizing aspects of difference, such as the Cornish language or Cornwall's metal mining traditions, became important and formed a 'discourse of differentiation' by the 1820s that helped the Cornish to define their own industrial identity.[34]

Deacon argues that Cornwall's industrial identity had by 1820 'supplanted' a definition of Cornwall as 'West Barbary', which had been prevalent since the eighteenth century. The 'West Barbary' label existed because of reports of wrecking, smuggling, and rioting which reached the rest of England. It encapsulated Cornwall as 'a lurid and dramatic place populated by food rioters […] and heavy drinking roisterers who lived most of their lives underground', and Cornish people as 'a barbarian tribe'. This was an 'othering' of 'the primitive periphery by the civilised centre' and Deacon makes it clear that 'it was always restricted to a voyeuristic metropolitan market' and was never internalized by the Cornish themselves.[35] 'West Barbary' was, therefore, a captivating fiction for those outside Cornwall.

Crucially, by embracing an identity based on 'industrial prowess', in contradistinction to the 'West Barbary' moniker, the Cornish were able to take control of their own identity in the nineteenth century. Deacon argues that '[t]hey adopted it with some enthusiasm and in doing so also adopted, in retrospect, the image of West Barbary as a binary opposition. In the late eighteenth century the preferred myth became one of progress from darkness to light, from West Barbary to Industrial Civilisation.'[36] Such was the power of Cornwall's industrial identity that it emanated outwards until 'outsider and insider representations had effectively converged by the second quarter of the nineteenth century to be closer together than probably at any time since'.[37] 'West Barbary' had been trumped by a less derogatory and far more positive identity which originated with the Cornish themselves.[38]

In 2022, photographer Sally Mitchell branched out and started creating illustrations of Cornish places as artistic travel posters. The style is a contemporary take on the type of poster typical of the Great Western Railway's marketing campaigns in the early twentieth century (discussed further in Chapter Two). This type of modern poster, with a stripped-back colour palette and simplified outline of landscape features, is aesthetically pleasing, and immediately recalls the place for those who have been there. This style is currently very popular and versions are sold in local galleries and by tourist information centres in Cornwall. However, Mitchell's posters have a twist: they include phrases from one-star TripAdvisor reviews of the place that the poster depicts. Her collection, entitled *Overrated Cornwall* includes: Kynance Cove: 'Reminded us of the central line at rush hour', Padstow: 'Not as nice as we had hoped', Mevagissey: 'Smells awful and there is nothing to see or do', and Charlestown: 'This place is no longer Cornish'.[39] There have also been calls for Mitchell to create a poster for Perranporth using a review which complained about the sand being too wet.[40]

While these posters are a somewhat light-hearted response to such reviews, they also speak to a number of things about the Cornish experience of modern-day mass tourism. These posters have been popular with Cornish people, perhaps because laughing at such reviews is a way of taking back ownership of places that have become solely defined, from an outside

Figure 1: Mevagissey poster from Sally Mitchell's *Overrated Cornwall* collection (by kind permission of the artist)

perspective, as tourist destinations. One dimension of the TripAdvisor complaints is that Cornwall does not perform for the visitor in the way that they expect. For example, the inescapable realities of a working fishing port such as Mevagissey have interrupted their imagined version of that place. It is an outsider-derived version of Cornwall to which these places fail to live up. Equally, experiencing change clashes with a common outsider view of Cornish places, and rural places more generally, as fixed and unchanging. The posters themselves juxtapose the familiar aesthetics of Cornish coastal sites with comments which demonstrate that a preformed image of a bucolic Cornwall, and of an escape to the periphery, is destroyed by the sheer number of people who, ironically, are probably visiting for the exact same reason.

What these posters also signal is the dominance of a homogenous, outsider-derived version of Cornwall from within touristic-centred constructions of Cornish place, and, therefore, the difficulty of expressing and maintaining the presence of counter-narratives of place which do not fit the expectations of tourism. Mitchell's posters do not give us the counter-narratives as such but, in exposing the gap between outsider expectations of place, and their actual experiences of that place, the work also suggests the presence of local lived experiences of place, which are made manifest through finding humour in these reactions, and through buying and displaying the posters, even if those local versions of the same place are off the page.

What Nick Groom has to say, in his discussion of the relationship between urban and rural places within Britain, speaks to how Cornwall is expected to function as a tourist site. As I have written about previously with Charlotte Mathieson, Groom

> tracks the development of this hierarchical interaction [between urban and rural] as precipitating what he calls a 'contemporary pastoral' whereby the current extensive migration back into rural space from the cities is part of an aestheticization, politicization and appropriation of rural space by an urban elite acting out 'an urban fantasy of country life'. He argues that, as a consequence 'the English countryside now becomes the conservatory of the urban'.[41]

The TripAdvisor comments are produced by a clash between fantasy and reality, but also through an inability to see place other than how it has been initially imagined, and fixed. Ella Westland sums up the requirements of tourism when she says that '[t]he tourist industry depends on displacing Cornwall's past social history and present social condition in favour of a cluster of easily manipulated signs (Celts, cliffs, mines, wrecks) that stand for Cornwall'.[42] This book hopes to interrogate those signs, and go beyond them, to give space to alternative versions of Cornish place which challenge, or even destabilize, a touristic narrative of place.

The tourist industry in Cornwall had its roots in the early nineteenth century when the Napoleonic Wars made it necessary to holiday closer to home. Travellers had, though, been coming to Cornwall for centuries: travel diaries can be found from the sixteenth century onwards from the likes of John Leyland, Celia Fiennes, and Daniel Defoe. However, it is in the nineteenth century that Cornwall, like other areas in Britain, begins to be seen as a holiday destination for a wider section of the population, primarily for the middle and upper classes of society. Guidebooks on Cornwall, such as *Murray's Handbook*, are in common usage from the 1850s and go through a series of reprints as tourism develops and expands.

It is from the end of the nineteenth century that tourism shows signs of becoming Cornwall's future industry. In order to be economically viable, however, this emergent industry needed to reconstruct and repackage Cornwall for a tourist market. Cornwall's perceived difference from England, while still being part of England, was utilized in the recreation of Cornwall for consumption by outsiders. There is now an economic imperative to highlight Cornwall's difference, not in terms of 'West Barbary' or its industrial expertise, but as a Mediterranean-style holiday destination on the doorstep of England. Its warmer climate, which enables the growth of palm trees and other exotic plants that are not seen elsewhere in Britain, visually aided the reinvention of Cornwall as a foreign holiday destination on British soil. In order to entice visitors Cornwall was recast by emphasizing its exoticism, and through drawing upon romanticized versions of rural place where its beauty could be indicated. Great Western Railway's marketing campaign in the early twentieth century, including a poster which compares Cornwall with Italy, is often cited as the most visible example of this, and is discussed in more detail in Chapter Two.[43]

It should be noted that commentators outside Cornwall have often misrepresented the transition from mining to tourism, imposing a facile narrative which ignores the more complex power dynamic and interplay between insiders and outsiders underway as the dominant landmarks in Cornish culture are reconfigured. For instance, Payton has drawn attention to Maxine Berg's 'gross oversimplification' of this period in Cornwall's history in her book *The Age of Manufactures* which, despite being a lengthy study, mentions only that 'in the middle of the nineteenth century mining suddenly declined and the region was rapidly transformed into a holiday resort'.[44] While tourism was ultimately to become Cornwall's replacement industry, Berg's comments give the erroneous impression that this process is one coherent narrative, as well as falsely suggesting that the transition between mining and tourism was quick and straightforward. Her choice of words also suggests that Cornwall's transformation into a tourist resort was imposed solely from outside.

Similarly, that the collapse of mining in Cornwall created a 'semantic vacuum waiting to be filled by the representations of English intellectuals' has been described as 'flawed' by Deacon.[45] While the end of mining eventually produces a shift in the Cornwalls which dominate how Cornwall is represented and understood, it does not enable a void or absence of culture simply to be filled by new cultural constructions of place. Working-class, industrial culture does not disappear like the smoke from the mine stacks, but it does stagnate, becoming insular, acting as a raft to which the Cornish working class cling in the storm produced by mining's failure, comforted by the familiarity of established cultural identifiers, such as Methodism.[46] That this cultural identity loses its dynamism, its energy, and also its confidence to project an identity outward to those beyond Cornwall, as it had done previously, enables other cultural versions of Cornwall to dominate instead.

So, who are the progenitors of cultural change during this time? The emigration from Cornwall of some of its local population, due to economic blight, can be contrasted with the influx of outsiders as visitors, writers, and commentators. Incomers were particularly enamoured with the notion of Cornwall as a romantic territory: England's Celtic 'other' could be an inspiring landscape. The burgeoning art scene brought artists to certain locations to capture Cornwall on canvas. Similarly, Cornwall was being recreated on the page by well-known writers such as D.H. Lawrence, Thomas Hardy, and Virginia Woolf, who produced literary versions of Cornwall read (and still read) by a wide audience. As mentioned above, outside interests such as the Great Western Railway played an active role in the cultural shift underway by promoting tourist-friendly images of Cornwall as an exotic, Celtic 'other' that was at the same time familiar, and part of England.

However, it would be too simplistic to see the post-mining era as solely the purview of outsiders, imposing their version of place onto a region in economic and cultural turmoil. Deacon asserts that those who understand the cultural dynamic in this way do so because they 'find it difficult to escape a dominant English nationalist discourse of the "discovery" of the periphery'.[47] Instead, we can see outsiders' and insiders' input in the reconfiguration of Cornish culture at the end of the nineteenth century, as well as points of connection between both groups. It is the Cornish revivalists who from the early twentieth century are most self-consciously reconstructing Cornish culture from within in the aftermath of mining's collapse. They desired to direct Cornish culture back to a pre-industrial, Celtic, Catholic (pre-Reformation) era.[48] Their presence demonstrates that there were still those within Cornwall actively involved in its post-industrial cultural reconstruction, which is evident in the involvement of the Cornish revivalists with the Great Western Railway.

This brief overview hopefully provides a sense of the complex cultural geography of Cornish place within which literary versions of place from the nineteenth century to the present day are 'enmeshed'.[49] The chapters which follow are not intended as a survey of literature in English set in Cornwall; rather, they begin with either a place, group of people or alternative reading as a starting point for alternative Cornwalls which require discussion. Chapter One, 'Mining Class and Gender', focuses on class and gender in Cornish mining literature. What about women's experiences of Cornish mining? How and where are they represented? Such material is rare. One of the only literary texts known of is Salome Hocking's novella about a balmaiden, called *Norah Lang: The Mine Girl* (1886), which is read here in relation to mining novels which privilege a male perspective: R.M. Ballantyne's *Deep Down* (1868), *Tin* by Edward Bosanketh (1888), and *Wheal Darkness* by H.D. Lowry (1927) and C.A. Dawson Scott. This chapter provides a gendered reading of the historical, cultural, and immediate literary context, central to which is the collapse of the mining industry in the second half of the nineteenth century. Such a reading enables us to understand the absence of the balmaiden in Cornish mining novels, and concurrently the emphasis on masculine achievement in the same novels. A particular narrative of mining comes to dominate how Cornwall is viewed from outside the region during the nineteenth century and beyond. So, while this chapter explores female perspectives of mining, it also does not simply set up narratives of mining and masculinity as the dominant other. It is necessary here to consider gender and class in relation to each other so that, even while mining can be cast in terms of 'industrial prowess', and even while this chapter argues that this is a gendered construction of mining, the experiences of working-class Cornish miners can also be eliminated.[50]

Chapter Two, 'Beyond England', takes us into a space which challenges tourist-friendly versions of Cornwall that remain within safe boundaries. From an outside perspective, even a sense of wildness, used to excite and entice, must ultimately be governable. This is often achieved through a sense of English control of the exotic or Celtic elements of Cornwall's make-up, even while Cornwall's difference and un-Englishness is part of its attraction. In contrast, there also exist Cornwalls which can be read as positioning Cornwall geographically and culturally beyond England, and beyond Englishness. Such Cornwalls are unfettered from or defiant of control, or they destabilize the concept of control or containment. Therefore, in such versions of place, there is a far greater sense of danger, hostility, and instability. In this context, crime fiction can be read as registering ungovernability, and so providing versions of place which challenge the more familiar positioning of Cornwall as a safe harbour in the escapist fantasies of romantic fiction. The crime, mystery and espionage fiction considered in this chapter includes: Emma Stonex's *The Lamplighters* (2021), Wilkie Collins's *The Dead Secret* (1856), John le Carré's *The Night Manager* (1993), Agatha Christie's *Peril at End House* (1932), Nicola Upson's *Angel with Two Faces* (2009), Arthur Conan Doyle's 'The Adventure of the Devil's Foot' (1910), and Katherine Stansfield's Cornish Mysteries trilogy, *Falling Creatures* (2017), *The Magpie Tree* (2018) and *The Mermaid's Call* (2019). It culminates with an examination of the portrayal of barbarity in Noel O'Reilly's *Wrecker* (2019) and anarchy in Daphne du Maurier's *Rule Britannia* (1972).

The Cornish coast dominates visual and literary representations of Cornwall. Chapter Three, 'On the Edge', investigates alternative ways in which the edge can be read that go beyond the aesthetic. The edge of the land is a geographical boundary, but it can alternatively be read as a point of connection to other land masses beyond, which contradicts the more common positioning of Cornwall as rural, peripheral and remote. This chapter is also interested in the notion of being both physically and psychologically on the edge, and how this connects to the physical geography of Cornwall. In some narratives, Cornwall becomes a space where people in emotional turmoil end up because it is as far as it is possible to travel, in one direction at least, on mainland Britain. The idea of Cornwall as a place to which to escape, which tourist marketing makes so much of, can therefore have a darker meaning. Often, in narratives where the physical edge of the land corresponds with being emotionally on the edge, or driven to the edge by illness, Cornwall is the space within which a psychological journey must be enacted. The texts discussed here are: Thomas Hardy's *A Pair of Blue Eyes* (1872–73), Virginia Woolf's *To the Lighthouse* (1927), Raynor Winn's *The Salt Path* (2018), Helen Dunmore's novels *Talking to the Dead* (1996), *Mourning Ruby* (2003) and *The Lie* (2014), Wyl Menmuir's *The Many* (2016), Charlie Carroll's *The Lip* (2021), and Katherine Stansfield's *The Visitor* (2013).

Chapter Four, 'Urban Cornwall', spends time experiencing literary versions of Truro. Truro often sits outside a touristic promotion of place, and is seen as somewhere simply to pass through, because it is urban (of a sort), inland, and its aesthetic is not relevant to a 'sun, sea, sand' promotion of Cornwall. Literary representations of this inland port are examined in Winston Graham's twelve-book *Poldark* series (1945–2002), Alan M. Kent's *Dan Daddow's Cornish Comicalities* (2016), and Jack Clemo's *Wilding Graft* (1948). Set in the late eighteenth, nineteenth, and mid-twentieth centuries, these texts all de-aestheticize Truro. In both *Poldark* and *Dan Daddow* the built environment of Truro enables the performance of wealth and power, but it is also a stage for subversive displays which challenge class and the authority of the state. In all the novels discussed in this chapter, characters have to negotiate their visibility within the urban landscape.

The final chapter, 'Moor and Clay', takes us inland into the open cast china clay mines of mid-Cornwall and onto the windswept terrain of Bodmin Moor through the novels of Jack Clemo, Daphne du Maurier's *Jamaica Inn* (1936), Rumer Godden's *China Court* (1961), Katherine Stansfield's *Falling Creatures* (2017), A.L. Rowse's *A Cornish Childhood* (1942), and Daphne du Maurier and Arthur Quiller-Couch's *Castle Dor* (1936). These locations are part of Cornwall, just as much as the coastal sites that are so familiar. One of the only remaining areas of Cornwall with an extant mining industry, the necessities of the extraction process visually define the landscape of the clay country. Clemo's novels register this distinct, inland region of Cornwall as industrial, harsh, and antithetic to tourist sites nearby, whilst simultaneously in a dialectic with those other worlds on the horizon. Both Clemo and du Maurier create worlds which are palimpsestic in a way that must be negotiated by the characters inhabiting them. Here we are invited to appreciate a different aesthetic of place, one which finds beauty in landscapes that do not straightforwardly fit the mould.

Chapter One

Mining Class and Gender

A mine spread out its vast machinery.
Here engines, with their huts and smoky stacks,
Cranks, wheels, and rods, boilers and hissing steam,
Pressed up the water from the depths below.
Here fire-whims ran till almost out of breath,
And chains cried sharply, strained with fiery force.
John Harris, 'The Mine' (1874)[1]

Imperilled on the edge stands this gaunt stake
Amid the hummocks of abandoned scree,
Where plaintive seagull and the mournful sea
Their dirge of this forsaken claim awake.
But plundered lode yields now no ore to break,
And empty engine house, of clamour free,
With smokeless stack in idle company
But phantoms on the wild horizon make.
William Orchard, 'Wheal Coates' (1973)[2]

Ghosts
of the Tin Kingdom
when King Tin was mighty
as Ozymandias, rich
as tin seams in limestone
under chill sea.
King Tin built fine houses
for mine owners and 'cappens,'
Guest houses now
for tourists who drive out

Alternative Cornwalls

> *to photograph the stone bones*
> *of King Tin.*
> Brian Daldorph, 'King Tin' (2000)[3]

The extracts above encapsulate the historical and cultural shift that is central to this book. These poems depict the eminence and demise of Cornwall's mining industry, and the emergence of tourism, seemingly as a replacement industry. Cornish industrialization and its decline is visibly played out on the landscape. It is the engine house which characterizes the Cornish landscape, changes that landscape, during a period of intense industrialization in the eighteenth and nineteenth centuries. 'The Mine' demonstrates the extent of this impact, both visually through the 'smoky stacks', and auditorily through the 'hissing steam' and the cry of chains under strain. This scene would have been repeated across significant swathes of the Cornish landscape, the smoke and the noise of industry dominating over the natural landscape.

In contrast, William Orchard's poem laments the loss of mining. Here work has ceased and the engine house stands empty. The scene, so noisy in Harris's poem, is now 'clamour free'. Harris's 'smoky stacks' have become Orchard's 'smokeless stack'.[4] Already in Orchard's poem we can detect the romanticization of mining's visual remnants through both nostalgia for a lost age of industry and, paradoxically, through the absence of smoke and noise which this industry created. Once the engine house is no longer in use, it is aestheticized. The ruined engine house against the sea, continually reminiscent of what has been lost, becomes an iconic image central to the romanticization of the Cornish landscape.

In Orchard's poem, the wound of industrial failure is still fresh, for the seagull is 'plaintive' and the sea 'mournful', but in 'King Tin' by Brian Daldorph the romantic aestheticization of the landscape is complete, in the eyes of the tourist at least. The engine house, the 'stone bones' of mining, is now an inherent part of the landscape scene as something to be photographed, but it is increasingly divorced from its original function.[5] This is not a poem which itself romanticizes the scene; instead it registers this process taking place through the incorporation of the engine house into the touristification of the Cornish landscape.

The centrality of mining to the history and culture of Cornwall and to Cornish identity cannot be underestimated. The actual nature of its contemporary resonance is perhaps harder to assess. It is omnipresent, its visible remains etched onto the landscape (a landscape protected since 2006 as a World Heritage Site). It is woven into songs and represented, through the body of the miner, alongside fishing on Cornwall's crest. As depicted in 'King Tin', mining is encapsulated within, rather than replaced by the romanticization and aestheticization of Cornwall that is intensified by tourism. The global success of the 2015 reboot of *Poldark* has brought a representation of Cornish mining anew to the public consciousness, and to further generations of television viewers. With Wheal Crofty, Cornwall's last working mine (aside from clay mining) closing in 1997, mining's position within Cornish culture is celebratory, whilst simultaneously carrying with it the scars of a decline which began in the mid-nineteenth century.

As discussed in the Introduction, in the nineteenth century mining is pivotal to how Cornish people define themselves, and how they are viewed by the rest of the world. In his history of Cornwall Philip Payton argues that mining had become the 'central plank of the Cornish identity' by the mid-nineteenth century and that miners were viewed as 'the chief repository of Cornish distinctiveness'.[6] It is a positive identity based on expertise and technological know-how which trounced earlier negative characterization of the Cornish, largely derived from stereotypical tropes of Celtic peoples as savage and indolent. It is an identity which outlived mining's decline at home to promote Cornish miners as desirable experts (and exports) in mining concerns all over the world.

This chapter argues that mining is also a gendered and classed discourse whereby Cornish identity is tied to metalliferous industrialism, masculine achievement, and the masculine toil of working-class miners. Cornish nineteenth-century identity is centred on the body of the working-class miner at work, as a repository of heroic masculinity. This sits within the wider British nineteenth-century context of a shift in definitions of gender and work which placed a greater emphasis on masculinity and work, and work as a specifically masculine endeavour.[7] This shift coincides with Cornwall becoming nationally and internationally more visible as an industrial powerhouse. It is, therefore, unsurprising that Cornwall's mining industry took on, and reflected to others, the Cornish miner as an exemplar of physical masculine work and achievement, whilst the industry faced decline.

Such constructions leave little cultural space for Cornish women. Balmaidens, women who worked on the mine's surface breaking and sorting mineral ore, are consistently absent: culturally, historically and in literature of mining.[8] This chapter is interested in the nature of that effacement and the problematics of balmaidens' presence, on the mine's surface, and when they do appear in Cornish literature and culture. It refocuses on the scarce narratives where balmaidens do appear, reading them within the wider contexts of Cornish mining culture and literature of mining. Balmaidens are a route into thinking about mining through the lens of class and gender. This chapter is concerned with nineteenth-century social and cultural anxieties attached to gender and class, anxieties of the female worker and the working-class miner, which it looks to understand within the specificity of the Cornish context in Victorian Britain.

The novels which provide the context of Cornish mining literature in this chapter are *Deep Down* by R.M. Ballantyne (1868), *Tin* by Edward Bosanketh (1888), and *Wheal Darkness* by H.D. Lowry (1927). Lowry's manuscript was completed by C.A. Dawson Scott, after his death. The dates of publication of these novels span the time from the beginning of industrial collapse in Cornwall to the new post-industrial era which witnessed the rise of tourism. These texts provide the literary context against which a feminist counter-narrative is explored in later sections of the chapter, with Salome Hocking's novel *Norah Lang* (1886) as the primary focus.

Balmaidens are not completely forgotten today. Freed from anxieties over their visibility in their own time, they occasionally surface into modern Cornish culture in positive and interesting ways. In Mark Jenkin's film *Enys Men* ('Stone Island' in Cornish), released in 2023 and set in 1973, apparitions of balmaidens appear behind The Volunteer, played by Mary Woodvine. The film delineates an insider-derived relationship with the Cornish landscape which harnesses its strangeness, its eeriness, and the palimpsestic nature of the present's relationship to those who have lived and worked within that landscape in the past. The balmaidens here are both present and not present, visible and not visible, even though they loom over The Volunteer in the shot, and this is a suitable starting point for understanding their historical and cultural positioning in their own time, and today.

In the early 2010s Rebel Brewing Company changed the name of their 'copper coloured quaffing bitter' from *Barrow Boys* to *Bal Maiden* in order to commemorate Cornwall's mining heritage.[9] Seth Lakeman's song 'Bal Maiden', released on the album *Word of Mouth* in 2014, honours the

Figure 2: Balmaidens appear behind The Volunteer in Mark Jenkin's *Enys Men* (ENYS MEN—Courtesy of Bosena © Steve Tanner 2021)

memory of balmaidens and their work by imagining in stark terms their quotidian existence:

> Waking from the creeping dawn
> From the background of our valley torn
> Our maiden leaves a bed of stone
> Two hungry mouths to feed at home
> In a ruffled dress, in a bodice bound
> All tarnished boots, they weigh her down.[10]

Cornish folk band Dalla have a song on their album *Rooz* called 'Bal Maidens' Chant' that was developed from a rare surviving historical snippet of a folk song balmaidens may have sung as they worked. It goes,

> I can buddy, and I can rocky,
> And I can work like a man,
> I can lobby and shaky,
> And please the old Jan.[11]

Such modern-day appearances not only give balmaidens a continuing presence, but also depict them displaying a strength and confidence that they must surely have needed to work in the world in which they worked, and in the time in which they worked.

As part of the tinth (10th) anniversary of the Cornish Mining World Heritage Site, artists Jesse Leroy Smith and Bernard Irwin were commissioned to produce artwork as part of the 'Picturing the Mines' project. Smith's series of twenty oil-on-copper images includes depictions of the subterranean male torso and an image entitled *Bal Maiden*. It is a strong rendering of a female worker, not at work, but in a familiar portraiture pose, her cropped head and shoulders almost filling the entire copper canvas. The red background is in tune with the wisps of fire-red hair creeping out from under her gook (a white bonnet worn as protective headgear) and framing her face. The black of her outfit contrasts starkly with the white of the gook (which dominates the central third of the painting in a swathe of white). She bears a look of gritted determination, but the red used around her facial features turns to purple around her eyes, suggesting the hardness of her lot.

The choice of a working-class female worker as artistic subject matter is reminiscent of van Gogh's paintings of peasant women. *Bal Maiden* is particularly akin to van Gogh's *Head of a Peasant Woman* in the positioning of the head and the slightly off-centre look of the subject. As with van Gogh's working women, the act of posing a balmaiden in a familiar portraiture pose, one that is usually reserved for those with some level of social importance, is a subversive act. It calls for the same respect and reverence for the balmaiden that a portrait signals for its more usual subjects. It also declares her existence, her visibility, something that would have been fraught with anxiety in her own time.

In 2018 o-region and Palores Productions staged 'Hireth'.[12] Written by Edward Rowe, directed by Simon Harvey and featuring the music of Seth Lakeman (including his song 'Bal Maiden'), it was performed at St Just Miners' Chapel. At this location near to Geevor mine, they were depicting on stage the experiences of Geevor miners recruited as tunnellers during the First World War. While the play is primarily about male experience, balmaidens are important to the narrative and often, literally, take centre stage. Edna Trevenan is described as being 'proud and strong' and Mildred Rodda as 'formidable'. Mildred is often in search of her mislaid 'bucking hammer'.

Figure 3: Jesse Leroy Smith's *Bal Maiden* (by kind permission of the artist)

Similarly formidable are the balmaidens in Nick Darke's play, *Ting Tang Mine*, first performed at the National Theatre in 1987. The play opens with balmaidens Ysella, Senara and Gorlos arriving at the count house steps carrying long hammers, alongside miners with picks, gads and boryers.[13] They are all concerned that men from the nearby Brigan mine are going to get work at Ting Tang mine. The balmaidens are very vocal in a tense stand-off with the Brigan miners, telling the Ting Tang miners to '[a]rm yourselves!' and the Brigan men to 'emigrate' if they need work.[14] Such depictions of balmaidens as individuals gives them the kind of presence that we often cannot glean from historical records, and only very rarely from literary works from their own time.

What historical material is available has been unearthed by Lynne Mayers, who in 2004 published the first comprehensive history of balmaidens. She estimated that between 1720 and 1920, around 60,000 women had been employed within the mining industry in Cornwall and Devon, but revised this up to 80,000 for the same period on her website. Numbers of women employed peaked in the mid-nineteenth century but declined rapidly from this point onwards as such workers were replaced by both technology and out-of-work miners.[15] Even these kinds of statistical estimates are difficult, given that the nomenclature of *balmaiden* was deemed a local term and so was not allowed to be used in census records. Balmaidens therefore appear under a range of terms, such as 'mine maiden' and 'bucking woman'.[16]

Mayers herself stresses the need to imagine what balmaidens' lives might have been like. We are left with little choice but to do so, due to a dearth of existing or surviving accounts from the women themselves. There are currently only four known sources of such material, and these women also pop up only fleetingly in historical documents. They are sometimes mentioned in documents written by mining engineers, but as Mayers states they, 'either received no attention at all, or at best, very limited mention "in passing"'.[17] Commentaries, such as that by George Henwood, were biased by Victorian anxieties over working women which saw these women as unfeminine because they had veered outside their natural sphere of domesticity.[18] Their visibility working on the surface of the mine, as opposed to the concealment of the miners below ground, is reversed in the cultural and historical centrality of working-class miners and the invisibility or absence of balmaidens in the same contexts.

Mining Masculinities

Shifting Victorian attitudes to gender and class in relation to work is the British context for understanding a specifically Cornish masculinity centred on mining and the miner, both in prosperous times and during the collapse of the industry. While class and gender are understood to be distinct, they intersect in relation to the Cornish miner in specific ways which this section intends to elucidate. What this means for working women, in particular balmaidens, will be discussed fully in the next section, but it clearly sets up a cultural context in which working women are at best social pariahs, at worst a perceived threat to masculinity and to the very fabric of Victorian society.

Martin A. Danahay points out that, from the 1840s, '[t]he equation of men and work was part of a redefinition of the division of labor in gender terms in the nineteenth century'.[19] While work in general was increasingly seen as an exclusively male preserve, it was male working-class labour which came to epitomize both an ideal of work and of Victorian masculinity. Michael Roper and John Tosh identify 'a marked shift in the codes of manliness […] during the latter half of the nineteenth century—from the moral earnestness of the Evangelicals and Dr Arnold to the respect for muscle and might so prevalent at the close of the Victorian era'.[20] Such a shift inevitably, therefore, provides a new emphasis on the male body: its physicality and as the source of production.

The identification of the male working-class labourer as the embodiment of both work and masculinity, as well as excluding women, also problematizes masculinity for men who do not fit into the category. As Danahay states, '[i]f the symbolic heart of work lies in manual labor then the intellectual is marginal to the industry of Victorian society'.[21] This therefore becomes an intellectual problem for writers and thinkers such as Thomas Carlyle and John Ruskin. While both understand the male body at work, its purpose, in slightly different ways, they both overlook the reality: the degradation of the male body as the inevitable outcome of an, often short, life of manual labour in unfavourable conditions.

Norma Clarke characterizes Thomas Carlyle as a man trapped between two types of masculinity: the inactive, cerebral writer, and the active, working-class labourer represented by his father.[22] The product of a working class family, Carlyle strove to make a living from literature.[23] Yet once that is achieved, his position as an intellectual has removed him from the very sphere in which he perceives masculinity to reside. Ultimately, it is the working-class man that Carlyle feels to be truly masculine. He writes, 'it is only among what are called the *un*-educated classes (those educated by experience) that you can look for *a man*'.[24] As a consequence, Carlyle romanticizes physical labour, but as a route to a higher state beyond the physical, which therefore minimizes the experience of undertaking physical labour.

John Ruskin also romanticizes manual labour. He is more attentive to the potential for manual labour to destroy male bodies, but he pursues a belief that the right kind of manual labour would enable men to reach the ideal of masculinity, and the ideal strong, healthy body. Danahay comments that Ruskin 'idealized manual labor and the working classes, especially the image of the heroic "man at work" wielding a shovel'.[25] He documents Ruskin's digging projects whereby Ruskin encouraged Oxford undergraduates to take up digging in order to become '"real" men'.[26]

In this context, it is not at all surprising that the feats of the working-class Cornish miner, allied to industrial success, produced a confident, masculine, Cornish identity. Danahay explains that '"[w]ork" could be used as a category to define national and racial identity as well as masculine identity'.[27] This was most certainly the case within the Cornish context. Victorian investment in the heroism of the male worker, its relevance to mining, and the centrality of a gendered narrative of mining to Cornish identity enabled the Cornish to redefine their identity by divesting it of Celtic stereotypes. Such stereotypes painted a typical Celtic population as idle. This new identity centred on male labour, could instead define itself contrastingly as physical, active, and productive.

The identity derived from Cornwall's mining success in the first half of the nineteenth century was the antithesis of the previous perception of Cornwall as 'West Barbary'. 'West Barbary' was an identification defined by outsiders, which drew on prevalent Celtic stereotypes to produce an image of Cornwall and the Cornish where wrecking, smuggling, and rioting was seen as inherent.[28] The ensuing reputation contrasted distinctly with this first and was an identity over which the Cornish had more control. It centred on industrial achievement, and a pride in that achievement, rather than being characterized as backward, barbaric, or uncivilized as the 'West Barbary' moniker implied. The Cornish were now leaders in industrial technological advancement. According to Payton there was a 'redefinition of Cornish society as modern and progressive', and this signalled a major shift in the way that Cornwall defined itself and was viewed by Britain and the rest of the world.[29] While this buoyant, confident identity had been generated from the successes of Cornish inventors and engineers, its bedrock was working-class miners, their expertise and bodily labour, who were portrayed and promoted as the best at their trade, particularly at the height of the Great Emigration when the Cornish miner was seen as taking his expertise to mining concerns all over the world.

Both Bernard Deacon's and Payton's work has provided the framework through which we understand the dominant nineteenth-century

Cornish identity as a product of industrial success. That identity is highly gendered. It is a masculine identity, based on male achievement and male work, which is accessible to nineteenth-century Cornish men and exclusionary to women, even to the women who worked on the mine's surface. There is no room within this identity for a female perspective, or for an appreciation of the achievements of women within Cornish mining. Indeed, such inclusion has the potential to threaten the very tenet of heroic masculine achievement on which the identity is based. This is the Cornish context of the four mining novels discussed in the following sections.

The Cornish Industrial Novel

Alan M. Kent notes that the novel flourished comparatively late in Cornwall, possibly due to Methodism's censure of the form, but that by the second half of the nineteenth century, it was being used by writers, both visiting and Cornish, to depict life within Cornish mining communities.[30] There is no doubt that the industrial prowess identity was seductive to writers such as R.M. Ballantyne, whose work displays a fascination with Cornwall's technological acumen, as well as a gaze that celebrates and reverences the body of the working-class miner at work. Such works feed off the cultural zeitgeist and enable it to perpetuate.

In Ballantyne's novel *Deep Down*, Oliver Trembath, a young expatriate Cornishman, returns to St Just to take up the post of doctor at Botallack mine. Oliver's love interest is Rose Ellis, an adopted niece of Oliver's uncle and, after love rival George Clearemout flees when his villainous plot to sell fake shares in Wheal Dooem mine is foiled, Oliver gets his girl. The Wheal Dooem plotline is reminiscent in some ways of Edward Bosanketh's *Tin*: both are concerned with the shares and money dealing of mining ventures.

It is *Deep Down* which is most representative of the Cornish 'industrial prowess' identity.[31] The novel demonstrates the author's knowledge of the technical detail of mining so that the text is stuffed with realist detail. By setting *Deep Down* in the early nineteenth century, Ballantyne has selected the historical moment of industrial success and confidence in Cornwall. This is certainly a text which buys into Cornish promotion of their own 'industrial prowess', and this is demonstrated through the way in which the mine, events, and miners are portrayed. At times, the narrative breaks away from the fictional storyline to sections that sound more like a mining journal, but which are tailored to inform audiences unfamiliar with this world. This level of detail gives substance to a narrative tone which often expresses wonderment at the scene described. While knowledgeable, the narrator looks on as an outsider who has come to learn about Cornish mining and is truly fascinated. For example, Botallack is first described as follows:

> From whatever point viewed, the aspect of Botallack mine is grand in the extreme. On the rocky point that stretches out into the sea, engines with all their fantastic machinery and buildings have been erected. On the very summit of the cliff is seen a complication of timbers, wheels, and chains sharply defined against the sky, with apparently scarce any hold of the cliff, while down below, on rocky ledges and in black chasms, are other engines and beams and rods and wheels and chains, fastened and perched in fantastic forms in dangerous-looking places.[32]

Kent argues that it is in sections such as this that '[t]he prowess is mainly achieved', because they demonstrate 'Ballantyne's fascination with Botallack mine [...] and how extraordinary a work of engineering it is'.[33] The wonderment and delight of the narrative gaze is clearly detectable here, in the choice of words but also the rapid cumulative presentation of images, which conveys excitement as well as a visual gorging by the narrator on the scene laid out before him. Ballantyne couples wonderment with facts which convey the engineering feats required for Botallack to exist and to succeed in its purpose.

Equally, Ballantyne's *Deep Down* is a manifesto for the physical feats of the individual miner. The novel gazes at the physical form of the miner, often observing miners at their arduous work below ground, and presents them as a species well adapted to their environment, and to the level of work required of them. For instance, we first meet David Trevarrow 'pursuing his toilsome work' in Botallack mine:

> Chip, chip, chip—down in the dusky mine! Oh, but the rock at which the miner chipped was hard, and the bit of rock on which he sat was hard, and the muscles with which he toiled were hard from prolonged labour; and the lot of the man seemed hard, as he sat there

in the hot, heavy atmosphere, hour after hour, from morn till eve, with the sweat pouring down his brow and over his naked shoulders, toiling and moiling with hammer and chisel.

But stout David Trevarrow did not think his lot peculiarly hard. His workshop was a low narrow tunnel deep down under the surface of the earth—ay, and deep under the bottom of the sea![34]

That the miner is suited to his role is demonstrated in this passage by the repetition of the adjective 'hard'. The rock is hard but so are 'the muscles with which he [the miner] toiled'. He is, therefore, at one with his environment. As well as exhibiting masculine characteristics which appeal to the Victorian understanding of 'true' masculinity, the miners' physicality is also perceived as inherently Cornish. These miners are seen to possess 'that stern Cornish spirit of determination to face and overcome great difficulties, which has doubtless much to do with the excessive development of chest and shoulder for which Cornish miners, especially those of St. Just, are celebrated'.[35] The physical capacity of the miner is continually registered in *Deep Down*.

The narrative perspective on the working-class miners' bodies is aligned with John Ruskin's belief that the right kind of manual labour creates a healthy male body which 'promotes an ideal of the muscular male body at work'.[36] David Trevarrow is described in *Deep Down* as being 'of herculean mould'.[37] Significantly this enables him to remain productive, for '[w]hen his right arm grew tired, he passed the hammer swiftly to his left hand, and, turning the borer with his right, continued to work with renewed vigour'.[38] The intent gaze at the miners is such that they are individually distinguished:

> [T]hey were of all sizes and characters. Some were robust and muscular; some were lean and wiry; some were just entering on manhood, with the ruddy hue of health shining through the slime on their smooth faces; some were in the prime of life, pale from long working underground, but strong, and almost as hard as the iron with which they chiselled the rocks.[39]

While not brushing over the hardship of working below ground, as in this extract, the text's optimism that such work ultimately leads to strength and health is engrained in its attitude to working-class male bodies.

What happens to those bodies when constant work saps their health and strength, when work wastes rather than builds up working bodies? In Émile Zola's *Germinal* (1885) work below ground inevitably degrades miners. Bonnemort, for example, coughs up coal from his saturated lungs which forms black foam at his lips.[40] Zola's primary objection is to the wealthy mine owners whose actions force the miner below ground to make his profit. Repeatedly throughout the novel, the mine is described as a 'voracious beast' swallowing its prey, and, if they survive, spitting out damaged, broken men when they are no longer fit enough to work.[41]

In *Deep Down*, while Botallack is once described as 'some awful sea-monster', crucially it is not enemy territory, but the true and proper home of the miner.[42] As mine doctor, Oliver Trembath takes us into the houses of men broken and dying as the result of both accidents and overlong exposure to the foul air of the mine. David Trevarrow, for instance, is born to be a miner and, while such a life will inevitably lead to an early death, in life his physical feats ennoble him. Trevarrow meets with '[a] long illness' as the result of working in the mine, but, crucially, he is able to rebuild himself and regain his spirit for work through his Methodist faith. Methodism supported and promoted the notion of individual achievement which was at the heart of Cornwall's new identity. *Deep Down* therefore venerates the physical prowess of the miner which is not dimmed by the ravages which will eventually tell on the body. Instead Trevarrow 'excelled and suffered'.[43] To maintain a gendered identity built upon the working-class body at work requires a reshaping of the devastating toll of manual labour to extend heroic masculinity beyond the usefulness of the body. It is a fudge which *Germinal* does not countenance.

As seen above, the narrative gaze in *Deep Down* intently views and describes the white working-class male body at work underground. Such a gaze goes further than admiration though. In the passages above, and again here, it is a desiring gaze. For example, a miner called Maggot is described as follows: 'As he stood there, naked to the waist, holding the borer with his left hand, and plying the hammer with all his might with the other, his great breadth of shoulder and development of muscle were finely displayed by the candlelight, which fell in brilliant gleams on parts of his frame'.[44] The gaze of the narrative perspective casts an eye up and down the various examples of male bodies in the text, resting upon muscles and registering sweat pouring down over torsos. Danahay sees the presence of desire here as the inevitable consequence of Victorian attempts to banish it through work. He says that,

> [t]he forces of pleasure, represented most powerfully by sexuality, reasserted themselves at the margins of representations of sweaty, muscled labor as the ultimate in masculine productivity and troubled the serene assertion of Victorian masculine values […] [and] the stability of Victorian masculine identity. Men's bodies at work are 'unstable' because like women's bodies they are subject to desire. The Victorian discourse on work is intertwined with the Victorian discourse on sexuality no matter how much authors like Carlyle may have wished to banish it to the margins, or at least to the tropics. The history of work in the Victorian period is, therefore, the history of the attempt to define work as masculine and the male body as productive and free from the threats of the feminine, idleness and sexuality.[45]

In later sections this understanding will further help us to comprehend a series of instabilities inherent in the Cornish masculinity upon which the 'industrial prowess' identity is based, as well as anxieties around balmaidens' visibility in a mine environment.[46] Such understanding helps us not simply to contrast male and female workers, but also to understand ways in which they are both read on the basis of their class position.

Crises

Cornish mining was in crisis from the end of the 1860s onwards. Its decline was swift and led to the eventual collapse of the entire industry, in both tin and copper production. Tourism became a feature of the Cornish economy from the second half of the nineteenth century and grew until it became (and remains) Cornwall's principal industry. Through a continuing gendered analysis, the collapse of mining also portends a crisis in masculinity. Cornwall's 'industrial prowess' identity was wholly masculine, and wholly reliant on a buoyant and successful mining industry.[47] It is within this context that we can more fully understand the emphasis in novels such as *Deep Down*, published during the crisis, on the prowess of the miner, and, as discussed in this section, a lack of literary engagement with the decline of mining in Cornwall. It also begins to explain the elision of balmaidens within Cornish mining novels, which is discussed fully in the next section.

Roper and Tosh argue that while 'the idea of a "crisis in masculinity" may be an invention of the 1980s [...] its relevance is clearly not confined to the present', and that such a crisis may be characterized as a 'contradiction between experience and expectation'. We can certainly apply this to the collapse of mining in Cornwall, for industrial success had produced a belief in Cornish 'industrial prowess', confidence in that ability, and an expectation that the success of the industry would perpetuate. The experience of industrial failure contrasted so completely with this: both culturally, and practically, in terms of the individual miners' experiences of unemployment. Combined, these were, then, both economic and psychic crises.[48] Unemployment, and the necessity of taking on surface work previously done by balmaidens, can be seen as proof that the 'industrial prowess' identity was unstable by the 1860s. In the division of labour, surface work was by precedent a female role that did not carry the same pay, and was not seen to require the same level of skill as was needed below ground.[49] This situation can be read as a perfect storm for a concomitant crisis in masculinity, given the centrality of heroic masculinity to Cornwall's industrial identity in the nineteenth century.

Crucially, however, confronting mining's collapse is impossible precisely because it is also a confrontation with a crisis in masculinity, with the fallibility and instability of masculinity itself. Therefore, the Great Emigration becomes the means of extending the 'industrial prowess' identity beyond mining's demise in Cornwall. As Payton comments,

> [a]t the time, the Great Emigration was seen as the culmination of the Cornish experience, the highpoint of Cornish achievement that—having established Cornwall in the forefront of technological advance—now took its energy and expertise to the four points of the compass. The reality, of course, was tragically more complex, for emigration was also a symptom of Cornwall's flawed industrial base, and the mechanism by which Cornwall was shorn of the most skilled and brightest and youngest elements of its population.[50]

Cornish miners, in reality their industry at home no longer able to support them, became the travelling experts, applying their superior knowledge to the world's mining ventures.[51]

Emigration is the perfect vehicle for this Cornish industrial identity, which no longer has a base at home. As Phillip Mallett says, '[e]mpire men were manly men'.[52] This is something which is often overlooked. The Cornish are more typically understood as the colonized, but in the nineteenth century they are very much part of Britain's imperial expansion, the settlement of countries with native populations, and the extraction of mineral wealth from these countries. Roper and Tosh point out that '[d]ominant ideologies of masculinity are [...] maintained through asserting their difference from—and superiority to—other races'.[53] This is certainly a characteristic exhibited by the Cornish miners abroad who asserted their racial superiority through contrast and active contention with the Irish, identifying themselves as 'Ancient Britons', the first and therefore the best.[54] It is within this arena that the Cornish 'industrial prowess' identity could perpetuate in the face of industrial failure at home.[55]

The novel, which had been embraced as a medium to delineate the Cornish experience of industrial success, could have provided the arena within which the end of mining, the crisis of masculinity, and the dawn of tourism was articulated and interpreted. Instead, much in the same way as the promotion of emigration, the novel artificially extends the 'industrial prowess' identity. All of the novels under discussion here are written during or following the time of crisis in Cornish mining.[56] By the time that Bosanketh and Lowry produce their novels, Cornwall is already deindustrializing in both tin and copper mining, albeit with momentary resurgences. *Deep Down* grasps for the security of the past in the form of the early nineteenth century, when Cornish mining was at its peak. At no point in the narrative is there any hint at what will happen some sixty years later. However, in order to demonstrate 'industrial prowess', Ballantyne does break the chronological boundaries in which his narrative exists.[57] *Deep Down* includes a description of the Royal Visit to Botallack Mine by the Prince and Princess of Wales in 1865 in order to explain the gig contraption then in use to enter the mine.[58] Reference to contemporary events is indulged, therefore, when they relate to a narrative of industrial progress. Ballantyne's retreat to a golden age of Cornish mining precludes an acceptance of industrial crisis and enables him to celebrate and marvel at Cornish industrial achievement without reservation.

In Edward Bosanketh's *Tin*, a novel published in 1888, twenty years after *Deep Down*, there is greater equivocation about the future of mining, yet it is still ultimately optimistic about the industry's future. Set contemporaneously, it is aware of the falling price of tin, and the consequent closure of mines. At the shareholders' meeting Walter Baxter, Esq. addresses the room, declaring, '[w]e have passed through a period of great depression [...]. We all hope, and some of us believe, that we have seen the worst.' The tone is optimistic, but Baxter has given the same speech at every meeting for the last thirty years. Mr East, the purser, is also optimistic; the mine is in profit and while '[t]he price of tin, it is true, is still very low, [...] there's every prospect of a rise'. Rather than viewing mining interests in Australia (to which Cornish men have emigrated) as succeeding local ventures, he believes their prospects 'cannot be said to compare favourably with those at home'.[59] There are more realistic opinions openly expressed by other characters. For instance, Captain Eady does not 'believe that things will ever be much better', and thinks it fanciful that Cornwall can ever compete with the mining potential in Australia.[60] However, ultimately the narrative perspective validates Mr East's optimism via an epilogue which terminates any notion of uncertainty. Camruth and Redborne remain 'much the same as they were before our story was written'. Redborne Consols is even 'one of the richest mines in the county'.[61] While displaying concern at the state of Cornish mining, *Tin* ultimately postpones any deeper recognition of its decline.

Wheal Darkness is the last novel to be published of those discussed in this chapter. It was found amongst Lowry's papers when he died in 1906 and was then completed by Dawson Scott and published in 1927.[62] Lowry and Dawson Scott had the greatest benefit of hindsight, writing at a time when mining in Cornwall on any significant scale was truly finished. The novel does register the turmoil of economic uncertainty. Set midway through the second half of the nineteenth century, when the major blows had already struck both tin and copper mining, it depicts the gravity of the situation. We hear of mines closing and its consequences. Mr Trevalga, Lord Dunstanville's steward, admits to John Pilgrim, the newly arrived vicar of Tallywarn, that 'mines have lately been closed; many are being worked at a loss, and may close at any moment [...]. Everyone is poor.'[63] The consequences of mine closures are visible in streets peopled by idle, out-of-work men. There is also a sense of the scale of emigration: Mr Trevalga's two sons are happy and doing well in mines in Mexico, but he and Mr Pilgrim witness a train leaving the local station 'heavy-laden with the sad hopes of women and the reluctant hearts of men', bound for 'foreign parts'. Wheal Darkness is the saviour: the mine still working while others nearby have closed.⁶⁴ However, even Wheal Darkness is put into jeopardy at the climax of the novel when an underground collapse occurs, spelling financial ruin for investors. Of all the novels, it is *Wheal Darkness* that is most open-ended regarding the state of Cornish mining. However, while there is no direct assurance, there are seeds of possibility sewn into the ending of this novel, both literally in Mr Trevalga's garden where 'everything is sprouting and growing', and concurrently in the lives of the protagonists as we leave them.⁶⁵ Nat Rescorla is saved from ruin by a rich acquaintance keen to go into partnership with him, so '[r]enewed hope had trodden so sharply on the heels of failure'.⁶⁶ Ultimately, sustained, realistic engagement with mining's demise is once again deferred.

Balmaidens

'What are you doing gooked up there?' To be 'gooked up' is a Cornish dialect phrase, the equivalent of 'sticking out like a sore thumb' with a suggestion that the nature of the standing out is somewhat ridiculous.⁶⁷ As mentioned above, a gook is a piece of structured cloth headgear worn by balmaidens to protect themselves from the sun. It is white, quite large and projects out and over their forehead and over the sides of their head and back of their neck. The term actually derives from the Cornish language word *kogh*, meaning bonnet, but it would seem that its usage within Cornish dialect is steeped in Victorian anxiety about the visibility of balmaidens as working women. There are some photos of French nurses from the First World War wearing similarly styled head coverings, as well as various orders of nuns. More recent comparisons can be drawn with the white winged bonnet worn by handmaids in Margaret Atwood's *The Handmaid's Tale*, made more prominent in the past few years by the very successful Hulu television adaptation of novel, and the co-opting of the handmaid's bonnet to protest for rights for women around the world. In the novel, Offred says that '[t]he white wings [...] are to keep us from seeing, but also from being seen'.⁶⁸ The balmaidens' gook is purely practical, but it has the opposite effect to the handmaid's bonnet: the white structured headgear made them stand out, public, visible, and visible in a way in which the men working below ground were not, in terms of the environment of the mine.

Even in a chapter such as this, which is looking to give due prominence to balmaidens, it is easier to write about their absence, and the reasons for this, than to write their presence back onto the page. This section aims to do both, and as much of the latter as possible with the limited amount of historical and literary material available that is specifically about balmaidens, and which gives them voices of their own on this page. It is within the context outlined above, of Cornish Victorian masculinities and their crises, that we begin to understand how balmaidens challenge every aspect of Victorian definitions of acceptable femininity, and, consequently, the absence of balmaidens from both Cornish mining history and literary representations of Cornish mining. Balmaidens not only induce Victorian anxieties about women; they are also a threat to constructions of gender, exposing them as such, and to the very assumptions upon which Cornwall's 'Industrial prowess' narrative was built. [69]

As I have argued elsewhere, balmaidens' history is one of problematic visibility on the mine's surface and subsequent invisibility in terms of historical records, and the absence of surviving material written by them.[70] Balmaidens should be seen within a wider context of working women within Victorian Britain and, especially, other female mine workers (there were, for example, pit brow lasses working at collieries in northern England).[71] We can draw parallels between the way in which balmaidens are viewed and these other mine women. Balmaidens worked on the mine's surface at a range of tasks—sorting, breaking, and refining the mineral ore brought to grass (to the surface). This was an arduous and dirty job which took place in all weathers under minimal protection from the elements. It required skill and considerable strength, one of the tasks being to break up the ore with hammer blows.

So much of what balmaidens had to do for their job, therefore, was problematic within Victorian culture. The influence of separate spheres in Victorian society, and its demarcation of spaces along gender lines, 'redefined the nature of femininity and of what was considered as acceptable women's work'.[72] As Danahay argues, '[f]or women to work was often represented as releasing a dangerous sexuality rather than repressing sexual desire'.[73] George Henwood, writing in *The Mining Journal* in 1858, provides one of the few snippets of contemporaneous information we have about balmaidens, but his is a middle-class male gaze, which exhibits many of the anxieties being discussed here. For instance, he fears that '[t]he indiscriminate association, in their employment, of the sexes naturally begets a want of modesty and delicacy, so important in the formation of character'. They were likely to be corrupted morally it was thought, but also made unfit for more suitable feminine tasks, such as maintaining a home and bearing children.[74] Upper-class women of the time went to great lengths in order to prove that they did not work, such as keeping white, soft hands.[75] Consider the rules of proper dress and comportment that were thought to show 'proper' femininity and then contrast this with the physical movements necessary to swing a heavy hammer down onto rock, and the dirt and sweat involved. We begin, therefore, to understand their absence.

Balmaidens are also notably absent within novels of Cornish mining, including those already discussed in this chapter. Angela V. John asserts that 'accounts of mining communities have not only forgotten the single woman and the widow, but have internalised the male miners' "eye-view"'.[76] The novels of Cornish mining by Ballantyne, Bosanketh, and Lowry all exhibit this viewpoint. In *Deep Down* the narrative eye rests only briefly on balmaidens, and in some scenes they have been scrubbed out completely. The novel gives the impression that the tasks carried out on the surface of the mine are primarily masculine ones: 'Here the large pieces of ore are broken into smaller ones by a man with a hammer.' The balmaidens are confined both to the traditionally female role of washing, and to a brief historical reference which misleadingly suggests they are an anachronism. We are told that '[i]n old times the tin was collected in large pits, whence it was transferred to the hands of balmaidens (or mine-girls) to be washed by them in wooden troughs called "frames"'.[77] While out-of-work miners did eventually usurp balmaidens' surface role during the industrial decline, this novel is set at the height of Cornish mining prosperity when women still carried out this role at the mine's surface, yet their contribution, breaking the ore with hammers, is effaced. This is surprising given the focus of the novel and Ballantyne's three-month study of Cornish mining, which enabled him to write a text which, in all other respects, is stuffed with mining details.

The balmaidens' absence enables Ballantyne's description of the mine's surface to be made consistent with the subsurface workings, with men dominating every aspect. Below ground, Cornish miners 'chiselled the rocks'.[78] At grass men wield hammers to break up the ore which is fed to the stamps. The novel describes the tin leaving 'the rough hand of the miner', from which it reaches the tin-smelter.[79] At Oliver's side we witness the smelter, 'a sturdy man […] with brawny arms bared to the shoulders', pouring forth the liquid metal from the bowels of the furnace. Ballantyne describes this man as 'begrimed and hairy—like a very Vulcan'.[80] The absence of balmaidens enables Ballantyne to produce a wholly masculine environment responsible for the entirety of the mining and refining process, which reflects the gendered 'industrial prowess' identity that the text embraces.[81] More detailed consideration of balmaidens and their role on the mine's surface is therefore impossible because they interrupt the coherence of such an identity, as well as drawing attention to its fallibility.

Where balmaidens do appear, *Deep Down* conforms to stereotypes. When describing the Royal Visit of 1865, Ballantyne comments that 'balmaidens donned their holiday-attire, and Johnny Fortnight took care, by supplying the poor mine-girls with the latest fashions, that their appearance should be, if we may be allowed the word, *splendiferous*!'[82] The tone is light-hearted, even mocking, and is divorced from the more sober sections of technological narrative, or from hard work at the mine. This attitude echoes one more generally held that balmaidens were excessive in their desire for fashionable clothes, and were consequently distasteful. Henwood comments that

> [t]o see the "bal maidens" on Sunday would astonish a stranger; whilst at their work the pendant earrings and showy bead necklaces excite the pity as well as the surprise of the thoughtful. All desire to save a few shillings [...] is discarded, and nothing but display is thought of.[83]

Their perceived showiness is distasteful, pitiable, unchristian, and profligate, according to Henwood's critical eye. Sharron P. Schwartz notes that, in fact, such dressing up 'challenged the social order, as it threatened to erode accepted class divisions'.[84] In multiple ways, then, balmaidens challenge established social rules attached to both class and gender.

In *Wheal Darkness* there is a more considered portrait of balmaidens than can be found in *Deep Down*. In the prologue, as part of John Pilgrim's reverie of his childhood in Tallywarn, he remembers that

> the women, when they were young, they rose early, and were off to the mines or tin-streams before the rest of the world was waking. They wore huge boots, short skirts, with coarse, white aprons, and linen sun-bonnets. At night they returned in little companies, singing very sweetly as they passed home-ward through the ill-lighted streets. On Sundays, or when choirs and Sunday Schools had their outings, they went gaily dressed. Later, these same women ceased from labour at the mine, and seemed to disappear from view—so

engrossing are the cares of a family to a wife who counts herself unusually fortunate if her husband earns a pound a week.[85]

There is time taken here to describe their apparel, giving them more of a physical presence on the page, even though appearing only in a memory. While John describes their 'huge boots' and 'short skirts' he does not pass judgement on their attire. There is also some understanding of their plight; once they have ceased their mine work they are enclosed by domesticity and shoulder the responsibility of nurturing a family on meagre subsistence. There is still some recourse to the stereotypical pastoral portraits of balmaidens that Mayers has identified, which sees them as always happy and singing, but it is a more thoughtful portrait overall.[86]

Crucially, however, *Wheal Darkness* never returns to the balmaidens in the main narrative. While the novel is named after the mine, and while it is at the mine that the denouement of the story takes place, the focus is predominantly with Tallywarn and its Methodist community. The mine is ever at a distance, the reverberating sound of the stamps a reminder to the villagers of the mine's presence, to and from which the miners tramp. Like the miners, in the prologue balmaidens are seen coming to and from the mine, rather than at work on the mine's surface. They journey to work before anyone is awake to witness them. They return through dark, ill-lit streets which once again cloak them from view. They are heard because of their singing, rather than seen, except in Pilgrim's mind's eye. Yet for the balmaidens this journey foreshadows their invisibility within the walls of the marital home. It is only when they are not dressed for the mine, but gaily attired, that they are seen, and then at 'outings', a different kind of public arena, the very opposite to their role at the mine, which is here rendered invisible through its location at the outer confines of the text. The text registers that, once they cease to be balmaidens and traverse from the public to the private realm, it is then that they 'disappear from view', but in fact their invisibility as balmaidens has been suggested all along. This passage therefore functions to uncover the balmaidens, describing the women that were usually unseen, yet the rest of the text serves to reinstate their invisibility and so this passage becomes, once again, no more than a fleeting glimpse.

Norah Lang: The Mine Girl
It is within this context that a novel such as Salome Hocking's *Norah Lang: The Mine Girl* is important. Hocking's narrative focuses on the very aspects

of mining that other writers have effaced. We can contrast the invisibility of the balmaiden in the texts above with her visibility in Hocking's text. Norah appears in almost every scene of the novel, and we as readers experience her point of view. The act of focusing on her brings to this work aspects and experiences not found within other novels of Cornish mining. We see Norah negotiating both the domestic space of the home and the public space of the mine. *Norah Lang* also provides a literary depiction of events that we regularly find in other mining novels, such as the mine accident, but here we experience the event from a previously unconsidered point of view. Balmaidens are given a literary space within Hocking's text that is denied elsewhere, and this opens up new literary horizons.[87]

Hocking's starting point is an ordinary but good young woman, still living within the family home where she must deal with her unlikeable stepmother. Through Norah the novel dispels the typical attitude to balmaidens and provides a counter-narrative. Norah's features are described as showing 'strength of character and firmness of will'.[88] She cares for her invalid sister Philippa, and works as a balmaiden at the St George Mine, where her father also works. There is awareness, confronted early in the novel, of balmaidens' unsavoury reputation: Norah 'knew that by being a mine girl she should fall in the estimation of a certain class of people'.[89] Yet Norah overturns the stereotypical beliefs of other characters in the novel. For example, Mr Newton 'heard with surprise that she was a mine girl, but he saw that far from letting her work drag her down, she had ennobled it'.[90] Hocking does not over-angelicize Norah, but she does hold her up as a bastion of goodness and moral worth.

Norah Lang appears against the more typically extreme characterizations of balmaidens by observers, or in other fictional texts (in the fleeting moments when they are shown to us). Lucy Fitzgerald, travelling in Cornwall in 1825, expounds the stereotypes described above; she describes the balmaidens she saw as 'all singing hymns which sounded so beautiful', and as looking 'so blooming and healthy'.[91] In stark contrast, Richard Ayton, visiting a colliery in 1813, commented that the women working there 'lose every quality that is graceful in women, and become a set of coarse, licentious wretches, scorning all kinds of restraint, and yielding themselves up, with shameless audacity, to the most detestable sensuality'.[92] In Zola's *Germinal*, we see a fictional representation of such licentiousness. Catherine, a fifteen-year-old haulage girl, succumbs to the predatory Chaval. She is by no means an exception. Old Mouque lives in a shack in the ruins of an old mine and

[e]ach time he ventured forth from his lair, he could not put a foot forward without treading on some couple in the grass, and it was worse still if he was [...] at the far end of the enclosure; for then he saw the sensual noses of all the Montsou girls popping up one by one, and had to be careful not to trip over legs stretched out across the paths.[93]

This is the version of working women that Victorians most feared—for them it was inevitable that unsuitable work unleashes unsuitable desires.

Rebecca Harding Davis's *Life in the Iron Mills* registers the physical warping of the female form by the industrial environment. The protagonist, Hugh Wolfe, immortalizes this form in a sculpture made of korl (the refuse from the ore refining process) which is described as 'a light, porous substance, of a delicate, waxen, flesh-colored tinge'.[94] The flesh colour of the material suggests that this is a lifelike reproduction of the female form. Yet it is also grotesque and startles the men visiting the mill when out of the darkness appears 'a woman, white, of giant proportions, crouching on the ground, her arms flung out in some wild gesture of warning'. The men are horrified by this artistic representation of a working woman, described as follows: 'There was not one line of beauty or grace in it: a nude woman's form, muscular, grown coarse with labor, the powerful limbs instinct with some one poignant longing. One idea: there it was in the tense, rigid muscles, the clutching hands, the wild, eager face, like that of a starving wolf's.' Rather than an anomaly, the figure is representative of the female mine worker. Dr May defines the sculpture as '[a] working-woman—the very type of her class'.[95] Deborah, a female worker, is described in similarly ghastly tones to Hugh's sculpture. We are told that '[t]here was no warmth, no brilliancy, no summer for this woman; so the stupor and vacancy had time to gnaw into her face perpetually. She was young, too, though no one guessed it; so the gnawing was the fiercer.'[96] Deborah, like the sculpture, has been transformed by her environment and the necessities of work.

As I have argued previously, in *Norah Lang* such a dichotomy is resisted. Hocking's balmaidens are ordinary young women, and in so being they counter the typical extremes inherent in the balmaidens' portrayal.[97] These balmaidens are not radically transformed or corrupted by their experience of the mine, either physically, morally, or with regards to their 'proper' role within the home. This is not achieved by disassociating Norah from her role as balmaiden—indeed the novel's subtitle identifies her as a mine worker—but by demonstrating continuity of character and ability within the domestic and work environments. Norah's function within the home, her care for her invalid sister, for instance, subverts the notion that industrial work made women unfit for the domestic sphere. Norah carries out her work at the mine and attends to duties in the home, and she is seen doing both as part of a typical day. For example, though Norah has spent all day at the mine, she brings home meat from Craddock the butcher and sets about cooking the evening meal.[98] That her stepmother had failed to ensure there was any food in the house, or that the fire was lit for Philippa, further highlights Norah's role.

The woman worker exposes, as John argues, 'the dichotomy between the fashionable ideal of womanhood and the necessity and reality of female manual labour'.[99] The reality of female labour is a direct challenge to social constructions of femininity and so the response is to label those workers as immoral and unnatural. This obfuscates the need for their labour, the impossibility of working-class women living up to upper-class ideals, and the artificiality of social constructions of gender against which such workers are being judged. In this context, to normalize balmaidens by portraying them as capable of demanding physical work and domestic tasks, to show them as not representing either extreme of their stereotypical portrayal, is a subversive act. It not only counters the negative judgements hurled at them, but also destabilizes and exposes gender itself as socially constructed.

As seen above, Norah provides continuity between the mine's surface and the home. Whereas in *Deep Down* the mine's surface is analogous with the mine workings below, *Norah Lang* both normalizes women's presence on the mine's surface, equal to the home, and defamiliarizes that surface as a masculine domain. Here, the mine's surface is a place of female interaction. The rather ordinary conversation of the balmaidens while at work are given space to be heard. The scene is not idealized; indeed two of the other balmaidens are vexed by Norah refusing to join their unauthorized breaks.[100] It is also not stereotypically portrayed as bitchy gossip: a range of opinions are aired, many of which are considered and show their knowledge of and understanding for each other, gained over time, in this space.

Inevitably, those in charge on the mine's surface remain male. However, just as the balmaidens are rendered peripheral in other mining texts, in *Norah Lang* it is the Cap'n who remains on the outskirts of the narrative's focus, and as supplementary to it. He is seen talking to another miner, but the reader does not hear him speak. Instead, the focus is given to the unofficial hierarchy amongst the balmaidens, and so Betty takes position within the group as a mature voice of reason and compassion. Although only in a small way, the women succeed in subverting the power of the Cap'n through their unauthorized break. While they are almost caught at rest by the Cap'n when they should have been working, they return to their tasks before he notices their transgression.

In *Norah Lang* there is no focus on female bodies at work. We are told that Norah is 'busy at work' and that they are all on the 'floors'.[101] Later, when the mine captain returns, all girls turn 'hastily to their "recks"', which are described as 'a kind of table on which the tin is cleaned'.[102] Unlike the descriptions of miners' bodies at work in *Deep Down*, the balmaidens' physicality does not define them; rather, these women are created through conversation and interaction with each other. Hocking blinds us to the conditions of their working environment and, significantly, to the dirtiness of their job. Only a reader supplying information from their own knowledge can imagine their undoubtedly ore-stained clothes as they carry out the cleaning of the tin and talk with each other. In doing so Hocking is keeping out of the picture something which would have had negative connotations for Victorian audiences and which may have compromised her sympathetic portrayal of balmaidens. In the nineteenth century there were associations made between female dirtiness—dirt and grime as the result of work—and moral standing. Visual signs of dirt on working-class women, therefore, became a symbol of ills beneath the surface, as well as a disruption of acceptable femininity. As Liz Stanley explains, '[f]or the Victorians, "femininity" demanded "appropriate" behaviours, aptitudes, activities and styles of dress; and failure to display these led to the withdrawal of approbation and so in a sense unsexed a woman. If she failed to achieve femininity she became "not a woman"'. Working women's bodies can therefore be unsexed and simultaneously viewed as oversexed (as in *Germinal* above). In *Norah Lang* the narrative eye is not able to gaze at the bodies of the balmaidens at work, which speaks to the problematics of the cultural meanings attached to women's bodies in the act of physical work.[103]

The opposite, of course, is true for male workers, for whom dirt could be a symbol of hard work, and a symbol of 'working-class difference and working-class power'.[104] Within a Cornish context it is also a symbol of 'industrial prowess': dirt visually indicating the toil and stamina of the Cornish miner.[105] For example, in *Deep Down*, the description of David

Trevarrow discussed above, which focuses on his body at work in the mine, also mentions that 'his colour from top to toe was red as brick-dust, owing to the iron ore around him'.[106] Dirt enhances the status of the Cornish miner—daubs on his body are evidence of toil to successfully extract mineral ore from the bowels of the earth. For a balmaiden to be similarly begrimed endangers her reputation. Balmaidens were likely aware of this, evidenced by the care they took to wear clean aprons to and from work. While at work, though, as in *Norah Lang*, it was impossible not to become visibly stained, and so to also be trapped within the system of signs that takes this innocuous cue as evidence of moral degradation. This helps us to see the basis upon which the commentary of balmaidens, such as that by George Henwood in *The Mining Journal*, could be formed, and why Hocking might try to extract her fictional balmaidens from such a reading, and to emphasize their womanliness through their talk.

Balmaidens' very presence, and in particular the way in which Hocking feminizes the mine's surface, disrupts the continuity of mining as a solely masculine process. It also, therefore, has implications for the 'industrial prowess' identity built upon the heroic masculinity of the Cornish working-class miner.[107] Balmaidens, when present on the page, challenge this identity. They expose the constructedness of gender and the Victorian rules of gender conformity as problematic, for both working-class men and women. Perhaps most interesting is the ways in which balmaidens are being reinterpreted today, through art, literature, and song. Freed from anxieties over their presence and what it signifies, contemporary Cornwall can celebrate balmaidens' incredible strength, in all aspects of the word, and begin to rewrite them back into Cornish culture.

Chapter Two

Beyond England

There are some travellers who think when they cross the Tamar, over that fairy bridge of Brunel's, hung aloft between the blue of the river and the blue of the sky, that they have left England behind them on the eastern shore—that they have entered a new country, almost a new world.

Mary Elizabeth Braddon, *Wyllard's Weird* (1880)[1]

I suppose you took a monthly tourist's ticket at Paddington (wonderfully cheap they are), and 'broke your journey' at Bath. Then you probably stopped at Exeter and Torquay, and, indeed, at so many places, that the Lizard and the Land's End very nearly had to be given up altogether. Somehow you did manage to see both our southernmost and most westerly promontory; and now, with the help of a few photographs and a good deal of make-believe, you can astonish your friends by talking about the Logan and Tol-Pedn and Kynance Cove, as glibly as if you lived within a score of miles of them.

Anon., 'On the Way to the Lizard' in *All the Year Round* (1876)[2]

What is the significance of crossing over the border into Cornwall? Mary Elizabeth Braddon's characterization strongly suggests that to traverse the watery border of the Tamar (which along with the sea on three sides makes Cornwall almost, but not quite, an island) is not to enter another county of England at all, but to cross into another country, one so starkly different to England, that it can be referred to, and is experienced as, another land altogether. In 'On the Way to the Lizard', that sense of difference is also present: in the place names derived from the Cornish language, and in the ability of travellers to astonish their friends with tales of their excursions in the furthest southern and western peninsulas of the British Isles. Such places are mysterious because of their distinctiveness, and so they form the basis of fantastical retellings of the explorers' adventures in Cornwall.

At the same time, however, that sense of difference from England is held in tension with a newly minted understanding of Cornwall as accessible. Cornwall had only been part of the national rail network since Isambard Kingdom Brunel's bridge over the Tamar was completed in 1859. Therefore, while the anonymous contributor to *All the Year Round* notes the many stops en route to Cornwall, that newfound sense of connection between London and Cornwall, along the rail network, is palpable. The travellers do make it to the Lizard, and to the Land's End, and they do so without great expense (in the eyes of the writer at least). Cornwall here is both affordable and accessible to willing tourists, whilst retaining its divergence from England.

Cornwall's relationship to England has always been complex, and open to a variety of interpretations. James Vernon explains that 'Cornwall had always existed on the margins of Englishness, both a county of England and a foreign country'. He goes on to express his interest in 'this ambivalent position in the English imagination, and of England in the Cornish imagination—of the Cornish as English, but not English'.[3] How literary texts exploit the ambiguity of this relationship, and challenge the dominance of an English perspective, is where the alternative Cornwalls are to be found in this chapter. There is not space here to cover all of Cornwall's varied and 'so often contradictory and paradoxical' history, which is so closely tied up with its English neighbour, but it is important to recognize that the trajectory from being its own kingdom to, ostensibly, an English county is not by any means straightforward or, for many, a status that is even now settled.[4] Philip Payton's work demonstrates the shifting nature of that relationship over time: it did not always play out as we might expect. In medieval times,

> [t]he relationship between England and Cornwall, *Anglia et Cornubia* [...] was complex and has yet to be teased out fully. But everywhere there are hints and clues [...] [which] intimate a unique relationship that was close but where Cornish distinctiveness was important, and where, paradoxically, behind the power-nexus of superior and subservient, coloniser and colonised, there was on occasions a sneaking English respect of (and indeed reliance upon) Cornish attributes.

The Duchy of Cornwall was first instituted in 1337 (and remains extant today) for the maintenance of the Heir Apparent to the English throne, an institution which bound Cornwall tightly into the needs and imperatives of the English state and yet at precisely the same moment was a powerful mechanism of constitutional accommodation which allowed Cornwall a considerable degree of political autonomy. Cornwall was therefore [in medieval times] tied closely to the English state but in an important sense was not actually integral to it.[5]

Another constitutional difference was the existence of the Stannaries (Stannary law and the Stannary parliament) which historians think originated with rights awarded to tinners, and which was both linked with the Duchy and a rival to it at different points in history.[6] Tension between Cornwall and England, or indeed at times actual fighting, often came about when Cornwall felt that the uniqueness of its constitutional rights was being eroded through greater encroachment of centralized English control, or when it perceived its cultural uniqueness, such as its own Celtic language, to be similarly under threat.[7] Both of these factors precipitated the Cornish rebellions against the crown in 1497 and 1549. As part of the 1497 rebellion, the pretender to the throne, Perkin Warbeck, was crowned at Bodmin. Cornwall directly challenged the right of the centralized state to rule over it.

In a varied historical record, therefore, Cornwall's relationship to England has rarely been fixed, and in different moments in different centuries, Cornwall has been more in line with central rule, in outright revolt against it, or somewhere in between. These issues are by no means fully resolved today. As Rachel Moseley states, 'Cornwall [...] remains tied to and dependent upon England in a complicated and contested relationship'.[8] Beyond the constitutional aspects discussed above (the Duchy remains; the Stannary is no more, apart from momentary attempts to revive it and its quasi-independent power) is a sense of Cornish difference and Cornish identity which has persisted over time. In the 2021 census almost 100,000 people recorded their nationality as Cornish or Cornish and British, up from 66,000 in the previous census.[9] For many these differences are cultural. For some this will be learning, speaking, and studying a revived Cornish language. For others there remains an imperative for Cornish independence: Mebyon Kernow—The Party for Cornwall has been a feature of the Cornish political landscape since 1951. Others are fighting for devolution in Cornwall similar to that already in place in Wales. In 2014, the Cornish were awarded National Minority Status under the Framework Convention for the Protection of National Minorities (FCPNM), giving Cornish identity the same status as that of the Scots, the Welsh, and the Irish.[10] Therefore, that sense of difference persists, is celebrated, and is now also protected, and it influences Cornwall's relationship to England, and the relationship of Cornishness to Englishness.

Of course, while the relationship to England may be, historically, unique, and while aspects of constitutional difference to other counties do still exist, Cornwall is still treated as a county, and does not in any sense have autonomy from Westminster. To date, the funding promised to Cornwall post-Brexit does not come anywhere near to the EU funding previously accessed by Cornwall. Despite the same status for Cornish identity as other Celtic nations of the UK, through the framework convention (FCPNM), Cornwall does not get to make its own decisions that would help protect that identity, and is largely reliant on the pot luck of sympathetic ministers in Westminster. Colonized further in the past than Ireland, for instance, or Scotland, Cornwall's claim for independence is often forcefully shouted down. Cornwall's size is regularly cited as justification for maintaining the current relationship with centralized power: opponents argue that it is too small for independence or indeed even for devolved powers.

In order to understand further how this relationship plays out, in her book *Picturing Cornwall* Moseley considers Cornwall in relation to Michael Hechter's work on the Celtic fringe, which thinks about England's relationship to those Celtic territories as internal colonization. To understand Cornwall as a colony takes us into the complexities of the relationship between Cornwall and England which the designation of 'county' largely expunges, and enables us to understand why the unequal power relations between these two places cannot solely be explained as the power of central governance of the peripheries, and why the centre must, to some extent, continually reiterate that power. It is for similar reasons that a postcolonial perspective helps to initiate a writing back against, often outsider-derived, stereotypes of place.

However, what has been discussed in this chapter so far about the relationship between England and Cornwall is primarily from an insider perspective, one that accepts Cornish difference, both constitutional and cultural, as incontrovertible. Other perspectives, largely from outside Cornwall, reveal that it remains a contentious topic, and for some a controversial assertion, regardless of Cornwall's history. In 2014, when Storm Brigid severed the railway line between Cornwall and England, temporarily taking Cornwall back to pre-1859, Cornish writer, actor, and comedian Edward Rowe (also known as Kernow King) wrote a piece for the *Guardian* newspaper asserting that '[i]t's England that's cut off from Cornwall, not the other way round' and using the moment to express that 'we've always felt different in Cornwall. […] The majority of us don't feel especially English.'[11] Online, the piece received 953 comments below the line, a high proportion of which were angry replies to this confident assertion of identity. Despite its official protections, to claim a Cornish identity in place of an English one remains very difficult within a wider national context.

Even within contexts where Cornwall might expect to find a sympathetic home, such as with the Celtic nations, Cornwall has, within the period of time under study in this book, not met the criteria for inclusion. Colin H. Williams states that 'over the years […] Cornwall has asserted and has been accepted as one of the six constituent Celtic nations of these isles', which suggests progress from the early twentieth century when activists within Cornwall were attempting to gain acceptance by the Celtic Association.[12] Part of stirrings within Cornwall to embrace a pre-industrial, Celtic Cornwall (which became the Cornish Revival and is contextualized by the wider Celtic Revival of the nineteenth and early twentieth centuries), the Cornish Celticists were rebuffed by some within the Celtic Association because Cornwall did not meet the specific criteria of Celticity, including language, that the association had outlined.[13] Similarly, Alan M. Kent points out that

> for the most part, the very discipline of 'Celtic Studies' has given Cornwall short shrift in the past; either ignoring Cornish literature and culture completely, or else being 'critical' of Cornwall for somehow not offering the kind of mythological or epic literature found in territories such as Wales and Éire. Put simply, Cornwall has been viewed as not being 'Celtic', or not 'Celtic enough', when certain scholars were basing their conceptualisation of what was or was not Celtic on only narrow and restrictive models.[14]

Cornwall's relationship to territories outside itself is, therefore, inherently ambiguous.

This ambiguous position as England-but-not-England is exploited by tourism from the nineteenth century onwards. It is Cornwall's othering through its perceived difference, its foreignness, that provides that thrill for the English visitor, but ultimately, and crucially, it must be a safe thrill. Cornwall is wild, strange, exotic, and Celtic at the same time as it is accessible, English, familiar, and safe. During the nineteenth century, Cornwall attracted many visiting writers, such as Charles Dickens, Algernon Charles Swinburne, Alfred, Lord Tennyson, and Thomas Hardy. This tradition continued into the twentieth century with writers such as Virginia Woolf and D.H. Lawrence. Many wrote about their experiences in diaries, travelogues, or the fiction they were to produce. Cornwall was commonly seen by such visitors as a Celtic 'other'. John Lowerson explains that Cornwall appeals to visitors because it 'offers a peculiar meld of geographical and temporal remoteness, a partially accessible strangeness'.[15] The overriding aim in the way in which Cornwall was promoted was to emphasize Cornwall's difference in an attractive, alluring way for the visitor, while at the same time promoting its accessibility.

The Great Western Railway played an active role in crafting the Cornwall that became familiar to potential tourists from the early twentieth century onwards. Paul Thornton and Philip Payton explain that the Great Western Railway promoted Cornwall as exotic, foreign, and un-English.[16] Chris Thomas asserts that the railways enabled 'new imaginations of territory' and we can see this happening both with regards to how Cornwall's remoteness is perceived post-1859, and the versions of Cornwall that are created around that.[17] Keith Robbins argues that, after the completion of the Brunel bridge, Cornwall managed to 'remain remote yet also become accessible in its remoteness'.[18] Contiguous with but now stretching beyond the collapse of mining, Cornwall was being repackaged in this new phase of burgeoning tourism.

Thomas argues that 'one of the most enduring imagined geographies of Cornwall' centred on the Great Western Railway's promotion of the Cornish Riviera, through which they disseminated a vision of exotic Cornwall. Thomas believes 'the concept has shaped our understanding of Cornwall, both as a place to visit and as a landscape in the mind ever since'. *The Cornish Riviera* was the name of the first express train from Plymouth to Penzance in 1904. A guidebook of the same name, by A.M. Broadley, was published by GWR to coincide with the introduction of its steam-driven namesake, with another book of the same title, this time by S.P.B. Mais, being published in 1928.[19]

The Great Western Railway's most significant medium for their marketing of Cornwall was the poster: a visual representation of place for a metropolitan audience. Thomas calls the construction of Cornwall through such posters the 'domestic exotic' or 'the-other-we-are-comfortable-with'.[20] In the 1907 poster 'See Your Own Country First', the land masses of Italy and Cornwall are positioned side by side with considerable artistic licence at play in the way in which the two places are drawn, so as to invite comparison and emphasize the similarity between the two holiday destinations.[21] A poster designed in about 1925 by Louis Burleigh Bruhl also entitled 'The Cornish Riviera' presents Cornwall to visitors as 'the warmest place in Britain […] a land of legend, superstition and romance, the home of the wild and imaginative'.[22] Here all the aspects of Cornwall it lists are romanticized, yet all are ultimately within reach, and without the hassle of travelling abroad.

In this discussion so far of what it might signify to go beyond the border with England into Cornwall, the possibilities can be divided into insider-derived experience of place and outsider-derived construction of that same place. However, as Payton and Thornton establish, in the early twentieth century, 'there was a high degree of collaboration, sometimes overt, between the Great Western Railway and the Cornish-Celtic Revival in which a significant section of Cornish society colluded in the creation of touristic images of Cornwall'.[23] The Cornish revivalists were seeking to reinvigorate Cornish culture by reaching back to a pre-industrial age. The Great Western Railway was looking to entice customers to Cornwall. A re-emphasis of Cornwall's Celtic and Arthurian heritage was useful to both, and formed the basis of common ground. In this moment, economically viable versions of place within tourism were also of value culturally within a certain section of Cornish society.

Tourist-friendly versions of Cornwall must remain within safe boundaries. In this context, even a sense of wildness or foreignness, used to excite and entice, must ultimately be governable. This is often achieved through a sense of English control of the exotic or Celtic aspects of place, even while Cornwall's difference and un-Englishness is part of its attraction. In contrast, however, there also exist portrayals which can be read as positioning Cornwall geographically and culturally beyond England, and beyond Englishness. Such Cornwalls are unfettered from or defiant of control, or they make visible the impossibility of control. In such versions of place there is a far greater sense of danger, hostility, and instability.

Such texts play with the ambiguity of Cornwall's relationship to England to destabilize the certainty of containment, and to realize the possibility of postcolonial resistance. If we think of Cornwall's positioning as England-but-not-England not simply as two overlapping, simultaneous identities, but rather as a continuum, then, for Cornwall to be wholly 'not England', and its consequences, is always in play.[24] This chapter will firstly explore this premise through a number of crime fiction novels set in Cornwall. Crime fiction narratives can play out in a way which confirms the control of the state, or which registers ungovernability. It will then examine Noel O'Reilly's *Wrecker* (2019), which provides a nuanced counter-narrative to the popular myth of Cornish wrecking, and Daphne du Maurier's *Rule Britannia* (1972), a novel which delineates an overt and specifically Cornish and Celtic resistance to outside control.

Cornwall as Escape

Cornwall has long been seen as a highly suitable site for romantic fiction, or as Ella Westland puts it, as 'the passionate periphery'.[25] The sheer amount of romantic novels set in Cornwall that are published each year is testament to the number of readers who wish to experience Cornwall in this way. The romanticization of the Cornish landscape, particularly beaches, cliffs, and the sea, creates a context in which Cornwall is an appropriate site for romantic storylines to play out.[26]

There is not space here, especially given the vast amounts of this type of literature of Cornwall, to analyse these narratives in detail, but it very quickly becomes evident that romantic fiction regularly constructs Cornwall as a rural idyll to which both female protagonists and readers can escape, and that this is also, therefore, central to the way in which such novels are marketed. For example, Phillipa Ashley's summer romance novel is titled *A Perfect Cornish Escape* (2020), and the book blurb, before anything else, entices us to '[e]scape to Cornwall'. Jenny Kane's novel is similarly titled *A Cornish Escape*. Helen Pollard's *The Little Shop in Cornwall* (2020) is marketed as '[t]he perfect summer holiday escape', and the book blurb for Holly Martin's *Ice Creams at Emerald Cove* (2021) entreats potential readers to '[e]scape to the Cornish coast'. Cornwall is certainly not unique in this respect: other places traditionally viewed as remote perform a similar function, usually in opposition to a metropolitan location where the main character starts her literal and emotional journey.

As Kerstin Fest explains, 'London is destructive, whereas the countryside is presented as a healing site where the heroine's crippled femininity can be restored'.[27] The geographical framework for such stories, then, relies on stereotypical and familiar characterizations of centre versus periphery, and of city versus country. The escape is rarely without some trials and tribulations along the way: secrets to be uncovered or aspects of the life they have left reappearing. Yet, ultimately, everything is most often resolved and Cornwall does indeed provide a safe harbour where not only can healing take place, but true fulfilment, romantically and professionally (there seem to be a high prevalence of little cafés, kitchens and bakeries in more recent publications), is achieved within a beautiful, rural environment.

It is already easy to see, therefore, that such literature is in lockstep with the tourist industry with regards to the versions of Cornwall that are most prevalent, and which are promoted as accessible, for protagonists and readers-cum-holidaymakers. Phrases such as 'perfect escape' are synonymous with the marketing of books and holidays. With more prominent authors, there is sometimes a more overt crossover between the marketing of publications, and of Cornwall as a holiday destination. I have mentioned elsewhere that when Virago Press republished Daphne du Maurier's works in the early 2000s, there were stickers advertising holiday breaks in Cornwall on the front cover.[28] 'Du Maurier country', like the more recently employed 'Poldark country', becomes a shorthand for a limited set of signifiers of place that can even replace the toponym Cornwall.[29] Once these terms are established, they crop up in all kinds of marketing material so that, for instance, Debbie Johnson's novel *Pippa's Cornish Dream* (2015) can be endorsed as '[t]he perfect summer story [...] set in glorious modern-day Poldark country'; Rena George's *The Loveday Mysteries* (2013–22) series are similarly billed as being 'set in Poldark country'. The expectation is that readers will already know the version of Cornwall to which this refers, without any further explanation being needed.

We remain, then, within a safe, familiar, idyllic version of Cornwall. The fact of it being specifically Cornish is important to conveying the romantic version of place, so that 'Cornwall' or 'Cornish' appears in many of the titles, and invented place names are made to sound, sort-of, Cornish. However, this is not a genre that sets up Cornishness as a challenge to Englishness in any way. To do so would disrupt the idyll that the narratives require of Cornwall for their decamped protagonist in search of healing and fulfilment. In many romantic and 'chick-lit' novels, such as those mentioned above, a sense of difference is focused onto contrasting the city with Cornish rurality.

As a final example of everything covered in this section so far, I want to briefly discuss the Rosamunde Pilcher phenomenon in Germany, where 160 dramas for television have been adapted from her oeuvre of romantic novels and short stories set in Cornwall. They remain hugely popular, with new shows being filmed, in the German language, in Cornwall each year. These shows present an uncomplicated Cornwall located within a cosy, nostalgic recent past where Cornwall is read straightforwardly as England, and indeed as the epitome of Englishness. Fittingly, one of the *Guardian* newspaper's articles on this topic is titled 'Escapist Dreams: Why Germans Love TV Romances Set in Cornwall'. In the piece, Michael Smeaton, producer for FFP New Media, who works on four to six Pilcher adaptations per year, puts their success down to the escapism that they provide to German audiences, and because '[t]hey evoke romantic ideas of English traditions that don't exist in Germany'—'[r]ed phone boxes, sheep and cream teas were a must' to sustain a fairy-tale televisual experience that is not encroached upon by the trappings of 'modern life'. The piece refers to the use of 'Pilcher country', yet another toponym for Cornwall derived from romantic fiction and the main draw for the pilgrimages of thousands of German tourists to Cornwall each year, some of whom so fully expect to experience the idealized England served up to them on screen that they are surprised when it is not perpetually sunny.[30] This is the epitome of Cornwall as safe harbour, a place into which to escape *because* it is English and familiar. The next section on crime fiction explores what happens when this construction of place is no longer stable, and can no longer be relied upon to endure, where crossing the border may at first seem like an escape, but where threat is always present.

Cornish Crime Fiction

This is a hideous and a wicked country,
Sloping to hateful sunsets and the end of time,
Hollow with mine-shafts, naked with granite, fanatic
With sorrow.
John Heath-Stubbs, 'To the Mermaid at Zennor' (1922)[31]

John Heath-Stubbs's poem about Cornwall strips it completely of the aesthetic appeal that is so central to romantic fiction and to the promotion of Cornwall by the tourist industry. Here, the landscape itself is laden with dangerous potential. It is also markedly not England, not home, but another country. To return to the England-but-not-England continuum, this is a version of Cornish place that is furthest from the accessible, rural idyll available as an escape destination. This poem catches the spirit of place that is accessed by crime fiction set in Cornwall. Crime fiction has the potential to negate the safe harbour of romantic fiction by exploiting other available versions of place ever-present along the continuum of Cornwall's ambiguous identity. In this respect, Cornish crime fiction is analogous to Cornish Gothic fiction which, as Joan Passey explains, also exploits 'Cornwall's simultaneous differences from and proximity to England—its Englishness and its not-Englishness—to provide a sense of the uncanny threat of the foreigner closer to home than initially thought, or within the home all along'.[32] In crime fiction, the nature of the threat can also be uncanny (as will be seen below), but it is foremost actual and bodily. By utilizing and subverting the rules of the crime fiction genre, in conjunction with the unstable potential of Cornish place, crime fiction can inhabit Cornwall's beyondness, destabilize the constancy of English control of the periphery, and turn escapist fantasies into nightmares.

To date, there is no understanding of Cornish crime fiction as a body of literature within the wider genre of crime fiction, or as part of a context of British, or Scottish, Irish and Welsh fiction of this type. Within Cornish Studies, there has been no study of Cornish crime fiction to date. This is perhaps surprising given the size of the body of extant work, and the fact that, from the nineteenth century onwards, many well-known crime and mystery writers have chosen to set their stories in Cornwall. The list includes Wilkie Collins, Arthur Conan Doyle, Agatha Christie, John le Carré, W.J. Burley, and P.D James. Sherlock Holmes and Hercule Poirot have both been detecting in Cornwall. This section is not intended as a comprehensive survey of Cornish crime fiction, but it does attempt to provide a sense of the different ways in which the genre both uses Cornwall as a location, and defines the nature of Cornwall's status beyond England.

The city has most often been seen as the most appropriate place for crime fiction. One of the most prevalent ways of understanding the city versus the country is as a 'den of vice, chaos, and social disorder'.[33] Crime writers can effectively utilize the city: the nature of urban living en masse, the greater possibility of anonymity, the greater potential for violence, and the dramatic potential in uncovering its 'darker underbelly'.[34] It follows from this characterization of the city as a locus of criminality that, as Lisa Fletcher has pointed out, 'most spatially oriented studies of crime focus on urban settings'.[35]

This is not to say, though, that rural environments are always configured simplistically as safe, nostalgic sites in counterpoint to the city. As the list of writers to have set fiction in Cornwall demonstrates, rural locations have long been used as spaces where criminality is at work. The 'country village whodunit' is a familiar staple on bookshelves and television screens.[36] As a subgenre, cosy crime fiction sometimes makes use, in a similar way to some romance fiction, of the stereotypes of bucolic rurality, which are then dramatically interrupted by horrific crimes. However, this is not the only way in which non-urban locations appear. Stephen Knight emphasizes the connection between rural and urban spaces within crime narratives, the travel outwards from a metropolitan centre that many detectives make in the search for answers. Indeed, it may even be the journey itself which leads to the discovery of a crime. Location is not just backdrop, but rather the relationship between rural and urban space creates meaning. As Knight argues,

> a sense of region, especially provincial against metropolitan, interacts consistently to define the forces at work upon and through the people in the story—including the detective. Place and region as issues and as signs are deep-laid voices of meaning in crime fiction, especially […] when they are apparently most silent.[37]

This section intends to uncover those deep-laid meanings of Cornish place within crime fiction.

If the city is already tagged as a place of sin and vice, then there are also aspects of remoteness, and of Celticity, which feed into a fear of criminality within rural and peripheral locations of Ireland, Scotland, Wales, and Cornwall, and a concomitant understanding of the requirement of the English, the centre, or the state, to exert control, along with a fear of the difficulty of maintaining control. Anne-Marie Kilday, in her work on the history of crime in Scotland, suggests that conceptions of an 'innate primitiveness' of the Scottish people became established over time as a negative stereotype which could be wielded when needed by those with vested interests. She further states that '[c]learly this notion of Scotland as a lawless, uncivilised and savage nation contrasts sharply with the inoffensive tartanry and romanticised shortbread-tin history propounded by elements of the Scottish tourist industry'. Perhaps such contrasting versions of place can exist simultaneously due to the concurrent need to characterize the Scottish people as 'primitive, uncivilised' but also, crucially, as 'easily subjugated'.[38] Such a need suggests that the actual fear is located in the possibility of not maintaining control, something which became manifest in the eighteenth century with the Jacobite rising.

Aspects of this positioning are common to all the Celtic countries and territories, and so there are many resonances here with Cornwall. At the fin de siècle, Matthew Arnold, the Victorian poet and thinker, includes the Cornish alongside the other Celtic territories of Britain (which included Ireland at that time) as the 'diminished remains of this great primitive race'.[39] The oxymoron here is indicative of his view of the Celts as imaginative yet primitive. He is insouciant about any threat of resistance because, according to him, by the second half of the nineteenth century, this race (save the 'insignificant exception' of Brittany) 'belongs to the English empire'.[40] Cornwall's lack of a living language is taken as an indication of its absorption, its 'swallowing up' into an English whole.[41]

Just a few years later, Henry Havelock Ellis, in his piece on 'The Men of Cornwall', aligns Cornishmen with their Celtic cousins, and in doing so registers their difference from the English. Like Arnold, he equates Celticness with primitiveness, and with savagery.[42] Carrying out a physiognomic type assessment, he concludes that Cornishmen 'belong to a lower race'.[43] This positioning suggests a need for control by their 'betters'. Yet Ellis also characterizes the Cornish as possessing an ancient democratic instinct and, because feudalism was not seeded there in the same way as elsewhere, as being 'distinctly averse to […] subordination and unquestioning obedience', specifically to 'social superiors'.[44] Here is the threat of resistance, and indeed criminality, which crystallizes around the construct of Cornwall as 'West Barbary' that is tied to specific aspects of a Cornish Celtic race. As Philip Payton points out, and as discussed earlier in this book, even into the eighteenth and nineteenth centuries '[t]o external observers, Cornwall was still "West Barbary", an unsavoury and potentially dangerous land characterised by wrecking and riot and smuggling'.[45] No amount of tourist-washing can eliminate this threat, and it is this that provides fertile soil for the crime fiction which plays contrasting versions of place off against each other.

The Possibilities of Remoteness

In Emma Stonex's *The Lamplighters* (2021), Cornwall's remoteness, and specifically remoteness created by the sea, is important to the mystery aspect of the narrative, in terms of both causation of events and the difficulty of uncovering what has happened. This is a locked-room mystery: the disappearance without trace of all three lighthouse keepers from the Maiden Rock Lighthouse, a tower built out of a rock in the ocean off Land's End. It is a fictional lighthouse which has a number of real-life Cornish counterparts—including the Longships, Wolf Rock, and Bishop's Rock lighthouses, all also located off Land's End—and close namesakes in the Maidens lighthouses in the North Channel off County Antrim, Northern Ireland. Prefacing the narrative, an author's note explains that the mystery is inspired by the actual unexplained disappearance of three lighthouse keepers from a rock lighthouse in the Outer Hebrides. Remoteness is the key signifier in this novel, beyond any other aspects of place. The text periodically reminds us of the extreme remoteness in which the plot plays out: this is not just the Land's End, but a location beyond it.[46]

Cornwall's remoteness at first seems easily transferable from and to other similarly remote locations and in some ways, it is. Yet the narrative also leans into aspects of remoteness existing in the collective consciousness about Cornwall, in order to heighten the mystery, and to deny the kind of resolution that is inevitable in Agatha Christie's Cornish murder mystery (discussed below). Discussing her choice of location in an interview, *The Lamplighters'* author Emma Stonex confirms that, once she had decided to set the story in a lighthouse, it had to be located off Cornwall. This location makes sense because of the number of lighthouses off Cornwall which act as real-life doubles to her fictional tower, but it is more than that. She recognizes Cornwall as a place 'steeped in sea mythology and rick folklore, [so that] Cornwall and her treacherous offshore reefs are as important characters in *The Lamplighters* as any of the keepers'. She understands that the 'sea towers exist in this in-between space' and so within the narrative, the already existent ways of reading this space imbue the remoteness that is key to the story with malign and mysterious possibilities.[47]

It is primarily the sea which imbues the remote location with aspects that feed the plot, so that this feels like a place where awful or unexplainable events are more likely to take place, therefore opening up a wider range of possibilities for what might have precipitated the men's demise.

When the narrative opens, three lighthouse keepers—Vince, Arthur, and Bill—have been missing for twenty years. As well as the very existence of the lighthouse as an epitaph to the danger of the sea off Land's End, we are kept aware of the threat it poses: that it is 'fickle and unpredictable, and it'll get you if you let it'.[48] The lighthouse keepers can still find beauty in it too but Helen, Arthur's wife, de-romanticizes the sea through her attitude to it. For Helen, when living on the cliff edge looking out across the vast expanse of water, the lighthouse too far in the distance to be discerned, there was too much sea. She felt 'surrounded' by 'a grey thing', a blankness on which nothing happened and which made her feel nothing beyond the sense that she was 'living in a fish bowl'. It is a claustrophobic, monotonous presence, and after Arthur's disappearance, she retreats inland to an urban location.[49]

For the lighthouse keepers, the sea is not such an inert presence as it surrounds them on the rock. It changes colour and temperament, and they are constant witnesses to its unpredictability.[50] As readers, we are aware of the uncanny potential of this environment, and that it might be influencing the mental state and actions of the protagonists. Here, then, it is about a malign influence of the environment, rather than the innate evilness or criminality of a people or individuals. Unable to get off the tower to begin his period of leave, Bill goes mad, imagining visitors to the lighthouse and eventually killing Vince and Arthur, and then himself. This potential in the location is present in the collective cultural consciousness, so that possibilities are opened up for what people think may have happened. Along with the more practical hypotheses, that they killed each other or were kidnapped, are fantastical theories of aliens, pirates, smugglers, ghosts, and sea serpents.[51] Rather than dismissing this conception of place, the novel sustains the possibility both of uncanny forces at work, and of lighthouse life as destabilizing to the mind. Bill describes himself as being 'infected' by the sea.[52] We learn that life on a lighthouse is not a normal state of being, that it 'takes its toll' and that long stretches on the job make it more likely someone will snap. Bill himself tell us that '[t]here are keepers who stay so long on towers they start to hear mermaids'. This adds tension to Bill's log of his days on the tower, especially when the storm keeps him trapped there beyond his release date. In the full flow of his delusion, but constructing his alibi for when he reaches land, he projects onto Arthur, as his patsy, exactly what has happened to him. He expounds: 'Years, Arthur has been living and dying out here on this rock, slowly losing his mind. It was bound to get to a bloke, after all. Couldn't put up with it, sick and tired of it, sick to death of it, the lights, the bloody lights.'[53] This remote, uncanny place breaks Bill in the end. Remoteness also ensures concealment of the truth: what actually happened, whilst known by us who get to eavesdrop on life in the tower, is never accessible to the lighthouse keepers' families, or to investigators. There is no closure here for those who need to know, and therefore no reassurance that the malign properties of this space beyond the land have been vanquished.

Cornwall as a sinister location is used by other crime, mystery, and espionage fiction and this chapter now moves on to discuss Wilkie Collins's *The Dead Secret* (1856) and John le Carré's *The Night Manager* (1993). As Emma Stonex comments in relation to her novel, Cornwall acts as another character.[54] Landscape is rarely inert. Much urban crime fiction looks to uncover the 'festering underbellies' of that space and, as Martin Priestman explains, this is an 'enthralling discovery', because it is the flipside of a touristic version of place that is being revealed.[55] This holds true for rural crime fiction set in Cornwall too, where the underbelly exposed is anti-romantic and anti-escapist, and can define itself in opposition to touristic renderings of the same space. Remoteness is reconfigured as threat and, as we have already seen above, as the potential for secrecy, and the potential to keep nefarious deeds from discovery.

The Dead Secret utilizes the familiar positioning of Cornwall as remote from London. This is the starting point for registering both a sinister sense of difference which masks over the landscape's aesthetic potential, and the location's suitability as a place to bury secrets. The novel emphasizes the geographical remoteness of Porthgenna Tower, the house at the centre of this mystery novel. This is further heightened by the 'unfinished state of the railroad at that time' so that, whilst other places are already more connected thanks to this new mode of transport, at Porthgenna it still takes two days for an answer from London.[56] This sets up a sense of beyondness out of which a more sinister, uncertain portrayal of place can be constructed.

The novel also reverses the familiar understanding of Cornwall as a suitable place for recuperation due to its climate. Mrs Treverton 'thinks the soft air of Cornwall makes her weak' and is ordered by her doctor to 'go away out of this damp, soft Cornwall climate, to where the air is fresh, and dry'.[57] The environment is referred to as wearying multiple times in the novel.[58] Its enervating qualities reveal the negative interaction of the environment with the bodies of the characters, and make visible its malignancy. As in a number of the novels under discussion in this section, the weather and features of the landscape possess a sinister portent which influences events. Dampness, mist, and fog are all signifiers that this is not quite the idyllic safe harbour we have been made to expect. In *The Dead Secret* the dynamics of the relationship between these two versions of place is displayed via weather and landscape so that, often, mist and fog blocks or smothers something that could be beautiful, making it something ugly and also unnerving. For example, Rosamond describes the view from the Myrtle Room at Porthgenna Tower to her blind husband Leonard Frankland as follows: 'Away to the left, there is a peep of white sea and tawny sand quivering in the yellow heat. There are no clouds; there is no blue sky. The mist quenches the brightness of the sunlight, and lets nothing but the fire of it through. There is something threatening in the sky, and the earth seems to know it!'. Similarly, the couple arrive at Porthgenna with 'the booming of the surf sounding threateningly near in the dense obscurity of the fog'. At other times an aesthetic view is allowed to show itself, but the environment's threatening and wearying abilities remain latent.[59]

The dance that the weather performs of smothering over the sun is reflective of the status of the secret at the centre of the mystery. The house is aligned with the outside because it also possesses a sinister potential. Upon entering the Myrtle Room, Rosamond admits to Leonard that 'a certain distrust of the room still clings to me'.[60] This is a suitable reaction for Rosamond to have here because it is within the Myrtle Room that the secret of her parentage (that she is actually the daughter of her mother's servant, Sarah Leeson) has been written down and hidden within a locked drawer. The house has held onto the secret for fifteen years, and it is Rosamond who uncovers the truth of her birth from within it, which puts into jeopardy her and Leonard's right to live there. Cornwall's remoteness, particularly the difficulty of disseminating news, had perhaps suggested that this was a place where secrets might be more permanently kept, yet remoteness is also threatening to those located there. While they get to remain there in the end, the portent of the house, its location, and the environment seem to have always been enabling such a secret to be hidden, whilst continually signalling the possibility of its revelation.

In *The Night Manager*, Jonathan Pine, newly recruited by SIS (Secret Intelligence Service) for an undercover operation to catch the arms dealer

Richard Roper, is sent to a village near Land's End to establish his alias as Jack Linden. From the beginning, then, this is not an escape to Cornwall to discover oneself, as seen above in romantic fiction, but instead to bury one's real self and emerge successfully inhabiting a false identity. Remoteness here provides necessary distance from his former life and actual identity, but both the Cornish people he encounters and the landscape itself refuse to allow anonymity. The moment that Jonathan, now Jack, arrives at Land's End, we are made aware that romantic notions of place are irrelevant here. Instead, this is a 'bleak' landscape open to the elements. He arrives on a day that 'had been sullen and damp' and the narrator draws attention to post mistress 'Mrs Trethewey's granite hedge [which] was hunchbacked from the southwesterly gales'. This hostile landscape is aligned with its inhabitants: '[B]umper stickers in the church car park told strangers to go home.' Jonathan's first encounter is with Mrs Trethewey who, while not as directly hostile as the automotive inscriptions, is by no means an easy mark. Indeed, she is a serious test for the verisimilitude of his cover. Mrs Trethewey is intelligent. She understands that the Cornish are stereotyped as a primitive people, but her assurance only that they are 'not *that* primitive' leaves a latent threat below her conversation with Jonathan. She immediately identifies him as 'a foreigner' and, accurately, as 'another of those migrant English souls who seem almost by gravity to sink further and further westward down the peninsula, trying to escape their secrets and themselves'. She surveils Jonathan intently, his body, his actions, and his words, and she interrogates him about his origins with a directness that is antithetically laced with endearments. Frustratingly, he remains '*elusive* [...]. Like soap in the bath'—yet this initial encounter, and his refusal to talk about himself, is the catalyst for an intelligence-gathering mission by the whole village using 'near-supernatural methods'. In some respects, their hypothesizing about the stranger in their midst actualizes Jack Linden, as his handlers intended, as a ne'er-do-well, but, like Mrs Trethewey above, who senses his very real need to escape himself, they also penetrate his cover to discover his innate goodness.[61] This is a place where he is continually watched and where remoteness never enables anonymity, or the chance to wipe the slate clean and start again from scratch.

However, this hostile environment also functions as a battleground on which he forges his new self for the approaching mission. Similar to *The Dead Secret*, mist, fog and wind, and their changeability are key features of a landscape imbued with dangerous potential.[62] Mist 'sticks to the sash windows like steam', and the wind's eerie stillness means '[a] footstep in the lane snaps like a broken neck'.[63] Warlike imagery invokes the acute hostility of this landscape: the wind 'made the slate roof chatter like an Uzi'. After the storm, Jonathan 'ventured outdoors to wander over last night's battlefield' and that evening he looks up at the night sky to see that '[g]rey bullet holes made a spray-pattern round the moon'.[64] This feels like an appropriate environment in which to stage a murder as part of his cover (so that Richard Roper will think him the kind of criminal worthy of taking into his arms operation). Strangely, though, the hostile environment also nurtures Jonathan, not just in terms of a credible cover, but in forging him into the kind of person capable of undertaking such a dangerous mission. Firstly, the cloaking effect of the mist and fog, and the assistance of the wind, heightens his other senses so that, for instance, when his handlers Leonard Burr and Rob Rooke pay him a visit on a foggy evening, he hears their approach in advance of seeing them, 'because alone on the cliff the close observer had learned to hear sounds in the making'.[65] Although this is an 'apocalyptic landscape' it is also for Jonathan 'the palace of his dreams'. This becomes his home and he does not want to leave it, but he also recognizes that it enables him to 'complete' himself.[66] Therefore, while his 'urge to be assumed into the landscape—hidden in it, buried in it—became almost unbearable', in allowing himself to be subsumed into and influenced by this environment, he also experiences a rebirth of sorts into the man he needs to become. 'The soldier in him was already polishing his boots for the long march towards the worst man in the world', and it is this remote, hostile, dangerous environment which has metamorphosized Jonathan Pine into Jack Linden, who is newly risen from its earth.[67]

The crime, mystery, and espionage novels explored so far in this chapter make use of well-established tropes of Cornwall as a remote location to access aspects of place antithetical to a romanticized, idyllic Cornwall. Such texts are largely accepting of versions of place that are already part of the cultural consciousness, and they play upon our understanding of those tropes to heighten the sense of threat or mystery through an active participation of the location, and of qualities of that environment, with events within the narrative, or even with the bodies and minds of their characters. In recognizing malign, even uncanny, aspects of place, there is an amorphous sense in these novels of something that might challenge the kind of control and containment that is needed when criminal events take place.

Reading the Detectives

This next section thinks about control and containment in a more concrete sense, largely through the role of the detective, whose job it is, of course, to solve the crime, bring criminal entities to justice, and thereby restore order. However, there are detectives in this section, even some very famous ones, who do not straightforwardly fit this by now familiar role; one which our culture is somewhat obsessed with on television, in novels, and in podcasts. We will encounter detectives in this section who are the nodal point of state control, and those who disrupt the very sense of control as something which can be reinstated or maintained. Sometimes both are the case for one character. This section will discuss the following crime fiction novels, and one short story, set in Cornwall: Agatha Christie's *Peril at End House* (1932), Nicola Upson's *Angel with Two Faces* (2009), Arthur Conan Doyle's 'The Adventure of the Devil's Foot' (1910), and Katherine Stansfield's Cornish Mysteries series, *Falling Creatures* (2017), *The Magpie Tree* (2018) and *The Mermaid's Call* (2019).

Peter Messent identifies a number of possible reasons for the increase in popularity of crime fiction, which all pertain to 'our (as readers) contemporary sense of identity and social agency'. He includes in his list 'the relationship accordingly played out between individual autonomy and the power of the state'.[68] In relation to Cornwall, we can layer into analysing this relationship the additional complexity of Cornwall's ambiguous status in relation to the state, and how a sense of beyondness informs our reading of assimilation into, or resistance to, England. Messent goes on to explain that

> one of the most productive ways of thinking about the genre is its relationship to the dominant social system: to the hierarchies, norms, and assumptions of the particular area, country, and historical period it represents, and to the power and authority of the state that ultimately upholds that system. To say this is immediately to recognize here a certain slippage. For, on the one hand I am referring to the internalization of a general set of social norms and values that condition day-to-day lives in any given culture: its generally accepted rights and wrongs, its patterns of social organization, and the relationships between the individual, the family, and the larger community. On the other, any allusion to the power of the state is a reminder of the coercive powers—the police, the secret service,

the justice system, and law—used by a dominant ruling class to discipline the larger social group and to keep anti-social and/or anti-establishment tendencies in check.[69]

Upamanyu Pablo Mukherjee opens his discussion of power dynamics of the state and its people out beyond the national in his study of nineteenth-century crime fiction and empire. Crucially, he connects the two, stating:

> First, that this language of crime or the juridical grew out of an intimate and symbiotic relationship between the colonizing/metropolitan and the colonized societies. We cannot understand why crime and policing assumed a particular importance in a particular way within imperial rhetoric unless we link it to the evolution of this strategy of power within the domestic boundaries of empire. Second, this strategy was necessarily ambiguous, releasing possibilities of dissent in the very moment of its articulation of authority.

This also means linking colonized peoples and domestic citizens, and he argues that 'the clearest connection between the colonized and the domestic oppressed […] is […] to be found in the signs of criminality attached to them'.[70] This is a useful framework, a way in to further understanding Cornwall as both domestic and colonized, and how this impacts the ways in which we might read the significances of strategies of power and resistance in Cornish crime fiction.

In Agatha Christie's *Peril at End House*, Hercule Poirot, one of literature's most famous detectives, visits Cornwall on holiday. Cornwall as a place is drawn in with a light touch. The novel makes use of Cornwall's peripherality to enhance aspects of the narrative specific to the crime and mystery genre, but refrains from interrogating Cornwall as a location for crime fiction, or the stereotypes of place that exist in relation to Cornwall. Elizabeth Leane in 'Unstable Places and Generic Spaces' talks of 'anywhere' locations:

> Icescapes, deserts, jungles, islands, oceans [where] –it does seem that the action could indeed be happening anywhere'. Crucially, though, '[t]hese "anywhere" settings, […] have something obvious in common: in the popular imagination, they signify remoteness, isolation, wilderness, excitement, and danger.[71]

The epithets for the anywhere places Leane identifies have all also been used elsewhere in relation to Cornwall. In some crime fiction, Cornwall is not quite as generic as an anywhere place, but its primary function is as a remote location that sits beyond, or at the furthest reaches of, England.

In *Peril at End House*, the remote location is cited in the name of the house at the centre of the mystery, and also, therefore, in the title. Yet it is always a remoteness that is kept within safe bounds, achieved through stressing the Englishness of the location at the same time as its peripherality, and through meta devices around the conventions of crime fiction. Poirot and Captain Hastings are sojourning at The Majestic Hotel in St Loo when they come to the aid of Magdala Buckley, known as Nick, whom Poirot thinks someone is trying to kill. There follows a succession of possible culprits from her friends and acquaintances, Nick's own death (a ruse at Poirot's behest for her own safety), the murder of her cousin Maggie, also called Magdala Buckley, Nick's Banquo-esque performance at End House in an attempt to expose the offender, faked wills and, eventually, the revelation that Nick has been the guilty party all along, murdering her cousin in an attempt to inherit Maggie's dead fiancé's vast wealth.

The opening pages of the novel gently register a foreignness through Poirot's equation of St Loo with the French Riviera, which is confirmed by the presence of palm trees and the colour of the sea as 'a deep and lovely blue'. Yet this is not a journey into another country for Poirot and Hastings. Cornwall is the best of England in its differences, rather than un-English. For example, in Hastings' opening narration he declares that '[n]o seaside town in the south of England is […] as attractive as St Loo'. Similarly, the sun is shining 'with all the single-hearted fervour an August sun should (but in England so often does not) have'.[72] Cornwall is part of England here, but a delightful, even exotic, example. This positioning is sustained throughout the novel. When Maggie is murdered, this is not a confirmation of Cornwall's potential as a site for criminality—in fact, just the opposite. Mrs Croft cannot believe this has happened: '[a]nd no lawless wild part of the world either. Right here in the heart of the old country'.[73] Mrs Croft is Australian and so the reference here to old country suggests she is referring to England. There is no indication here that she is of Cornish descent and that this refers to Cornwall as its own country. Rather, in being part of England, available understandings of Cornwall as wild or lawless are contrary, rather than apposite.

The positioning of Cornwall as England also means that certain qualities of the location connected to its beyondness do not challenge the 'rules' of detective fiction. Indeed, readers are reassured as the plot unfurls that this mystery will play out as we have come to expect: Poirot will discover the truth and all loose ends will be neatly tied at the story's conclusion. This is achieved due to our familiarity with this genre, but also by the metaness of the characters' interpretation of their situation. There are many instances of the characters expressing incredulity at events taking place by contrasting their reality with what happens in crime fiction. For example, Nick denies she can be the target of multiple assassination attempts because 'that sort of thing doesn't really happen. Only in books' and she is 'not the beautiful young heiress whose death releases millions'.[74] In jest, prior to being introduced, Nick addresses Hastings as Dr Watson, and, in admitting that he has entertained 'absurd suppositions' in attempting to find a motive for targeting Nick, Poirot fears he has 'adopted the mentality of the cheap thriller'.[75] These meta crime fiction references are expressed by the characters within this plot to distance what is happening to them from what happens in novels. However, for us as readers, it has the exact opposite effect: it reminds us that we are reading a novel that is part of a genre with distinct conventions. It reminds us what those conventions are, and in doing so, it reassures us that some kind of resolution will be present in the final pages. Crucially, though, the resolution does not involve the state's apparatus of justice; rather, Poirot, in full knowledge that Nick intends to kill herself, lets her go, judging it to be '[b]etter than the hangman's rope'.[76] He personally remains in control of seeing justice done here. This moment makes us aware of the additional latitude he has as a private detective: he can adhere to his own code of justice rather than that of nation states.

Resolutions of a sort are also forthcoming in Nicola Upson's Cornish crime novel *Angel with Two Faces*, but they bear a yet more complicated relationship to official justice. By the end of the narrative, all secrets are revealed, but no one involved faces prosecution. In this book set in the 1930s, the second in the series of Josephine Tey mysteries, Inspector Archie Penrose invites Josephine to his family's estate near Penzance for a holiday. Yet he is quickly burdened with unravelling a complex web of death and dark secrets, which involves his own family and friends, and the estate's workers. The story opens with the funeral of young Harry Pinching who is thought to have drowned himself in the lake by riding his beloved horse Shilling into the water. Later, Nathaniel Shoebridge is pushed off the cliff at the Minack Theatre, by Harry it turns out, who had faked his own death after murdering a stranger in a brawl. Harry's motive was, wrongly, believing that his twin sister Morwenna had been told by Nathaniel that Harry was sleeping with his other, younger sister Loveday. In fact, this is not the case; Nathaniel had known that Harry had set the fire that killed his own parents, but he had not known of Morwenna and Harry's incestuous relationship that had prompted him to do so, and he had not made up a lie about Harry and Loveday. In the course of events, Archie's own mother's sexual abuse at the hands of her brother is also revealed. In the middle of all the action, orchestrating her community's lives is Morveth, a creator and keeper of secrets, who sees herself as a kind of healer, and who tests Archie's dual responsibilities as part of this community, and as an instrument of the law.

In the opening pages of the novel, Cornwall is positioned as different from England, and as simultaneously subject to, and contained by, its connection to it. The distance required to travel to reach Penzance is registered when Josephine gets off the *Cornish Riviera Express* 'at the end of the line'. She is excited by the notion of 'getting as far away as you can' and, to her, '[t]he sound of Land's End had a distant, far-away feel which appealed to her fascination for foreign travel'. At the same time, this distance is mitigated by the sense of connection provided by the railway line Josephine has just travelled along, which provides ease of access to Cornwall for Londoners and others. Archie's cousin Ronnie bemoans the colonization of Newlyn by artists, so that, '[n]ow you can't move for easels clogging up the street and people in smocks trying to capture the "Newlyn style"'. While people flow down to the end of the line, goods (in the form of flowers from the Isles of Scilly) are transported in the opposite direction, making 'Penzance into a suburb of Covent Garden'.[77] Cornwall is contained here by being locked into a supply relationship with the rest of England, tied via the railway, and acting as both its riviera and its conservatory—and in both senses of the word: as cultivator of plants, and as a place where a way of life, from an outside perspective at least, is preserved.

The events at Archie's family estate, though, continually challenge a sense of control or containment at a state level, even with Archie Penrose, Inspector of Scotland Yard, on the scene. At first, Archie seems well placed to investigate events on his family's estate. As Carol Baraniuk says of Brian McGilloway's Irish detective, Benedict Devlin, '[h]is advantage is his native local knowledge'.[78] Archie's understanding of the place and its people is emphasized through contrast with Josephine, who looks at Cornwall, initially at least, through a touristic lens. She is 'surprised at how un-English everything seemed', finds it 'idyllic' and echoes an orientalist viewpoint when she assumes that 'daily life in this part of Cornwall […] had probably not changed very much in three hundred years'.[79] Fixing Cornish life in an ever-present past is a familiar romantic construct of peripheral and rural place in general, and of Cornwall specifically. Josephine, therefore, finds the beauty of the Loe Estate incongruous with her plan to work on her next murder mystery. Archie tries to complicate this stereotypical and simplistic vision of Cornwall, explaining that tensions exist below the surface here, but because she finds it such an idyllic place, even then, she continues to believe that this 'seemed to be that rare sort of place which encouraged the illusion that certain corners of England might never again be touched by conflict, the sort of place where a personal life undisturbed by politics might still be possible—and for that, she blessed it'.[80] She may have some awareness of it being an illusion here, but it is still one that is powerful enough to prevent her from engaging with Archie's more realistic version of the exact same place.

Archie's perception of and relationship to Cornwall is far more complex, and it means he is able to recognize both change and nuance. It is a synthesized perspective, combining his local knowledge and the viewpoint enabled by his time away. Where Josephine assumes stasis, Archie laments the tensions now present in a previously peaceful community.[81] He understands that, like London, Cornwall too has a dark underbelly, even if it is initially 'masked' by its beauty, and he intuits that this is because of 'the close proximity to death in which the people lived their lives here'.[82] His lived experience of the realities of rural life means he skewers as fiction the romanticized, cosy country cottage he so often sees hung on the walls of aspirational Londoners.[83] In contrast with Josephine's more straightforward romanticizing of her holiday location, when Archie is alone with Nathaniel's body on the cliff edge at the Minack, having been lowered down to him on a rope, he is aware of the overwhelming, 'elemental power of the sea' and its potential to shape Cornish people, including himself. We are told that 'Penrose found it hard not to resort to an age-old language of good and evil, to look for the imprint of the devil himself in Nathaniel's eyes'.[84] This moment indicates Archie's level of engagement with this place, but it also demonstrates the kind of challenge it mounts to the rational policeman inside of him.

As the devastating secrets are unravelled, because of his position as part of the community, Archie is increasingly compromised as an officer of the law, as someone entrusted with ensuring the application of justice on behalf of the state. Through Archie we see the difficulty of applying London-made law in Cornwall, and therefore, ultimately, the impossibility of containing criminality in the way that Archie's role and previous experiences as an inspector might suggest is possible. Ronnie informs Josephine that both Archie, and the law that he represents, are an awkward fit for Cornwall. She explains that 'Archie fits in rather uncomfortably—he's not the boss, but he's not one of the workers either. And of course a Cambridge education and a job at the Yard haven't helped bridge the gap. The law down here is very much a subjective thing, and something to be worked out privately.'[85] This is not a lawless place, but one where an informal kind of law, applied and agreed internally by the community, is at work.

Discussing literary detectives, Laura Marcus explains that '[w]here [Walter] Benjamin [...] blurs the distinction between pursuer and pursued, detective and criminal (a blurring which 'postmodernist' detective fiction will exploit to the limit), [G.K.] Chesterton places them on either side of the divide between civilisation and barbarism'.[86] The divide here is certainly blurred by Archie's role as both detective and community member, whose family's lives, and actions, are interwoven with those that he needs to pursue. Despite his 'uncomfortable' fit with his place of birth, Archie still sees himself as a Cornishman. En route with Constable Trew to interview Jago Snipe, he dismisses Trew's assertion that, because he is an undertaker, Snipe would no doubt tell them the truth. Archie retorts, '[h]e's a Cornishman, Trew, and what was it someone said about us? Beware the fluency of the Celts—it makes their lies more convincing than a Saxon truth.'[87] Even though the assertion here about Celts is a negative one, and one which speaks to how an internal law operates here as Ronnie mentions above, Archie speaks of 'us' not 'them', thus rejecting a straightforward divide between himself and the man he is about to interview.

The awkward position that Archie occupies muddies his ability both to uncover information, and to apply the law to those who have committed criminal acts. It is Josephine, rather than Archie, to whom people confide their secrets, which marks both her evolution from naive outsider and the extent to which he is compromised. For example, Morveth tells her about Jasper's past abuse of Archie's mother, and, when Archie finally learns the awful truth, he is shocked that Josephine was already privy to this closely kept family secret.[88] Yet he is too close to the events unfolding on the estate. People try to protect him by keeping information from him, but, because those events are so entangled with the lives of those who have committed criminal acts, it infringes upon his ability to fulfil his role as an officer of the law.

His own personal relationships with those responsible for the web of secrets and criminal acts also compromises his willingness to apply the law. This is most obviously the case with Morveth, who is at the heart of everything that happens within this community, as a midwife, healer, and confidante. More than anyone else, she operates her own subjective law of the type that Ronnie refers to above. Through rigorous secrecy, she keeps her actions and those of others private from the outside world, and from state law. For instance, she knows about Morwenna and Harry's incestuous relationship, and that he set the fire that killed his parents. She decides not to send him away because there would be no one to support Morwenna and their younger sister Loveday. Through her work at the Union, she gives Jago Snipe a young boy, Christopher, to raise after his wife and daughter die. Christopher has been given up by Joseph Caplin, and neither of the men know what Morveth has done. She bumps into Harry on the coastal path shortly after he has murdered the stranger. She cleans him up and advises him to run away.[89] She suspects he may have faked his own death by putting the stranger's body into the lake, and that he may have killed Nathaniel at the Minack.[90] Going to the law with this vital information is something Morveth would never do, and she only reveals it to Archie when he goes to her, and she is left with no other choice.

Archie, then, is left stuck between his community loyalties, and his responsibilities as an officer of the law representing the state. Ultimately, he becomes part of the system of secrecy operating within the community at the expense of state justice. In the name of friendship, he tells Morveth that he will not ask her if she did anything to bring on Loveday's miscarriage.[91] Yet while he pointedly tells her, in a direct articulation of his responsibility to enforce the law, that if she destroyed evidence of Harry's presence at the Minack (where he killed Nathaniel) it's '*not* something I can turn a blind eye to', her immediate confession elicits no arrest.[92] Indeed Morveth, operating in opposition to the law with her own informal system of secrets and solutions, is still walking free at the end of the novel. Harry, like Nick in *Peril at End House*, punishes himself by committing suicide. Events in this insular, secretive community are not containable by the law, even when one of its representatives belongs at its heart. What is therefore exposed is the inability of the state to apply justice in the form that it would wish in all corners of the nation.

In Arthur Conan Doyle's short story 'The Adventure of the Devil's Foot', the impossibility of containing criminality goes beyond the domestic, beyond national borders, to include parts of Africa as territories of the British Empire. It is in this context that Cornwall's ambiguous identity as England-but-not-England, but also as colonized and colonizer, is most palpable, and most problematic to British authority. Like Poirot and Hastings above, Sherlock Holmes and Dr Watson travel to Cornwall for leisure, as 'health tourists', but, inevitably, an incomprehensible crime occurs during their stay which they are called upon to investigate.[93] Siblings Owen, George, and Brenda Tregennis have been found dead, still sat around a table at which they had been playing cards, their bodies petrified in a 'very paroxysm of fear'.[94] As in many of the crime novels discussed in this chapter so far, and as Joan Passey points out, when '[a] terrible crime falls at their feet, [...] Cornwall is revealed to be even more barbarous than the city, its romantic beauties nothing more than a façade'.[95] This horrific crime (indeed, it comes to be known in the London press as the Cornish Horror) flips Cornwall from safe harbour to threatening periphery, exposing the instability of Cornish place, and the ambiguity of its Cornish actors.[96]

In order to understand what the implications are here for the policing of criminality, it is important to first establish how the paradoxical positioning of Cornish place, and its people, plays out in Conan Doyle's short story. As Passey has already pointed out, in addition to the health benefits of the Cornish air, Holmes and Watson are tourists of Cornwall's difference, looking for a mysterious Cornish Celticity in a palimpsestic landscape which they feel provides them with access to an ancient past.[97] Shelley Trower argues that 'Watson goes on to describe Cornwall as though it is not quite part of the modern nation' and that its construction here as 'un-English or foreign, [...] paves the way for the further leap into Africa' (we learn that the victims have been poisoned by their brother, Mortimer Tregennis, using devil's-foot root, stolen from Dr Leon Sterndale, who had brought it back from his explorations in Africa).[98] This English–foreign duality is extended to Sterndale who, in love with Brenda Tregennis for many years, enacts revenge on Mortimer Tregennis for her death, using the same poison. As Trower states, he is both an English gentleman explorer and as threatening as the Cornish landscape, which is registered in the animality of his forename, and his Cornishness. As Trower concludes, '[t]his dual possibility of identifying both with and against the Cornish in these stories reflects how Cornwall was perceived as foreign while at the same time being part of England'.[99]

Through Sterndale, Cornwall is also, therefore, seen to be part of the British imperialist project at the same time it is aligned with colonized Africa through its foreignness, and its Celticity (which, as discussed above, is identified with primitiveness and a potential for savagery). Cornwall is simultaneously colonizer and colonized here, and through this we can see how Cornish place (and by extension its people) exists simultaneously within the narrative as two opposing versions of itself. We can track this through mapping the acquisition and transportation of different kinds of resource within the story. Cornwall's utilization as a holiday destination, as a site being used by Holmes specifically to inhale its clean air to improve his health, is an example of outsiders infiltrating Cornwall, as an internal colony we might say, to make use of its natural resources.[100] Although the murders interrupt their plans, the archaeological interest Holmes takes in Cornwall demonstrates a desire for knowledge, but one which is gained by digging artefacts of Cornwall's ancient past up out of the ground.[101] Similarly, we learn that Mortimer Tregennis's motive for murdering his siblings is linked to the division of profits from the family's tin-mining venture at Redruth.[102] Although this is a Cornish family profiting from Cornish natural resources, we know that this is not always the case, either within Cornwall (indeed, who is the company to whom the family have sold their concern?) or within territories of the British Empire with which Cornwall has already been aligned.

Cornwall is also seen to be simultaneously both remote (Holmes and Watson are sojourning 'at the further extremity of the Cornish peninsula') and physically connected with Africa, along routes of passage taken by the explorer Sterndale.[103] Mortimer Tregennis tries to cover his tracks by suggesting 'devilish' causes for his siblings' deaths, relying on an already established cultural construction of Cornish place as one where supernatural occurrences are possible. Holmes dismisses this, looking for a practical solution, and once it is revealed that the poison has been transported to Cornwall from Africa by Sterndale, we see through it, and him, the network which enables the flow of British people to colonized territories, and the importation of resources from there to the British mainland.[104] Through Sterndale, Cornwall is very much an active part of that network, but also, because of its sea-fringed remoteness, its peninsularity, which the story emphasizes, it is not remote in the context of foreign travel, but is conveniently located for Sterndale's voyages by boat between Cornwall (via Plymouth) and Africa.[105] At the same time, the foreign poison both he and Mortimer Tregennis use to commit murder, although released by their hands, reverse colonizes the bodies of its victims. In addition, Trower explains, 'the mist or cloud [of the airborne poison] […] transcends national borders, invades and overpowers the domestic space, and threatens the lives of several people including the English hero Holmes himself' (who experiments with the poison and almost dies).[106] Cornwall, therefore, is always its own contradiction in this narrative: remote and globally connected, England and not England, colonizer and colonized, threat and health retreat.

That these characteristics of Cornish place always also entail their opposite destabilizes the construction of place in the narrative. This has implications for British authority, both domestically and by extension abroad. The poison cannot be contained, but equally, the law does not operate as expected, and nor do those tasked to uphold it. When Leon Sterndale is directly challenged by Holmes about the murder of Mortimer Tregennis, Sterndale warns him of the physical threat he now poses to Holmes himself because he has 'lived so long among savages and beyond the law' that he is now a law unto himself.[107] As Trower and others point out, this is a familiar characterization of explorers as having gone native.[108] Yet at the same time, there is a specifically English context here in terms of the operation of the law and its failure to ensure compliant subjects of the state. Sterndale's murder of Mortimer Tregennis was revenge for his murder of Brenda Tregennis, with whom Sterndale was in love. They were never able to marry because of what he calls 'the deplorable laws of England' which prevented him from getting a divorce.[109] Therefore, he is already primed to be contemptuous of the laws of his own nation. With Mortimer, he usurps the roles of both 'judge and executioner' rather than seek state-sanctioned justice.[110] Meanwhile, and perhaps surprisingly, prompted by sympathy for Sterndale's loss, Holmes steps back from ensuring the application of the law in relation to Sterndale's act of homicide. Although Holmes has never been an instrument of the British state he has, like Poirot, often assisted them to uncover criminal perpetrators in order to bring them to justice. In this moment, in this place (does it have anything to do, we might ask, with his perception of Cornwall's remoteness and difference?) he declares his investigation, and his actions upon the discovery of Sterndale's guilt, 'independent' and he allows Sterndale to return to Africa to continue his work without any form of punishment for his crime.[111] Here, both detective and criminal are a law unto themselves, and the state fails to extend its power into the furthest reaches of Cornwall, being simply dismissed by them both.

This has implications too for Britain's status as a colonial power. As already discussed above, both the previously colonized Cornwall and Africa can be aligned here as similar spaces, at the same time as Cornwall is also positioned as part of Britain. Mukherjee asks, '[c]ould the fictions of crime effect any meaningful interrogation of the ideology of British colonial authority?'. He goes on to argue that, within the English novel, the 'rhetoric of crime […], even as it came to play a central role in the construction of authority at home and abroad, […] could also provide an opportunity to interrogate the very premiss of that authority'.[112] Here, the failure of state control within Cornwall has already been established, and this can be coupled with the reverse colonization on British soil via the poison which Sterndale uses because he knows 'how powerless European science would be to detect it'.[113] Both Britain's domestic control and its imperial power are therefore put into question by the events which take place within 'The Adventure of the Devil's Foot'. Yet this is further complicated by Sterndale, as a Cornish subject unprepared to uphold English law, and who secretively smuggles the deadly poison onto British soil; his going native is representative of the failure of domestic control of the Celtic periphery as much as anything else, suggesting both the impossibility of control of colonial subjects abroad *and*, crucially, the unreliability of British citizens to act as representatives of imperial power in colonial territories. Therefore, the extension of state power, both at home and abroad, is compromised because containment of criminality is revealed to be impossible.

The final novels in this section on detectives are from Katherine Stansfield's Cornish Mysteries series. The three novels to date, *Falling Creatures*, *The Magpie Tree*, and *The Mermaid's Call*, cover three cases investigated by a female detective duo. The first case is an embellishment of the real-life murder of Charlotte Dymond on Bodmin Moor in 1844. It is here that those doing the investigating are themselves the furthest away from the state, and from assisting in any kind of official proceedings of justice. Truth is accessed differently here, in a way which has little to do with the law, is wholly internal to Cornwall, and cannot be replicated by outsiders. Anna Drake and Shilly (real name Charlotte but so nicknamed for her shilly-shallying at her farm work) are themselves social outcasts. Due to her gender, Anna has been rejected by Scotland Yard, and so plans to start her own detective agency in Cornwall. Poor, working class, and illiterate, and with an overfondness for drink, Shilly has been sold by her father to labour at a farm on Bodmin Moor. Shilly is aware that she is doubly minoritized by both her class and her gender, while she must also keep hidden her homosexual relationships, first with Charlotte Dymond, and after with Anna.[114]

With little social currency between them, Anna teaches Shilly how to craft false selves to give them the social access that they need to ask questions and uncover truths.[115] There are a range of characters 'fashioned from wigs and paints, and clothes with padding sewn inside to give […] new bodies'. Sometimes, this involves cross-dressing to pass as men because 'it was men who had the keys and decided who should pass'.[116] At other times, they pose as the heterosexual couple Mr and Mrs Williams, and as women and men of a higher social status, or as characters who have backstories that give them the confidence and agency they need to assume the role of detective. They are good at adapting their disguises to the situations in which they find themselves, and what they need to achieve, but we are aware that they can never be themselves, and must always assume some form of disguise to give them a cachet that their own, real, outcast selves cannot provide. Even when they both present to a potential client as women, as in *The Magpie Tree*, they craft a more palatable version of femininity, 'for show' and to foster the confidence, in both themselves and their audience, that they need. Anna introduces herself to Sir Vivian, a potential client, without using one of her pseudonyms, but she dresses in clothes which project wealth, and covers her cropped fair hair with a styled dark wig, so that Shilly suspects this is just another 'false self'. Shilly, too, is boosted by Mrs Williams's long red curls and make-up, taking her a long way from her actual self, and enabling her to become this widow who 'knows her own mind'.[117]

We can see why crafting such characters is vital. In *The Mermaid's Call*, the third novel, Captain Ians, calling upon Williams and Williams Investigations, is surprised to find that they are women (the advertisement of their services had provided no clue). Both Shilly, here playing Mrs Williams, and Miss Drake, as Anna introduces herself because she is not currently wearing any disguise, are quick to assure him that their sex, far from impeding their work, means that they 'are often able to move more easily than men, to pass in plain sight, for we are ignored, *dismissed*'. Shilly tells him that '[i]f someone doesn't see *us*, we see *them* all the better', but they also reassure him that they have ways of making themselves seen (and we can assume that they mean passing as men here). This sounds like the ideal kind of flexibility for a detective agency, yet we are also made aware that this response from Captain Ians is a familiar hurdle. Anna struggles to hide her anger here because she is once again encountering the sexism that drove her from London. Shilly reminds us of what is at stake: that securing work from men such as Captain Ians is what kept them 'safe from having to turn to men for our keep'.[118] We are aware, therefore, of the unusualness of what they are trying to do, its difficulties, and that, regardless of their temporary disguises, it continues to position them as social anomalies.

Whilst Shilly may be a social outcast in relation to cultural orthodoxies of gender, class, and sexuality, she is aligned with the supernatural. What she says above about seeing is particularly relevant to her because of her strange abilities. For Shilly, the veil between this world and that of ghosts and other supernatural creatures is a thin one, so that she can see, feel, and understand what Anna cannot. With Shilly lacking in life experience (she has never seen the sea, for instance, until they travel to Boscastle in *The Magpie Tree*), this is an instinctual knowledge.[119] She is illiterate in the conventional sense, but hers is a literacy of a different kind, one which is central to accessing truth in these mystery novels. Shilly sees her role as helping Anna 'with the in between' through skills which she understands as 'a kind of knowing. My kind'.[120] She is, therefore, clear about what she brings to their detecting partnership. She explains to the reader:

> Anna had asked me to work with her for I could see the parts of the world she couldn't. The parts that were hard to see for they had to be looked at askance. They were dark and strange, rooted deep in the earth where by rights they should remain. They were long ago deaths and deaths still to come. They were devils and unquiet souls. Where Anna saw the cuts a knife made in a young girl's throat, could tell the kind of knife it was, I felt the dead girl's anger like a hot brand on my own breast. When Anna saw things that could be touched and smelt, I saw beneath them.[121]

Supernatural agencies are not the cause of the crime here—they are the route to uncovering the truth, for which we need Shilly as our interpreter.

For example, in *Falling Creatures* Charlotte Dymond's murderer is discovered through a combination of traditional detective work, and Shilly's supernatural connection to her after her death. Daniel Carwitham's confession is compelled by Charlotte's ghostly presence in the room, which he cannot see or feel himself, but for which Shilly acts as intermediary. She 'could feel her close to me [...] could taste her blood' and the immediacy of this, fuelling his terror and remorse, leads him to speak the truth.[122] Shilly's abilities, and the way in which they enable the discovery of the truth, 'resist "the linear logic of clue added to clue", and challenge "normative Western conceptions of knowledge"' in detective fiction.[123] This is an unusual brand of detecting which plays by none of the rules with which we are familiar.

Shilly's kind of knowledge is tied to her Cornishness and embedded with her intimate relationship to the landscapes in which these stories play out, which on the surface seem to be simply hostile. For example, in *The Magpie Tree*, Anna and Shilly are tasked with investigating the disappearance of a young boy in ancient woodland surrounding Saint Nectan's Glen. The wood is anthropomorphized by its inhabitants, and by Shilly. Mrs Haskell warns that '[t]he woods are troubled', and Shilly knows that '[t]he trees put forth malice like other, more ordinary plants would put forth buds'.[124] Anna's lack of seeing or feeling in the right way is accentuated in this environment; she 'didn't feel the woods' strangeness' and she mocks Shilly's presentiments as superstition, looking instead to rationalize unexplainable events that befall them and others in the woods.[125] Yet this world requires an embrace of the irrational, of the supernatural, and it is partly Shilly's Cornishness which brings her affinity with both the wood and its inhabitants. When Mrs Haskell starts to tell Shilly about the sacred Magpie Tree, and the mysterious happenings when people cut it down, Shilly is glad that Anna is not present because '[s]he had no heart for the ways of the people of my country'. While Anna has dismissed Shilly's knowledge here, Mrs Haskell recognizes her wisdom.[126] It is a wisdom that enables Shilly to instinctually believe what to Anna is simply ludicrous, and so arrive at the correct understanding that, in the woods, the women have the ability to turn into birds, the tips of the feathers pushing out through their skin.[127] It is Mrs Haskell, in her changed form, who has murdered one of the German women whom the community suspected of taking the boy (it turns out that it is actually the squire who has taken him). Without Shilly's understanding, this revelation of the truth would not be possible. Neither would Shilly's rescue of Mathilde (the surviving German woman living in the woods) have been possible without her ability to commune with the ancient woodland environment. At the story's denouement, the squire tries to murder Mathilde (who is his daughter, it turns out) in the river by the waterfall. To get to her in time Shilly communicates with the wood, lightly touching the trunks as they run past and 'speaking in a soundless tongue' that Mrs Haskell had also used, for the trees to '[t]*ake us to her*'. She can still feel the wood's anger, but she chooses not to shrink from it and consequently Shilly tells us that '[t]he roots made way for us. The path stayed true for us.'[128] She knows that this is something she could never fully explain to Anna. Shilly had previously thought she needed to be in drink for her powers to manifest, but here we see that she can harness her intimate relationship with the place and its people when it is most needed.

Shilly's supernatural affinities, and those of the Cornish people and places she communes with, is a knowledge which resists outside intervention, and which is unintelligible to and uncontainable by outside authority (and more definitively so here than in any of the other detective narratives we have discussed in this chapter).[129] Anna cannot learn how to see like Shilly, she can never fully understand it, but she does in the next novel come to be more accepting of its necessity to detecting in Cornwall. Peripheral locations like Cornwall are often seen as places where the potential for supernatural occurrence is greater, through a palimpsestic landscape (see du Maurier's *Jamaica Inn*, for instance, discussed in the final chapter) and through ancient customs and traditions. From the outside, the frisson of danger such versions of place provide are laced with the inability to keep control. Shilly's is an insider knowledge, a language that can harness the power of the supernatural in a way which will never be decipherable to outsiders.

Barbarity

Set around ten years after the Napoleonic Wars (1803–15), Noel O'Reilly's *Wrecker* is not a crime novel, but at the centre of the narrative is a shipwrecked body of a woman, washed up on the beach of Porthmorvoren Cove, whose earlobes have been chewed away in order to pilfer her earrings. Significantly though, this is not a novel which recreates popular myths about Cornish barbarity and wrecking. Instead, it produces a nuanced portrayal of a community which undertakes wrecking activities; it interrogates what is classed as criminal behaviour, and the discriminate ways in which this applies to the upper and lower classes. In this story everyone is flawed, no matter what class they come from, but what is revealed is the hypocrisy of the 'bettermost' and their religiosity, which fuels a zeal to reform 'the country people'.[130]

Our place in the narrative is alongside Mary Blight, a young working-class member of the Porthmorvoren community, who works whatever manual jobs she can—packing pilchards, mending fisherman's nets, 'smashing lode-stuff' as a balmaiden—in order to survive.[131] She steals the boots of the cannibalized woman before realizing what has been done to her ears by someone else. Consequently, Mary is erroneously suspected of committing the horrific act, and of murdering the woman, by Aunt Madgie, when she encounters Mary by the body with blood on her lips (from hitting herself in the face with one of the boots when prising them from the woman's feet).[132] Later, Mary's heroic rescue of Gideon Stone when he is also shipwrecked brings him and his fervent Methodism into her life, and into the community, until the village turns against him, and against Mary once Aunt Madgie finally reveals her suspicions.[133] At the novel's close, Gideon and Mary leave the village by boat for an unknown future.

Like O'Reilly's novel, Cathryn Pearce's important study of Cornish wrecking sets out the mythos surrounding this activity and juxtaposes a historic account which deconstructs much of the wrecking folklore that exists in our cultural imagination.[134] Cornwall becomes infamous as a shipwreck hot-spot even though, in reality, the East of England saw a higher number of wrecks off its coast. Cornwall's reputation for wrecking is tied to an understanding of Cornwall's remoteness, and a belief in the innate Celtic barbarity of its people and landscape.[135] Even though there is no evidence that ships were deliberately wrecked by false lights luring them onto rocks, this remains a prevalent cultural myth, and one which appears time and again in literature and plays of the nineteenth century, and is typified in the twentieth century by Daphne du Maurier's *Jamaica Inn* (1936).[136]

The term wrecking actually encompasses a whole range of activities with different degrees of social acceptance, which often get subsumed under the predominant image of fiendish Cornish inhabitants deliberately wrecking ships, and murdering castaways washed ashore.[137] There is actually a 'popular morality' in existence within these communities which, while it may not match the official laws with regards to wrecking, did usually prevent the kind of all-out violence that popular myths substantiate.[138] Pearce makes clear that the harvesting of wreck goods (cargo or wood from a broken-up ship) from beaches is the most justified 'social crime' within the communities themselves.[139] Clothing was also taken from wrecks, or from bodies on the beach. Pearce places this activity within a wider context of garment theft in the eighteenth century, which was precipitated by poverty, the desire for unaffordable fashions, or the resale market for such items.[140] However, it should also be noted that the duty to carry out lifesaving efforts is also part of the 'social code' of these coastal communities, alongside these harvesting activities. Pearce also explains that wrecking was not the sole preserve of the lower orders of society, and its practice was not universally condoned within working-class communities.[141] Her work identifies 'a diverse population whose justifications and motivations for wrecking activity illustrate a more complex popular morality than has heretofore been recognised—a popular morality that also informed their behaviour during wrecking events'.[142]

Alongside this complex 'popular morality' is a social understanding of a right to salvage goods that wash up on Cornish shores, regardless of the vicissitudes of national laws and their enforcement throughout the eighteenth and nineteenth centuries.[143] Such was the extreme need in many of these communities that it was seen as a necessary supplement to meagre incomes, and, because of the prohibitively high duty payable on them, the only way to access so-called luxury goods such as tobacco, sugar, and alcohol.[144] Pearce argues that the extant moral code was 'later enhanced, by Methodism' when the non-conformist religion was 'syncretised into an existing Cornish culture that included the customs of wrecking and smuggling', and that it was therefore responsible for the decrease in wrecking and smuggling activity. At the same time, harvesting continued, and remained within Cornish culture as something to which inhabitants believed they had a natural right (an attitude which survives today). Crucially, though, Methodism was also responsible for the perpetuation of the big myths about wrecking, which still hold currency in our collective cultural consciousness.[145]

Pearce's work feels like a blueprint for the complexified portrayal of wrecking in O'Reilly's novel. In the novel, the upper-class characters still espouse all the stereotypes of the Cornish wrecker myth. From the perspective of the 'bettermost' (as the working-class characters call them) and echoed by the press, Cornishness, and its associated barbarous Celticity, is located within those of the lower orders.[146] Their attitudes and assumptions about what type of person inferior birth and Cornishness produces is reified for them by the activity of wrecking, and in particular, by the sensational deeds of the so-called Porthmorvoren Cannibal. The victim of the ear chewing is the wife of Lord S—, a Member of Parliament, collector of art, and owner of multiple plantations in Jamaica (which had been a stop on the soon-to-be-wrecked vessel's return to Liverpool). Lord S—'s civilized nature is registered in his involvement in the arts, and despite his involvement in slavery. Mr Dabb, whom Mary meets when she is invited to stay with Gideon and his wife as part of her instruction to be a Sunday school teacher, sets out the criteria for the murdered woman's goodness and pre-eminence. As if no further explanation is needed, he confirms that '[s]he was a religious woman [...], of superior blood, and [had been] presented at court'. In contrast, he pronounces that '[t]he mental darkness of these isolated villages is the shame of all Cornwall'.[147] Such darkness is seen to be a product of both isolation and Celtic savagery. This is something that *The Sherborne Mercury* picks up on and sensationalizes in their account of the shipwreck. They report that 'a parcel of Cornish Barbarians rushed forth to plunder the wreck, all checks of Conscience removed'. Elsewhere in the piece they refer to the wreckers as 'Human Vultures', 'Cormorants', and 'lawless villains', classing all inhabitants of Porthmorvoren as contemptuous of all laws. They align the Cornish 'with the Native Indians of North America in their Barbarism [...] unfit to be Citizens in a civilised country'.[148] The working-class Cornish are othered through their Celticity and positioned on the outer edges of society, something which mirrors their geographical location.

This understanding of the Cornish is bound up with wider, prevalent attitudes about the working class. Mr Dabb, Mrs Stone (Gideon's wife), and others treat Mary as a curiosity—an anomaly who, because she has been admitted by them to their gathering, is excepted from their remarks about the Cornish working class (even though she is a curiosity to them only because she is working class). Mr Dabb warns the ladies present against doling out alms, informing them that poverty is 'not [the] want of employ, or short wages or dear provisions'. His condescension, with which others present concur, originates from both a sense of the natural superiority of their social position, and an unexamined assumption, even in Mary's presence, that indigence is the result of an inherent weakness of character, rather than that of social inequalities.[149] This is a familiar nineteenth-century attitude to the poor, which is here wedded to and supercharged by an even darker understanding of the working-class Cornish as an innately barbarous race.

As readers, though, we get to go beyond the headlines to see that life within Porthmorvoren is far more nuanced than the 'bettermost' or the press would allow.[150] Popular myths of wrecking are deconstructed without turning so-called devils into angels. The opening sequence of harvesting on the beach, where we first meet Mary, is challenging for our modern-day moral compass. With 'all hands drowned', bodies lie on the sand whilst members of the village strip wood from the ship. Oranges (some of which Mary collects in her kerchief) are scattered amongst the corpses and 'gobbets of human flesh', and as Mary moves through the fog, she almost steps upon a dead child. In these surroundings, she covets the soft leather boots of Lord S—'s wife and works about prising them from her feet.[151] This behaviour, though, is contextualized in the novel by an understanding of what Mary calls a life of 'ceaseless toil and hardship', where goods offered up by the universe onto their own sand, often items they could never afford to buy, provide necessities for survival.[152] In addition, shortly after this opening scene we see that when there is the possibility of saving a life, it is also part of the village's code to attempt do so. Even though she cannot swim, Mary wades out into the sea, with her friend Tegan, to bring shipwrecked Gideon Stone to safety, and she then nurses him back to health at her home.[153] In addition, when Martha Tregaskis confesses to Mary that she is the Porthmorvoren Cannibal, unburdening herself because of the weight of her conscience, we can see her behaviour as a product of her own brutalization at the hands of her husband.[154] Her act is not representative of a barbaric Celtic race as the press have made out, but rather of one woman's violent maltreatment which she revisits upon the corpse on the beach.

Through Marget Maddern (Aunt Madgie to the whole cove) we see that there is a moral code at work within the village, and that elders like her assume the responsibility of imposing it. There is a careful calibration between what is decent, and making use of fortuitous wrecks to meet the practical necessities of an impoverished community. Observing on the beach in the aftermath of the wreck, she warns Mary that 'we must not cross the bounds of decency, or the cove will be infested with

Preventive Men'. She requires Mary to swear that she did not murder the lady before them, or desecrate her body, and she castigates Mary for her reputation for 'stripping clothes and jewels off dead women'. Importantly though, Aunt Madgie does not simply denounce the practice. Indeed, Mary shows her a waterlogged watch she has collected from another corpse and Aunt Madgie muses about getting it fixed in Penzance. Her justification is that '[w]hoever owned this won't need to tell the time where they're gone'. Those who have perished no longer have any use for worldly goods that in turn can assist this struggling community, and it is a sense of community, of 'One and All', that informs how villagers should behave on the beach. What Aunt Madgie dislikes is not necessarily the practice of harvesting itself, but Mary's wont for 'sneaking about' looking for items to satisfy her vanity, rather than joining in with the efforts to salvage items for the good of the community as a whole.[155] Everything is managed internally within the community according to their rules, and to protect them from the 'Preventive Men' looking to impose state law. Mary tells us '[i]t was One and All, and Aunt Madgie [...] never missed a chance to tell us so. We might stank [stamp] on our own, but we didn't hand them over to uplongers.'[156] When Aunt Madgie airs her suspicions to the rest of the community that Mary is the Porthmorvoren Cannibal, it is because she believes that she has broken their code of morality, which needs to be dealt with internally. There is no thought of seeking justice from outside.

When Mary rescues Gideon Stone from the water, though, she brings into the village an outsider who looks to impose his version of Methodism onto what he sees as an 'outpost of civilisation'.[157] This is a moment in time before Methodist belief has been fully assimilated into such communities, and Gideon's puritanical stance simply does not fit with the realities of life in the cove. The way in which Gideon frames his mission in Porthmorvoren aligns the inhabitants with slaves in Jamaica on Lord S—'s plantations, where although the news is that six Methodist chapels have been demolished and the preachers arrested, we are aware that they were built for the education of the slaves.[158] In Porthmorvoren, Gideon believes his mission is to 'break the chains of superstition and barbarous custom'.[159] Mary is more susceptible to Gideon's preaching, being consumed by fear of exposure and guilt connected to the woman on the beach. Others too join in, attend services, and are willing to assist Gideon, but ultimately Gideon is unable to comprehend that religion must be flexible enough to work with the existing culture of the cove. This sets up a number of major conflicts. Methodism sees wrecking as immoral, while the inhabitants see it as their natural right.[160] Gideon goes to the kiddlywink to sermonize against drinking, wrecking, cock fighting, and gambling. One of the men present declares '[w]e ain't wreckers; we're *salvors*', and points out that 'your doctrine is hard on poor men like we, whose only pleasure in life is to partake of a pot or two of porter', but Gideon is not prepared to listen.[161] Ultimately, just like the last parson, Gideon is driven from the village. Aunt Madgie's position exemplifies how it has to be when facing the harshness of life in the cove; we are told by Mary that '[t]he old dame was devout, but not when it took food out of the villagers' mouths—or tobacco out of their pipes'.[162] Mary's sister Tegan exposes Methodism's shortcomings in relation to their lived reality when she compares Nathaniel to Gideon, saying that 'Nathaniel might not make fine speeches and lay claim to saving people's souls, but he have saved dozens of people over the years, clinging to a rope while the waves rolled over his head'.[163] These are not barbarous Celts shunning religion for unrestrained acts of devilry, and at this point in time, Methodism has not bent sufficiently to incorporate their existing moral code, which is far more suited to the harsh realities of Cornish coastal life.

In any case, both Gideon and his circle are exposed as frauds and hypocrites, their pretensions to moral superiority a sham. Their unmasking exposes their derogation of working-class Cornish people as confected, and their assumed right to instruct and correct the lower orders as pompous and hypocritical. Firstly, Gideon, for all his sermonizing at the inhabitants of Porthmorvoren, is found to have a dark past and a capacity for extreme violence. Ironically, it is he, and not the wreckers, who has 'left a man with his skull cracked open and his life blood spilling out'. Yet he blames the incident on the woman he was involved with rather than atoning for his actions, as he is instructing others to do.[164] Resisting any admission of guilt precludes his own redemption. Indeed, two women from his Methodist circuit at Penwith have made complaints about his conduct in the present day of the narrative. Yet unreformed and unrepentant, he had presumed to instruct the Porthmorvoren community in righteous behaviour.[165] Once exposed as a fraud, he leaves Porthmorvoren in a boat with Mary, his reputation in tatters. Mary had not invited him to join her, yet their juxtaposition in this moment reveals his fall from the pedestal on which she had placed him. We are aware that, rather than Gideon saving

Mary as he had fanatically set out to do, if anything, it will be the other way around.[166]

The hypocrisy of the 'bettermost' is most evidently exposed when Mary goes to stay with Gideon and his wife.[167] Two items reveal both their sanctimoniousness and the performative nature of their moral position. Before a tea party with Mr Dabb and Miss Vyvyan, Mrs Stone places John Wesley's *Thoughts on Slavery* in full view on the coffee table. As we might perhaps still see coffee table books being used today, this placement is intended as a conspicuous expression of worthy values. Yet crucially, we learn that she has not read it. Instead, she places a pressed flower partway into the book to make it seem as if this is her current reading matter. Mrs Stone artfully constructs the scene in order to project her moral goodness to her guests.[168] However, at the dinner party which takes place a few days later, at which Mary is also present, a ship made of spun sugar is placed in the centre of the table to be broken up and consumed by the guests. Perhaps Mrs Stone has not understood the connotations of this display for a Methodist professing to be against slavery, and that is damning in itself. One of the wives present feels it would be 'a shame to eat it!', but as readers, we are invited to see this spectacle as shameful in more profound ways. John Wesley had asked his followers to abjure sugar (and many in Cornwall did) because of its connections to slavery. Just prior to the sugar ship's unveiling, the discussion had been about the abolition movement, and Lord S—'s stance against abolition in parliament. Mrs Vyvyan identifies herself as an abolitionist, and points out that Lord S—'s fortune had been made in the sugar trade on the backs of slaves. Moments later, though, they are breaking up the sugar ship to consume it. We are, therefore, left in little doubt as to the origins of the sugar from which the ship has been spun. In addition, the breaking up of the ship into the shards that they consume recalls the actual breaking up of Lord S—'s ship on Porthmorvoren beach, and the wood and food items which the villagers appropriate.[169] We already know that Mary herself was given a sugarloaf for her part in harvesting from the wreck, and so there is no facile distinction here which exonerates one class and demonizes another.[170] Yet the villagers are more honest about where their goods come from, and in their belief that wreck goods are their right. While Mrs Stone's circle look down upon the working-class Cornish for taking these goods, and not paying duty on them, we are simultaneously aware that the sugar she and her coterie consume has been harvested with free slave labour.

Anarchy

Rule Britannia (1972) is, as Ella Westland says, 'a Daphne du Maurier novel in disguise'.[171] Its content will be all the more disorientating for those who see du Maurier as simply a purveyor of pulp romance. This is a novel which realizes English fears over the controllability of the Celtic fringe. *Rule Britannia* manifests the historic threat of internal resistance to English rule and makes it inevitable by setting the events in an undefined future. It is a future where Britain's departure from the European Economic Community (EEC), which in reality it joined in 1973, has made it so vulnerable that the government of the United Kingdom has had 'no alternative' but to agree to combine the country with the United States to become USUK. In response, Cornwall, Wales, and Scotland rise up in outright rebellion, and we follow this insurrection through the people of Cornwall. Here, British citizens are given no say in the decision to create USUK, and everything that follows. Given Britain's actual decision to leave the European Union in 2016, there are new resonances to the Prime Minister of the novel explaining the need for the merger with America, announcing to the nation:

> The breakdown of our partnership with the European community and our withdrawal from it, due to no failure on our part, brought great economic difficulties, as I feared would be the case and as I warned you at the time, and our political autonomy and military supremacy were also endangered.[172]

The UK's withdrawal from the EEC (in the novel) creates an unstable situation in which fault lines created by colonization are exposed.

Firstly, it is clear that the situation created by leaving the EEC has been utilized by Britain's former colony to reverse colonize the UK. The Prime Minister tries to spin the new relationship between the US and the UK as an equal partnership: 'We are a great and common people', he claims; '[w]hat we have to give is theirs, what they have to give is ours'. However, he has already made clear that there was no other option for the UK, and that they are 'threatened no longer' only because of this merger. This undercuts everything that follows in the premier's speech, and the American Colonel Cheeseman's assessment that 'this is a very great day for our two countries'.[173] The assumption of greatness here echoes an older sense of Britain as an imperial power, but we are more likely to agree with Mad that the UK was already, and is now even more so, 'the laughing-stock of the world'.[174] In reality, the US intends to utilize the UK as a colony that it can exploit for its own benefit. Excited by the idea, Emma's pa (and Mad's son) tells her that the UK is 'to become the playground of the Americas' as they 'come here in search of the past'. This means performing tourist-lite versions of the island's complex history for American tourists: 'Mock battles, feudal customs, [...] maids in mob caps' and 'inhabitants tarted up in coloured stockings and pointed shoes'. Emma grasps that this would be 'degrading' but her father, understanding it as a purely capitalist exchange, has faith that '[p]eople will do anything for money'.[175] He is one of a number of short-sighted or grasping characters who cannot see, or do not care, that this is a relationship which looks only to extract from the UK its history in a form palatable to, and entertaining for, American visitors, and which subjugates UK citizens.

The reactive uprising foments exclusively within Britain's Celtic fringe, thereby exposing age-old fault lines between England and its previously colonized territories. The resistance takes the form of actual armed conflict by guerrilla groups within the Celtic territories of Cornwall, Wales, and Scotland. A newsreader recounts:

> Following explosions in the Falmouth area, there have been two more, one near Camborne and a second in the clay district, a mile from Nanpean. Other disturbances have been reported from South Wales. It is believed that Celtic factions amongst the population are taking this opportunity of giving vent to their dissatisfaction with the Coalition Government and the formation of USUK. Elsewhere the country is quiet.[176]

In the clay area dissidents have stolen gelignite from the clay works (used for blasting granite) to create bombs.[177] This is a response to actual American troops on the ground, taking over beaches and ports, commandeering holiday accommodation for their billet, restricting the movement of inhabitants, cutting communications during an imposed state of emergency, searching houses, and anchoring warships off the Cornish coast.[178] The American invaders respond to the unrest by arresting young men in the district. What ensues is an occupation-resistance situation reminiscent of France during the Second World War, with the community banding together to hide people, keep secrets, share food, and even murder soldiers.

Already existing attitudes, from an English-centric perspective, to the Celtic peoples of the UK are made more visible by the ongoing situation. Those assumptions are used to both explain the uprising and to provide justification for the merger. The Prime Minister calls out those resisting by criticizing their unwillingness to homogenize, and by dismissing any basis for their sense of difference. He says,

> I wish, too, to address myself particularly to some of our countrymen who live in the west country and who, because of their place of birth, imagine themselves to be different from the rest of us—and this applies also to the inhabitants of Scotland and Wales, where there have been reports of minor explosions.[179]

Similarly, Emma's pa, while he is the son of Mad who is involved in the Cornish resistance, exemplifies a condescending English attitude, which has already been authorized from the highest echelons of political power, and which privileges a London-centric way of life and world view as more civilized, and better, than a Cornish one. He maintains that civilization only begins once he is past Exeter en route to London, and that 'standards become lower every mile you travel west' so that Cornwall, as Ultima Thule, 'might as well be in Tibet'.[180] He sees the cultural plans as part of USUK as 'complete cock' when discussing them in private with his daughter, but also as the way 'Tibet [Cornwall] will become civilised'. As we have seen above, his is an attitude which also embraces the capitalist exploitation of citizens required to perform a pantomime of their history for tourists. He thinks that 'the native', 'the hoi polloi' of Cornwall has little choice but to take part given that, in his eyes, '[i]ndustry is finished here' and Cornwall has 'no future'.[181] Such attitudes, from Londoner and premier alike, always existed, but they are now at the forefront of public discourse in this moment of extreme upheaval.

In Cornwall, for those perspicacious enough, the increased visibility of their inferior positioning by the state, and its conformists, enables them to fully discern the extent of their existing and forthcoming exploitation, particularly with regards to tourism, which feeds into the defiant action undertaken. By setting her narrative in a dystopic alternate version of our world, du Maurier enables comparisons to be drawn with Cornwall's actual function as a site of mass tourism. What is happening in the novel through USUK's cultural programme is what Neil Kennedy and Nigel Kingcome, discussing tourism in the real world, call the 'Disneyfication of Cornwall', where 'commodified heritage' is dominant and '*ersatz* cultural artefacts and guide-book representations raise the spectre of a sanitised, Disneyesque, "Kernowland"'.[182] The events of *Rule Britannia* may make us uncomfortable because, in some respects, familiar aspects of our world are being reflected back at us. In the novel, the fisherman Tom Bate absolutely understands what is happening and demonstrates a sense of protectiveness, for his livelihood and for Cornwall, that gives us an insight into why others have taken up arms. He complains that the cultural plans for Cornwall are

> [t]urning us into a fair ground, with all this talk about going back to the old days. Before we know where we are, they'll have us all dressed up as smugglers and pirates and the like. I tell you one thing. If I catch any Yankee tourist in a frog-suit after my lobster-pots when the season comes around, I'll use him as blinkin' bait.[183]

There are others, of course, who are fully on board, fully sucked into a capitalist value system. Mr Libby, landlord of the Sailor's Rest public house, had already upscaled the pub, originally for local workers, to a trendy hangout for affluent visitors. When Cornwall is invaded, he is just as happy to swap those customers for the American military, because he can make more money, whilst showing no concern about the realities of the invasion.[184] Ultimately, though, there are enough people within Cornwall, and Wales and Scotland, who clearly see the power structures behind, and cultural impact of, this situation, and who are prepared to risk all in outright rebellion against the new state.

At the close of the novel Cornwall remains beyond England; it cannot be subsumed into USUK or subjugated by it. American forces have been routed in Cornwall, and the final image of the novel is of their helicopters heading east. Cornish youths have headed to Wales and Scotland to assist in their resistance, and an ill-tempered Pa informs Emma that what began in Cornwall is now 'spreading through the whole blasted country like an epidemic of smallpox'.[185] In *Rule Britannia* the fear of keeping control of the Celtic peripheries is made reality. Flirtation with a safe, 'sanitized' version of Cornishness for the sake of tourism has been quashed.[186] Ultimately, the seeds of that resistance have always been present, sown within fault lines of internal colonization, and only superficially covered over through the dominance of an English-centric homogenizing viewpoint. What is irreducible here is a sense of Cornish (and Welsh and Scottish) difference, which always poses an uncontainable threat to the power of the state.

Chapter Three

On the Edge

The sea here is real sea. It rises and falls with a loud noise, has a long, silky roll on it as though it purred, seems sometimes to climb half up into the sky and you see the sail boats perched upon clouds—like flying cherubs.
  Journal of Katherine Mansfield (22 May 1918)[1]

Katherine Mansfield's appraisal of the sea at Looe exemplifies both an understanding of Cornwall and its coast as more 'real', because of its wildness and the access it provides to raw nature, and as something surreal: to her eye the sea and sky form an optical illusion suggestive of fantasy beings. As the previous chapter has discussed, so often Cornwall is more than one thing at any one time—it is England but then not England, it is a place to which to escape and a hostile place. Literature set in Cornwall that goes beyond the stereotypical (that of idyllic retreat in romance novels, for example) often looks to exploit these perceived contrary qualities of place, where the drama of storytelling can be found in the unpredictability of the Cornish space. Like the previous chapter, this next chapter will explore Cornish literary worlds where physical and cultural boundaries are in play.

The cultural and economic importance of the sea and the coast to Cornwall is easily recognizable and understandable. A total of 422 miles of coastline encircles Cornwall on three craggy sides, its cliffs facing the Atlantic Ocean from the north and the west and the English Channel from the south.[2] There is a long history of maritime industry—fishing, ship building, trade—prior to and ongoing alongside mining and later tourism. Such is its dominance that Cornwall's coast, its edges, have, representationally, come to stand in for the whole of Cornwall. In her book *Picturing Cornwall: Landscape, Region and the Moving Image*, Rachel Moseley argues that it is 'the periphery of the periphery—which has continued to dominate the place-myth of Cornwall'. She identifies the cost of a fixation on the coast as a 'resultant "emptying out" of the terrain, in which the centre falls away and out of representation, [which] produces a set of exclusions around poverty and industry which have cemented a place-myth in which Cornwall remains rural, picturesque, archaic and unchanging'.[3] The predominance of the coastal site is as common in literary representation as it is in moving image. Chapters Four and Five go in search of literary imaginings of Cornwall's interior, that which has fallen out of representation on any kind of scale, but first this chapter looks to uncover less familiar ways in which the coastal site itself can be rendered and read.

This chapter looks at literary representations which pierce, challenge, and go beyond an aesthetic rendering of the Cornish littoral. Such versions of the coastal site coalesce around socially outcast characters: those pushed to the edges of society both figuratively and literally. Their occupation of 'the periphery of the periphery', their geographical location at or relocation to the edge, correlates with and externalizes a psychic edge, both of which they are in danger of going beyond to their destruction.[4] In such narratives the Cornish coast, therefore, becomes either the necessary or the inescapable site of crisis, rather than a space for aesthetic contemplation and leisure. This is not Cornwall as destination but Cornwall as the end of the line: as far as it is possible to go on land in one direction until the physical edge demands some kind of decision.[5] Therefore, the idea of Cornwall as a place to which to escape, a function it often fulfils in literary texts, is undermined.

In the Cornish language the word *glas* is used for a whole range of colours that can be found in nature, and in particular for 'sea-like' colours.[6] It is a word whose meaning recognizes the mutability of the sea 'as an ever-changing palette of greens [and] blues'.[7] Touristic renderings of the sea that surrounds Cornwall, and indeed many of our own personal photographs of the coast, are often attracted to a turquoise blue: to a clearness and vividness which has exotic connotations, especially when coupled with white sands. That this is actually Cornwall, when it could be mistaken for somewhere abroad, can be a source of pride within Cornwall, and a useful marketing strategy.[8] As discussed in the previous chapter, harnessing a Cornish exotic for touristic promotion is not that new. The Great Western Railway (GWR) poster campaign in the early twentieth century was impactful because it explicitly aligned Cornwall with Italy, a more typically exotic location, to promote it as an internal sun, sea and sand destination.⁹ Cornwall's dual identification as simultaneously home and other intensifies the attraction of the 'domestic exotic' aesthetic, which is a well-established construction of the Cornish littoral.¹⁰

The ubiquity of the Cornish coastal aesthetic (which of course has an economic as well as a cultural imperative) has implications for our ability to access what lies beyond it. The journey of the engine house from functional to aesthetic is our touchpoint in this book for the contextual shift from mining to tourism. Against the remains of engine houses perched on cliffs around Cornwall's coast we can map how the dominance of the coastal view can override more nuanced versions of the same space. The aestheticization of the Cornish engine house is an example of what Raymond Williams identifies as an emergent need of the observer to 'divide […] observations into "practical" and "aesthetic"' which are 'parts of a social history, in the separation of production and consumption'.¹¹ Engine houses are found all over Cornwall, both inland and on the coast, but it is those located on the edge, such as Crowns mine at Botallack or Wheal Coates near St Agnes, that have been fully incorporated into a Cornish coastal aesthetic. These shells of mechanical apparatus, decaying and crumbling remnants of production, and in some cases headstones of men entombed below the surface, are divorced from their original purpose and from that industry's demise.¹² Instead of monuments inscribing the death of mining, and the trauma associated with that, engine houses have become both part of the view and picture windows through which the sea can be framed and consumed.

Alain Corbin's in-depth study of the seaside enables us to understand how, by the end of the eighteenth century, the 'aesthetics of picturesqueness' are established.¹³ In a Cornish setting this is particularly relevant when the decline of mining and the development of tourism in the nineteenth century optimizes conditions, within the wider context Corbin outlines, for the incorporation of the engine house into an aesthetic visual 'grammar' of the coast, and for the rise in dominance of the aesthetic of the Cornish coast.¹⁴ Corbin explains that '[t]he picturesque journey also requires a model for appreciation of place. It dictates the choice of viewpoint, the one which most easily frames the natural spectacle in a picture.'¹⁵ Rather than looking down at what horrors may lie below, the engine house is just one element of the coast which enables a prospect view out and through it, which frames that view in a way similar to how television will later package similar coastal views.

Corbin maps the journey of our relationship to the seaside from a space which engenders repulsion and fear, to the more familiar cultural place that we would still recognize today, and that includes the aesthetic transformation discussed above. That transition has a long and complex history, of which Cornwall is a part and within which we can further understand the specificities of the Cornish situation. Until the middle of the eighteenth century, the fear Corbin identifies is located in a view of the seaside as 'irredeemably wild'. It was not a space over which mankind could exert its mastery. Yet a version of that fear is also central to the rehabilitation of the seaside as a site of beauty and leisure. Corbin argues that '[b]efore the sea-shore could enter the range of attractive places, the desire had to arise for visions of the sublime, and the therapeutic necessity had to make itself felt'. The seaside comes to be better understood as a place with health benefits, and, paradoxically, 'the sea became a refuge and a source of hope because it inspired fear'.[16] Quoting Edmund Burke, Corbin goes on to explain the aspects of the seaside that make sublime experiences possible:

> The shore easily provides the 'sort of tranquillity tinged with terror' that defines the aesthetics of the sublime. Walking along the edge of the abyss on the solid rock of the cliff, facing the rush of the wind and a feeling of dizziness (without real danger), venturing into dark sea caves under cicerone's guidance, climbing up and then rushing down the slopes of embankments, succumbing to the impact of the waves on a soft, smooth, sandy beach, or running the imaginary risk of being ambushed by bandits and pirates, all give rise to emotions in the soul that create sublime moments.[17]

There forms a hierarchy of beaches based on this new appreciation of what the seashore is, and Cornish beaches are included in this: Newquay provides bracing sea air and Falmouth is an appropriate site for convalescents.[18]

Cornwall's ambiguous position as England-but-not-England, exploited by tourism to offer a 'domestic exotic' or 'the-other-we-are-comfortable-with', can be aligned with the paradoxical nature of the sublime at the seaside.[19] The safe access to danger that the sublime enables is mirrored by the characteristics of Cornwall's home–other positioning. As discussed in the previous chapter, this duality of two versions of place held in tension with each other works to entice visitors to Cornwall who want an accessible, but ultimately safe, thrill. One can imagine that such proximity to the rest of England both heightened the thrill of the wild whilst simultaneously providing comfort that one was never in any real danger. This is exactly how Corbin describes the 'aesthetics of the sublime' in relation to sea bathing: 'It involved facing the violent water, but without risk, enjoying the pretence that one could be swept under, and being struck by the full force of the waves, but without losing one's footing.'[20] In Cornwall, then, the sublime of the beach space, how that space can be experienced in relation to the sublime, is heightened by and can be said to interact with a wider positioning of Cornwall as England-but-not-England.

Studying the Cornish Edge

The representation and symbolic significance of the Cornish coast and the sea is already of interest to a number of scholars in history, literature, and film and television studies, where the dominance of the edge in representations of Cornwall is recognized and interrogated. Such work already goes beyond a more familiar romanticized aesthetic of the coast, sometimes literally delving below the surface. Here, I provide a brief overview of work by Philip Marsden, Rachel Moseley, Joan Passey, Cathryn Pearce, Shelley Trower and myself which contextualizes this chapter. Scholars are interested in exploring the specificity of Cornish liminality, and the Cornish littoral as a space which entertains more than one possibility at any one time. Such work not only sets out to understand why the Cornish edge, in a twist on its geographical location, is so central to delineations of Cornwall; it also reveals the edge as a site of 'indeterminacy and possibility', connection and exposure.[21]

There is an alternative perspective to the more familiar rendering of Cornwall as remote and peripheral. Such characterizations are almost always made from a London-centric perspective, from which Scotland and Cornwall are indeed the furthest you can travel away from the capital on this island. However, such a viewpoint does not account for a Cornu-centric lens through which its coastal ports are seen as sites of connection. Philip Marsden's history of Falmouth, *The Levelling Sea*, reveals this port's role in a maritime revolution which begins in the sixteenth century. Citing Hendrick Danckerts' painting *A View of Falmouth Harbour* (c.1678), Marsden explains that the work 'shows the harbour entrance filled with a southern glow, borrowed from scenes of Renaissance Italy, and giving Falmouth and its waters not only a sense of light and hopefulness, but a hint of all those hot and distant shores with which it was now connected'.²² Here, Cornwall's own exoticism aligns it with foreign climes, which are accessible from Falmouth's own port.

These connections are not just notional; they exist because of Cornwall's position as an integral part of a global interchange of trade and commerce criss-crossing the sea. Marsden explains that Glasney College (an ecclesiastical site instituted in the thirteenth century and located nearby the port at Penryn, a little further upriver from what would later become Falmouth) was part of a 'network of ports and havens and anchorages which for thousands of years had been not so much on the land-fringes of European countries, as on the edge of a loose nation linked by the sea'.²³ Rather than these countries being cut off from each other by water, it is the sea here that enables contact, and via which an alternative set of relations are fostered.

It was not just Falmouth that was externally connected in this way. Cathryn Pearce sets out Cornwall's position as a key part of a maritime trade network, at least until the mid-nineteenth century. England was well placed geographically in this respect and 'sitting centrally along those trade routes was Cornwall'.²⁴ Here Cornwall is central, not peripheral. Pearce echoes Marsden in drawing attention to evidence of a long history of connection out into the world from the Cornish coast. She comments that 'Cornwall's trading ties with Brittany, Wales and Ireland, as well as Iberia and the Mediterranean, were part of a much older tradition going back thousands of years—perhaps initially stronger than that resulting from their land-based relationship with the rest of England'.²⁵ Such points of connection, looking out to sea from Cornwall rather than inland, turn on its head a hierarchy of location in Britain which posits its fringes as inherently remote.

This is an entirely different perspective, and one which is obscured when the eye travels via land into Cornwall, rather than out from Cornwall's many miles of coastline. Kneehigh Theatre's version of 'Tristan and Yseult', first performed in 2003, makes this alternative viewpoint into King Mark's rallying cry:

> Forget what you've been taught or think you know:
> The centre of everything's here—Kernow.
> We don't look inland, there's not much point
> Let Rome rule the Anglos, their foreheads anoint.
> No, outward lies the way!
> Inland there's little to write home about and much less to say.

With the assistance of a map produced onstage, King Mark's speech reorientates the play's audience. Cornwall here is the opposite of peripheral: it is the centre of the world. Such a viewpoint is a provocation, but it is also where, with Ireland threatening war, King Mark locates Cornish identity as something un-English, and thereby legitimizes his power and rights as king. This is reinforced by characterizing himself, Cornish people, and Cornwall itself as being forged by its watery elements:

> My soul is in the rock, my blood in the rivers
> This land a gift that the ocean delivers
> We are fashioned by the wind and the sea
> I'll not give up its freedom easily.[26]

This is a kind of origin story for Cornwall and its people, rooted in the uniqueness of its location and its relationship to the sea which surrounds it.

Increased connectivity spanning out from Cornwall's watery borders, whilst signalling a march for progress in the nineteenth century, could also be a locus for anxiety about the porosity of those borders. Shelley Trower's work on nineteenth-century sensation and Gothic fiction and non-fiction, from well-known writers such as Wilkie Collins, Arthur Conan Doyle, Thomas Hardy, and Bram Stoker, locates this anxiety at the cliff edge. She argues that 'cliffs function as a space that is almost but not quite detached from the nation, as part of the mainland of England but also semi-foreign'.[27] Trower points out:

> Cliffs are frightening, not only because of their physical dangers—as a cause of shipwrecks, or as precarious edges from which one can fall off, or in other words as lethal points of entry and exit—but in their embodiment of insecure national borders, as unstable, shaky boundaries that undergo the continuous onslaught of the elements.[28]

Cliffs are therefore also points of exposure, of vulnerability and danger, and of potential invasion, all made possible because of how the location connects outwards across the ocean. Such insecurity is heightened at the Cornish cliff edge due to Cornwall's ambiguous status as both England and not England, as part of the nation and as a potential threat to it.[29]

Joan Passey's work makes the case for a Cornish Gothic tradition in the long nineteenth century that, as happens so often with literature of Cornwall, has been missing from critical studies of Gothic literature. As she points out, this is the case even though many of the authors who pen Gothic novels and short stories set in Cornwall in this period, including those mentioned in the paragraph above, are canonical. Similarly to Trower's argument above, Passey explores how Cornwall's ambiguous position as simultaneously England and not England makes it an 'uncanny threat' to the stability of Britain, a potential enemy within, and therefore also a highly appropriate space for Gothic fiction.[30]

The coast and the sea surrounding Cornwall are an important part of the Cornish Gothic, particularly in the form of shipwreck narratives, which Passey explores. As Passey says, in the eighteenth and nineteenth centuries, Cornwall was 'imaginatively associated with its wrecks' so that '[t]he shipwreck is a Gothic master trope and essential to the construction of Cornwall as a Gothic space'.[31] Here too there is a concern with leaky borders. Cornish Gothic shipwreck narratives articulate nineteenth-century anxieties of invasion and the permeability of British borders, and what this means for Britain, its empire, and its own sense of its status as a maritime power. Ships that sink question that power, and instead demonstrate the might of the ocean as something which cannot be wholly mastered by man.[32] In these Gothic narratives, that which is hiding below the waves can be regurgitated to the surface and wash up on land: bodies, rats, and the remains of the ships themselves. Anxiety is heightened by a question mark over the Cornish people and whether, as perceived vestiges of primitiveness, they play a part in the death and destruction taking place at the coast, thus manifesting their internal threat. Shipwrecks off the Cornish coast, and the narratives set around such events, draw attention to the Cornish littoral as a liminal place because, as Passey concludes, it 'challenges the boundaries between surface and depth, life and death, sea and land'.[33]

Beaches, cliff edges, and coastlines have long been identified as liminal spaces, of interest due to their position at the edge of land, and because of the ambiguous, shifting nature of the beach space threshold as both land and sea, depending on the tide. Rob Shields in *Places on the Margin* opens up how this liminality, 'vis-à-vis the more closely governed realms of the nation', informs the sociological and cultural use of the seaside. The beach space is 'appropriate for specific behaviours and patterns of interaction outside of the norms of everyday behaviour, dress and activity'.[34] The coastal site is one of flux; it is destabilizing because, as McCormick states, it is a 'liminal place where paradox and ambiguity reign'.[35] The geographical liminality of the coastal site informs its social interpretation and use.

Rachel Moseley, in 'Women at the Edge', elucidates 'the specificity of the liminality suggested by the Cornish coastline' through an understanding of the liminality of the Cornish littoral as an 'intensification' of the liminality of Cornwall as a whole.[36] Not just through its geographical peripherality, but largely due to the contested nature of Cornwall's status and identity, Cornwall itself is 'a landscape both of indeterminacy and possibility'.[37] The heightened liminality of the Cornish clifftop and beach space informs the representations of women on screen, which Moseley reads in relation to Laura Knight's paintings of women on the Cornish cliff edge. Knight's women are 'anxious, uncertain' and positioned 'precariously close to the edge'.[38] The danger of the edge for Knight's women, and for those in film, is both literal and representative of other dangers facing modern women, and anxieties over social change, morality, and sexuality. Moseley identifies liminality itself as 'closely aligned with moments of crisis and uncertainty', which makes the preoccupation with the cliff space understandable in moments of 'national or personal' crisis.[39] This will be important, too, later in this chapter when we encounter characters from fiction who end up at the edge due to personal crisis (sometimes precipitated by national events). The films and television shows discussed by Moseley, including adaptations of Mary Wesley's *The Camomile Lawn* (1984) and Rosamunde Pilcher's *Coming Home* (1995), are set around the time of the Second World War. In these shows, the Cornish cliff edge is the appropriate site of 'instability, danger and uncertainty' against which 'sexual and social rites of passage and transgressions are pictured'.[40] This is not just an aesthetic space inhabited for the view—it has meaning as a specifically Cornish liminal site at which anxieties over women and sexuality play out, and are pictured.

In my previous work on Charles Lee's *Cynthia in the West* (1900) and Daphne du Maurier's *The Loving Spirit* (1931) and *Frenchman's Creek* (1941), I too have been interested in the liminality of the Cornish coastal site, and how this is informed by the ambiguity of Cornwall's characterization as simultaneously England-but-not-England. In *Cynthia in the West*, a novel that depicts the goings-on in the fictional Cornish village of Tregurda between the local fisherfolk and the incoming artists, the flux of the beach space 'unsettles gender codes', but not class structures.[41] A reading of the climactic scene in the novel, where fishermen bring in a pilchard catch whilst observed from a promontory by the painters, shows us that the initial misgivings of one of the male painters about his own masculinity, in the face of the activity of the toiling working-class men, is mistaken. The scene actually depicts desperation, in the face of fishing's decline, to haul in the catch, and much like the miners in Chapter One, the physical degradation, not supremacy, of such a life.[42]

As I have discussed previously, in reading du Maurier's Cornish novels, understanding the liminality of the Cornish edge and sea that some of her female characters inhabit enables a more nuanced reading of gender in her work than her pigeonholing as romantic novelist allows. Shields and other scholars above position the liminal space of the seaside as a site within the national that is, potentially, less governed, and therefore a locus of anxiety. As seen, this is a familiar concept in relation to Cornwall whose shift along the continuum of its England-but-not-England status has often been determined at any given moment by how much it is understood as an ungovernable (and remote and Celtic) space within, or antithetical to, the nation. For Janet Coombe in *The Loving Spirit* and Dona St Columb in *Frenchman's Creek*, because of its liminality and therefore distance from governance, the Cornish coast and its sea is the possible site of an escape from their socially prescribed gender roles. However, for these women, Cornwall's hybrid identity, simultaneously England and not England, means that such escapes are only temporary. In these novels, the rules of governed social space, of Cornwall as part of the nation, are ultimately reinscribed.[43]

Gender at the Cornish Edge

It remains of interest to me how the liminality, ambiguity, and shifting nature of Cornwall and its coast 'mediates gendered experience', and I want to expand this discussion here through an analysis of Thomas Hardy's *A Pair of Blue Eyes* (1872–73) through a Cornu-centric lens.[44] In 1870 Thomas Hardy visited St Juliot Church, near Boscastle, to carry out architectural work. Whilst there he met his first wife, Emma Gifford, who was the daughter of the church's rector with whom he was staying.[45] His Cornish novel, which was to appear just a few years later, is set in a fictional version of this location, including the rectory where the novel's protagonist Elfride, possessor of the title's blue eyes, resides with her widowed father. The novel centres on her courtship with two very different suitors, Stephen Smith and Henry Knight, neither of whom weds her, and her death in childbirth after her eventual marriage to Lord Luxellian. As would later become Tess Durbeyfield's burden too, Elfride's tragic trajectory is hastened by a Victorian obsession with reputation, of which the young, unworldly Elfride falls foul.[46]

The equivocal nature of Cornwall's positioning in Hardy's fiction as 'Off Wessex' echoes the ambiguous relationship of Cornwall to the nation, and is relevant to how we can read gender at the edge in A Pair of Blue Eyes. In most of the various maps of Wessex that were included in succeeding editions of multiple Hardy publications, Cornwall is present but not connected to Wessex itself.[47] For instance, on the first map entitled 'The Wessex of the Novels', first included in the seventeen-volume Osgood, McIlvaine collected edition of Hardy's work known as The Wessex Novels (1895–97), Cornwall is contained within a boxed-off section at the top left of the page, and with only Land's End and the sites relevant to A Pair of Blue Eyes named. Cornwall is on the page and off the page, included and excluded at the same time.[48]

Figure 4: 'The Wessex of the Novels' map first included with the Osgood, McIlvaine collected edition of Hardy's work (1895).

According to Alan L. Manford, Hardy drew a new version of the map for the collected works, known as The Wessex Edition, of 1912 (from which Emery Walker made a drawing for the etching). He asked his publishers to add his own revisions to this map on two further occasions, to be included in *A Changed Man* in 1914 and for the Melstock edition in 1919.[49] In this map, entitled 'Map of the Wessex of the Novels and Poems', Cornwall looms over Wessex. Out of proportion to the mapping of Wessex itself, it takes up almost half of the top left-hand side of the double-paged map, oversized, almost menacingly so, in relation to Wessex itself. It is still walled off, though, this time with an embellished double-thickness border. Island-like, and with the same limited places identified, in the 1912 version its geographical relationship to Wessex remains undefined. The rest of Cornwall is a blank space, as if unmapped territory. Its illustrative contour lines suggest rivers and terrain, but not civilization. Most of Cornwall, therefore, exists on the map as an unoccupied non-place, something heightened by its dislocation from the land mass at the centre of the page.

Given the revisions Hardy made himself and, as Manford states, that maps produced in various publications after Hardy's death can be hybrids of the two maps that originated with Hardy himself, mapped place in Wessex is never stable.[50] This is particularly so for Cornwall. On the 1914 revised version of the map, Cornwall is still quarantined in the top left-hand corner, but some of the large expanse of territory has been named. *A Changed Man* is a collection of short stories that includes 'A Mere Interlude', which is set in Cornwall. Hardy's names for Truro (Trufal), Redruth (Redrutin) and Penzance (Pen-zephyr) are therefore added to the map as they are locations in the story.[51] However, in all versions, especially when compared to the rest of map, the fictional version of Cornwall still looks like a largely unpopulated territory, with the majority of its small number of named places on its edges. Significantly, on the 1914 map, the walled-off Cornwall is named as 'Off Wessex'. Cornwall now has a Hardyan moniker, one that is stamped through the entirety of the narrow Cornish peninsula. In the 1919 revised version this is extended to 'Lyonnesse (or) Off Wessex'. However, with such a term, cardinal direction in relation to Wessex itself remains ambiguous and Lyonnesse is famously a mythical lost land. Cornwall is part of Hardy's fictional world, yet it sits apart. The appellation 'off' does not locate Cornwall in the same way as the maps do for the rest of the Wessex world, which is variously identified as 'lower' 'upper', 'north' or 'mid' Wessex. Cornwall is once again other, and less easy to define.

The relationship of Cornwall to the Wessex territories on the main map is echoed in the construction of Cornwall within the novel itself, and this has an impact on how we can read events that play out in the novel, particularly with regards to Elfride. Pamela Dalziel's note on the history of the text in the front matter of the 1998 Penguin Classics edition of *A Pair of Blue Eyes* cites a 'wessexisation' of the novel for its publication as part of the Osgood, McIlvaine Wessex Novels edition. This was part of a wider effort by Hardy to give a more consistent sense of the Wessex world throughout his work, as if he had conceived of Wessex whole from his first novel. His revision of *A Pair of Blue Eyes* makes fictional places in the novel more obviously based on actual Cornish locations. Cornwall is never mentioned, though, in the various versions of the novel and only in the 1877 edition do we have a single reference to a 'Cornish town'.[52]

However, the nature of Cornwall's 'Off Wessex' relationship to the Wessex of the other novels remains vague in the same way as it appears on the maps. In the 1873 edition of *A Pair of Blue Eyes*, the novel's front matter states the scene as 'chiefly near the coast of a western county'.[53] In later editions, this has become '[m]ostly on the outskirts of lower Wessex'. This is more than we have been given previously but the description still withholds a more specific placing of 'Off Wessex', other than to locate it beyond the border of Wessex proper. In an accompanying preface, written in 1899, Hardy plays with the relationship between the real and the fictional, and thereby with the reader, accepting that many people now recognize the actual Cornish location of his novel, including the 'enormous sea-bord cliff' of the story's dramatic cliff rescue (discussed below). At the same time, he refuses to confirm anything in a twisty piece of prose which backs away from a straightforward relationship between fictional and actual place. Instead, the preface maintains the ambiguity of 'Off Wessex'. Unlike the maps, it does provide a compass direction of 'the furthest westward' of all his fictional settings, but it is also 'near to, or no great way beyond, the vague border of the Wessex kingdom'. The border is 'uncertain', calling into question the identities of the territories on either side of it, and their relationship to each other. The ambiguity of location is heightened by the nature of the place as one of 'dream and mystery', the 'ghostly birds, [...] pall-like sea [...] frothy wind [and] the eternal soliloquy of the waters' suggesting another realm, impossible to locate on any map.[54]

Remoteness and disconnection suggest freedom, escape from everyday social rules and expectations. This is often how Cornwall is configured, as discussed elsewhere in this book and this chapter. In terms of Hardy's Wessex, the maps, and Hardy's own preface, both create and reinforce this understanding of place. In the novel itself, Stephen remarks upon 'the delightful freedom of manner in the remoter counties in comparison with the reserve of London'.[55] As I and others have discussed previously in relation to du Maurier's work, Cornwall can be configured, in literature and in life, as a place where it is possible to 'exercise [...] unfeminine freedoms'.[56] Cornwall's remoteness, its 'off the map', beyond the border ambiguity, enables an invention of place that positions it outside social rules and expectations, or at least where such rules are less rigorously applied. Accordingly, this is even more the case at the 'periphery of the periphery', at the cliff edge.[57] However, as discussed below, it turns out to be a far more complex and dangerous site for Elfride.

As a novel of the 1870s, *A Pair of Blue Eyes* is set in a moment of emergent tourism. In keeping with this, the presence of tourists at the coast is registered, but they are depicted Gothically 'haunting the coast', their presence as yet ethereal.[58] The coast itself is not aestheticized. The more lush, verdant spaces exist slightly inland, but the coast is described as 'the miserable skeletons of tortured old cliffs that would not even yet succumb to the wear and tear of the tides'.[59] This is a dark description, which personifies the cliffs as corporeal remains that are all too tangible, in contrast to the ghostly visitors. The reader's eye is drawn not out to the available prospect view, but down to horrific cliffs so etched with trauma that there is regret that their tormenter has not yet erased them. The sense of foreboding here is befitting, given the danger that the cliff edge presents in the course of the narrative, and its role in a train of events which lead to Elfride's death.

The cliff edge is most obviously dangerous for Elfride's suitor Henry Knight, who, in a dramatic scene, literally falls over the edge. Clinging perilously to vegetation, he is hauled back to safety by Elfride (it is thought that this is where the term cliffhanger originates). Yet the cliff space is ultimately more insidiously damaging for her, even though, as in other instances discussed above, it suggests itself as a space where greater social freedoms can be exercised. Prior to the accident (discussed below), the cliff edge is the site of her first kiss with her first suitor, Stephen Smith, and his proposal of marriage. While out in the open fields, Elfride had refused his request to kiss her because '[a]nybody might look; and it would be the death of me'. While it does not appear to be a plot on Elfride's part to kiss Stephen out of the sight of others, she leads him to the cliffs, and to a ledge halfway between the clifftop and the sea. They are doubly shielded here, below the cliff edge and within an alcove in the rock formation which is described as 'tempting'. It is an in-between place, barely on land, suspended above the sea, its vastness stretched before them. She allows her first kiss to take place here, and while she remains an awkward recipient of Stephen's affections, she does not draw back or chide him afterwards. Instead, she openly and directly confesses her love for him, in contrast to her previous hesitation and concern for the rules of social decency.[60]

At the exact same spot (and occurring after the cliff fall), she confesses both the kiss and the proposal to Knight, which ultimately leads him to reject her. The narrator reminds the reader that this is '[a] duplicate of her original arrangement with Stephen' and that, therefore, '[s]ome fatality must be hanging over her head'. Seated on the ledge, Elfride must respond to Knight's direct questioning of her past.[61] This and the other cliff edge moments demonstrate that 'Off Wessex' is not a dreamlike space for Elfride, as Hardy has suggested to us in his preface, but one of lived, gendered experience with social consequences which set a path to her death. The cliff edge is a location where events, such as the kiss and the later confession, must culminate because, literally, there is nowhere further to go, unless down to her immediate destruction.

Between the proposal and the confession, Knight accidentally falls over a cliff described as 'a hundred feet higher than Beachy Head'.[62] The moment demands immediate action from Elfride. Inescapably for her, such action requires that she 'disregards the Victorian social conventions of decency'.[63] Her initial rescue attempt takes her too over the cliff edge boundary; she clings tightly to Knight who holds precariously to the 'shaly surface of the incline' greased by the falling rain. Beyond the incline, and the piece of quartz against which Knight has wedged his foot, is 'sheer perpendicularity' and the 'dizzy depths'. In this moment of extreme peril, the relationship of her body to Knight's cannot remain within the bounds of respectability: he instructs her to '[c]lamber up' his body to reach safe ground. Knight fears she has 'endangered' herself in trying to effect this rescue, yet we later come to understand that the danger is social, and not physical.[64] The breaking of the boundary of the cliff edge symbolizes that transgression.

Her additional weight on Knight as she hauls herself up dislodges the quartz and he is left clinging to vegetation.[65] The increased urgency means that going for help is no longer an option. Elfride's dress, behaviour, and comportment are all in flux in this moment of jeopardy. She steps outside her socially prescribed gender role to become Knight's rescuer, signified by literally stepping out of her clothes. The under layers of her dress are exposed, stripped away, repurposed. Naked, she clothes herself with 'only her outer robe and skirt', fashions a rope from her undergarments, and hauls him back over the edge to safety. The narrative eye is drawn to her exposed body. Rain-drenched, her soaked clothing 'seemed to cling to her like a glove' because the water had reduced 'the protuberances' of her clothing.[66] We are reminded here of how important appropriate dress is to signal an individual's compliance with social rules of respectability by disguising contours of the female body and, therefore, why Elfride's déshabillé is indicative of her transgression.

Even in this moment of transformation, Knight is 'already resuming his position of ruling power' by shouting instructions up from the precipice, and, once he is back on terra firma, he immediately assumes full control. The text makes it clear that '[h]e was saved, and by Elfride', but in the same moment, she reverts back to a passive role, considering it 'a glorious crown to all the years of her life' to be 'slave of the greater than the queen of the less'. That Knight's 'peculiarity of nature' during their relieved embrace prevents him from kissing her is foreboding, as well as indicative of the re-establishment of social conformity in both their minds. Elfride breaks their embrace and reddens with shame at the same moment that Henry comprehends the origin of the rope. She flees the scene, 'like a pheasant [...] scampering away with a lowered tail', in order to be out of his sight, and to re-attire herself without delay.[67]

Ultimately, Elfride is punished for breaking the rules of acceptable feminine morality and decency during the cliff fall. Her physical exposure, and its implications, at the cliff edge foreshadows her moral exposure when she confesses her past with Stephen to Knight on the cliff ledge and, later, when Gertrude Jethway reveals her miscarried elopement to London to marry Stephen.⁶⁸ Knight ends their association in the stubble-field among the allegorical 'dead and brown stubble, [and] the weeds'. He commands her to remain there whilst he departs. Looking back, he sees 'a slight girlish figure in the midst of it—up against the sky'. Once again, she is exposed in the landscape.⁶⁹

The remoteness and ambiguity of the space had suggested that 'unfeminine freedoms' (epitomized by her horse-riding about the countryside unchaperoned) would be without consequence.⁷⁰ Yet the return to Cornwall of her body at the end of the novel, in a train carriage from London, dispels this myth. She is now literally boxed in, her corpse returning to be interred in the family vault of her husband (who is neither Stephen Smith nor Henry Knight). This is no dreamland. No longer dislocated from mapped place, the train is a definite, direct line of connection between Cornwall and London. Its remoteness, in that moment, is diminished as her body is borne home. The Cornish space, and especially the cliff edge, had suggested itself as extra-social, as a place where the norms of gendered behaviour were looser, of less consequence. Elfride's downfall and death shows us that this was never really the case at all.

The Emotional Edge

The second half of this chapter examines the relationship between the inner, psychic, and emotional world of literary characters, and the exterior location of the Cornish littoral. The characters included here are grieving, or suffer from mental health conditions or other illnesses. There is symbiosis between the nature of their extreme emotion, pushing them to the edge mentally, and the physical location of the Cornish cliff edge or beach space where their emotional, mental, and medical crises play out.

Emotions have a geography: they take place in time and they are 'placed'. Emotions, then, are 'unavoidably situated' and geography's 'emotional turn' prompts us to consider 'the spatiality and temporality of emotions, with the way they coalesce around and within certain places'.⁷¹ As Liz Bondi, Joyce Davidson, and Mick Smith set out, 'an emotional geography […] attempts to understand emotion—experientially and conceptually—in terms of its socio-*spatial* mediation and articulation rather than as entirely interiorised subjective mental states'.⁷² This chapter is interested in the specificity of Cornwall's coastal locations and the nature of their socio-spatial relationship to emotional and psychic experience.

No one is a tourist here. In all the novels examined, characters dwell at or arrive at the edge for reasons other than leisure: they are inhabitants, natives who return, or outcasts from lives lived elsewhere. For whatever reason, they have become peripheral to mainstream society. For some, a journey takes them to the physical edge of the Cornish coast, where something has to happen because they can travel no further. It is a stopping point, a line, one which forces confrontation with the self, or beyond it with death. In common with the previous chapter, therefore, the notion of Cornwall as a relaxing rural escape from stressful city life is problematized. As Joyce Davidson and Christine Milligan point out,

> [c]onsideration of rural spaces reveals a considerable body of work that can be used to challenge stereotypes and representations of "rural relaxation" versus "city stress". Such spaces can be characterized by emotional hardship for those without homes, those experiencing mental ill-health or marginalized from the mainstream.[73]

While the previous chapter discusses texts where an escape to an idyllic Cornwall morphs into something more sinister, here a touristic type of escape (or indeed any kind of escape) is not available.

In narratives such as those discussed below, the aesthetic of the coast is less relevant. The kind of looking we are familiar with as the 'romantic gaze' or the 'tourist gaze' is often overridden or absent, or interacts with a complex of emotions in the viewer. John Urry states that 'the pleasures of place derive at least in part from the emotions involved in visual consumption of place'.[74] Place is, therefore, not always pleasurable in these narratives. Consequently, place is not consumed in the same way but, in being consumed by emotion or suffering, the experience of place, even place itself, is created through it.

Virginia Woolf's *To the Lighthouse* (1927) is a study of the relationship between emotion and landscape. The Ramsay family's sojourn on the Isle of Skye is a literary recreation of St Ives and Godrevy Lighthouse, where Woolf's own family holidayed during her childhood. In the novel, we experience the intimate interrelation of Mrs Ramsay's interior emotional landscape with the exterior sites in the novel, particularly the sea and the intermittent beam of the lighthouse. Mrs Ramsay's relationship to her exterior environment goes far beyond looking and emotionally responding to a view. The lighthouse merges with her to enable an externalization of and, therefore, recognition and understanding of self. In the section of the novel entitled 'The Window', Mrs Ramsay sits looking out at the lighthouse beam 'coming regularly across the waves first two quick strokes and then one long steady stroke'. In this nocturnal moment, her caring responsibilities over for the day, '[s]he could be herself, by herself'. The veneer needed for society can be cast off, unnecessary in one's own company, and she feels 'one shrunk […] [to] a wedge-shaped core of darkness'. There is a sense here of Mrs Ramsay accessing her real self, the one held deep within and known only to herself. Within this moment the nature of her relationship to the lighthouse progresses from a sense of attachment or ownership—'the long steady stroke, the last of the three, […] was her stroke'—to one where the lighthouse beam anthropomorphically becomes her. It is a different kind of looking—intense, sustained, solitary—that leads her to feel 'she became the thing she looked at—that light for example'. The rhythm of the passage is dictated by the strokes of the lighthouse's beam so that when the third stroke, her stroke, comes around again, so does the same feeling. For Mrs Ramsay 'it seemed to her like her own eyes meeting her own eyes, searching as she alone could search into her mind and her heart'.[75] This externalization of self, so that what she recognizes as her own self is reflected back at her, is spotlighting her, indeed searches within her to cast light upon the dark wedge within. It also irrevocably breaks down the boundaries between internal and external, human and inanimate object, and as such complicates an understanding of the psyche as solely interiorized by positing it as spatialized.

Raynor Winn's memoir *The Salt Path* (2018) was her first publication, and was born out of an extraordinary real-life experience. It is the only non-fiction text in this section, but it directly and poetically portrays a moment of personal crisis, which pushes her and her husband Moth onto the South West Coast Path. A disastrous investment in a friend's business venture forces them to give up their beloved home in Wales. With all savings used up in the court battle, only seven days to vacate their house, and with Moth receiving a concurrently devastating diagnosis of Corticobasal Degeneration (CBD), a progressive neurological disorder, they decide to walk the 630-mile-long path from Somerset through Dorset and Devon and around Cornwall with £48 per week in tax credits to sustain them. The book details the hardship, but also the healing, that their engagement with the salt path enables.

As homeless people, they are cast out onto the headland, their social peripherality and the instability of their situation mirrored by the narrow stretch of coast path along which they walk. Winn recognizes and describes their change of position, recounting:

> Occasional people passed, but we were becoming observers, not participants. Crows crawked in the damp air, their calls eerily clear against the cliff face. Our world was changing, the edges fading as our journey drew us on between sea, sky and rock. Becoming one with the wild edge we inhabited, our fetch redefined by the salt path we trod.[76]

They no longer fit into society as citizens, yet at the same time, they move towards greater harmony with the natural environment which is now their home.

The change in how they are seen by others, or indeed the way in which they have become unseen, is starkly portrayed in the chapter entitled 'Homeless'. Whilst counting what money she has left outside a shop, and calculating what it is possible to buy, a melee between two dogs causes the coins to fall from her hands. Winn throws herself to the tarmac to try to catch the coins as they roll down the hill. A two-pound coin is snatched up by a small child whose parent allows him to keep it for ice cream, as if she is not there. Winn recounts that one of the dog owners 'prodded me with her foot' before exclaiming 'are you drunk? [...] You tramps should learn how to control yourselves.'[77] Such dehumanization at the hands of someone who clearly delineates between herself and the woman on the floor in front of her shows just how peripheral they have become. In Newquay, they bear witness to the presence of 'the invisible ones' lining the street, unseen by the holidaymakers milling about.[78] Other homeless people are now noticeable to them as fellow outcasts with whom they share their invisibility.

They occupy a very different position to Cornwall's tourists. It is an alternative kind of inhabiting of the cliff edge that, initially at least, does not allow space for aesthetic appreciation of their surroundings. Winn recognizes the contrast, saying that '[h]ad we not been so tired it would have been a day of endless photos and admiration of amazing views, but we could only focus on moving our feet'.[79] This is a tenancy of the cliff edge, but one without the right to dwell, which therefore impels them ever forward. The necessity to keep moving, precipitated by their homelessness, trudging along the cliff path in all weathers even when exhausted, distinguishes and removes them from those who access the coast as a leisurescape. Such people are there through choice, not exigency.

However, their journey along the coast path does not become an endless, joyless slog. Instead, they find themselves 'growing stronger with every headland'.[80] This change does not occur independent of the environment in which they walk. The very location at which they have ended up in desperate times is what enables their healing and renewal, and so their relationship to it goes beyond aesthetic appreciation. Initially, the coast path offers this by literally providing a route, when their lives have been thrown into chaos. With no plan other than to walk, the coast path becomes a certainty amidst turmoil. It is a 'dusty umbilical cord'. The path, stretching out ahead of them and mapped out in their guidebook, gives them something to 'instinctively' follow, headland after headland after headland.[81] The process of walking becomes akin to processing their grief for what they have lost. They are held by the path, couched within its narrow environs rather than trapped. Winn describes this progress towards new growth as they progress along the path as being

> drawn to the edge, a strip of wilderness where we could be free to let the answers come, or not, to find a way of accepting life, our life, whatever that was. Were we searching this narrow margin between the land and sea for another way of being, becoming edgelanders along the way? Stuck between one world and the next. Walking a thin line between tame and wild, lost and found, life and death. At the edge of existence.[82]

'Edgelanders' becomes the title of the sixth and final section of the book, which includes the chapters 'Alive', 'Accepting', and 'Salted'. Edgelanders is a positive identity, encompassing the hardship they have suffered, their survival, and the potential for a new life that has been arrived at on the path. Salted is another, equally positive identity. At Portheras Cove in West Cornwall, a passing dog walker recognizes that they have been what she calls 'salted'. 'It's touched you', she says, 'it's written all over you: you've felt the hand of nature. It won't ever leave you now; you're salted.'[83] This identity is taken up by Winn, and indeed closes out the memoir. It conveys their time spent so close to the sea, what being within that environment has done for them, and how it has marked and changed them. If we think of salting as an act of preservation, their time at the edge has preserved them in a moment of crisis, until they were ready for whatever comes next.

On the Edge at the Edge

The harbour town of St Ives is closely associated with the holiday trade, and with its aesthetic beauty, which draws people there to enjoy the views, to paint them, and to play on its beaches. Such is the dominance of its characterization as a tourist leisurescape that alternatives, such as the presence of a local population living there all year round, are much less visible. Helen Dunmore's novels *Talking to the Dead* (1996) and *Mourning Ruby* (2003) are both about the death of a child, and the reverberations of grief caused by such a loss. Fictional versions of St Ives feature in both novels, which offer up a lived experience of place that sits in an uncomfortable juxtaposition with, and contemporaneous to, the more familiar temporary visitation of touristic experience. The focus on death and loss in such a place exposes, and invites us to consider, this other experience of place, one which overrides the aesthetic or, at least, makes us aware of the relationship of the beauty of place to grief.

Talking to the Dead is narrated by Nina, who goes to live with her sister Isabel following the problematic birth of Isabel's son, from which she needs time to recover. Whilst there, Nina has an affair with Isabel's husband Richard, and when she discovers their liaison, Isabel commits suicide. The novel periodically cuts back to the sisters' childhood together in St Ives, one punctuated by the tragic death of their baby brother Colin. As it did for Virginia Woolf, the St Ives landscape of her formative years, its features, textures, smells, has imprinted itself on Nina's memory. She recalls a lived experience of place, one that is an embedding within and as part of place, a forming of self in and through a particular landscape. The family home looks out over Porthmeor Beach. Such proximity to the Cornish coast may seem idyllic, and indeed, comforted by its omnipresence, Nina is lulled to sleep by the sound of the sea in her childhood bedroom (a sound she tries to recreate from traffic noise as an adult living in London).[84] Yet it quickly becomes clear in the gobbet of memory below that there is also a sinister aspect to this environment that makes it challenging, even dangerous, to live in:

> The sea got into everything. Our leather school sandals were white with salt before we'd had them a week. Later they would rot at the seams, long before we'd grown out of them. There was sand in the carpets, sand in the grass. Every year my mother would slap paint on every window-frame she could reach, so that the sea would not eat down to the wood. Wind and salt scoured off paint and covered the windows with spray. Our hair was sticky, whipped into tangles until we couldn't get a comb through it. Each summer one streak bleached white over my forehead. In winter there were thick white mists that

clung to us like cobwebs, and the noise of a foghorn lowing; then the air would begin to move again and black humps of rock would slide out of the silence. When the fog was heavy I kept my mouth shut, frightened that it would get into my throat and choke me.[85]

The salting that preserves Winn and Moth here rots shoes and bestially devours homes. Just like their inanimate objects, humans who live there are coated in salt. Gothically, the coastal fog covers over the prospect view so that aspects of landscape loom independently, at the whim of the breeze. More menacing even than the salt, the vulnerability of her body is what Nina fears, its porosity to the fog, which she imagines is possessed with an anthropomorphic desire to suffocate her. Here, landscape is not just to be looked at. These coastal dwellers are embedded within a hostile environment, one which seems to possess the potential to embed itself within them.

In the passage above, we can feel the intensity and intimacy of Nina's relationship to St Ives during her childhood, and how this diverges from a touristic experience of the same place. Both *Talking to the Dead* and *Mourning Ruby* feature scenes within Barnoon Cemetery (it first appears in her novel *Zennor in Darkness* (1993)), which sits 'overlooking the sea'.[86] In *Talking to the Dead*, it is in these scenes that we see most starkly the contrast between how place is experienced by those visiting St Ives, and those living there through all seasons. As children, Barnoon is a place for Nina and Isabel to play 'up and down the little paths, visiting our favourite graves'. Familiarity is built through repetition. Nina distances herself and her sister from those she observes who are there on holiday (whilst pretending she has not paid them any attention at all). She recounts that '[b]elow us the sea glittered and the holiday people threw themselves in and out of the waves, but we took no notice of them'.[87] This 'them and us' dichotomy is set up early on in the novel through the two very different experiences of the coastal cemetery. For Nina it is her brother's resting place; she remembers both his 'tiny grave in a steep cemetery above the sea' and that '[t]here's a path through the cemetery which tourists use as a short cut down to the beach'. For one group of people, this is the quickest route to their temporary leisurescape. For inhabitants this is their eternal resting place, and where their presence on earth is memorialized. Whilst Nina and Isabel's family are living through the loss of Colin, tourists who respectfully pause to read his and others' inscriptions linger only briefly, and can then clasp their children's hands 'tightly as they walk on'.[88] Such tragedy is incongruous with their purpose for being there and they can move on to the beach. Here are two starkly different experiences of place, which is heightened by the 'holiday mode' of those wandering through Barnoon Cemetery. That same space is socially constructed very differently for both parties. For one, their emotion is 'unavoidably situated' there.[89] For the other, it is a place which they can temporarily consume.

In *Mourning Ruby*, Dunmore returns to Barnoon Cemetery once again. Inhabitation of this place is, as for Nina above, an embedding *within* place that shapes those who are a part of it. In *Mourning Ruby*, this relationship to place spans across familial generations, and across life and death, and Rebecca becomes a part of it via her husband Adam. In the chapter 'Barnoon is Heaven', Rebecca recalls visiting the cemetery with Adam, whilst pregnant with Ruby, to pay respects at his grandmother's grave.[90] By the end of this chapter, we learn the details of Ruby's death as a toddler in a tragic road accident, and understand that this informs Rebecca's memory of Barnoon, where Ruby is now buried, with Adam's grandmother, where Rebecca feels she is safe.[91] During that first visit with Adam, Rebecca is taken by Barnoon as a resting place and thinks she would like to be buried there. Adam informs her that there is competition for the plots, given the location.[92] The desire for an aesthetically pleasing resting place, in which you would be buried below ground, may seem somewhat odd, ridiculous even. The passage, however, reveals that this is not so and helps us to understand why Rebecca later feels Ruby is safe there. Adam's grandmother is interred within the landscape she has been embedded within in life. She remains a part of it in death. Rebecca remembers that her headstone had 'long ago lost the raw look of death. It was settled into the earth and the wind and light played around it in a jewel-like way I had never seen in any other graveyard. Most graveyards collect darkness, but this one collected light.'[93] The familiar world and daily life of St Ives goes on around the grandmother's resting place, and Rebecca thinks 'of the years she had been there with the smell of salt on the springy turf, and the sea sounding, and the boats sailing around the Island and out to the fishing grounds'.[94] Although slipping into a romanticized view of St Ives, one very different to Nina's memory of salt and fog above, it is the interwoven nature of place and family ties which is ultimately important to Rebecca. So much so that, on the visit to St Ives whilst pregnant, she translates unborn Ruby's movement inside her as excitement, and recognition of her belonging in this place, even before she is in the world.[95]

In contrast, in *Talking to the Dead*, Nina sees death as cutting her off from her own family history, with the line of the cliff edge acting as the metaphor for this. She laments that: 'When both your parents are dead great slabs of the past drop away like eroded cliffs. I want my past back. I need it now, to ask it the questions I never realized I needed to ask. But there's nothing. Silence, and the shining of the sea where once there was land.'[96] Nina's past is submerged and, like the wrecks which litter this coastline, it is now inaccessible. In *Mourning Ruby*, however, those ties to family history remain in place across generations and Adam's grandmother's grave, embedded firmly within the ground of St Ives, tended by family, is very much a part of it. The edge here does not represent the line between life and death, or between history and its erasure. As a foundling left in a shoebox at the back of an Italian restaurant, Rebecca is struck by how Adam's history is 'carried on in the bloodstream' and how he 'reached so easily into his past, and pulled down handfuls of history'. Typical for Cornish families who have lived in one location for generations, he knows the lives of his ancestors, where they lived, where they are buried; and he remains connected to fellow descendants. Rebecca realizes, standing in Barnoon Cemetery, seven months pregnant, that 'Adam's ancestors would be Ruby's, too. She would pass through my historyless body and come into her inheritance.'[97] Through Adam, Ruby and Rebecca too are part of the web of family relationships that are embedded within, and interwoven with, a particular place across time. It is only possible through being 'placed' across generations of lives. This is why Ruby is safe at Barnoon.

The relationship between internal feelings and the external environment in Wyl Menmuir's *The Many* (2016) and Charlie Carroll's *The Lip* (2021) goes beyond the embedding of each with the other. In these novels the trauma of loss is externalized through environmental disasters at the coastal sites the protagonists inhabit. The novels have much in common. They are both set in fictional versions of the North Cornish coast, and feature local people's distrust of incomers and their associated fears about the changes this imposes on their home.[98] Both protagonists, Timothy Buchannan in *The Many* and Melody Janie in *The Lip*, are grieving for lost loved ones, conscious knowledge of which they suppress, from themselves and from the reader.

The Many is set in a small coastal fishing village. The atmosphere of the world created in the novel is strange, eerie, and, as a number of reviews have characterized it, unsettling.[99] Ordered by the Department of Fisheries and Aquaculture not to fish beyond a cordon of container ships that have been anchored on the horizon, local fishermen go through the motions of fishing without any hope of a catch within the now barren cordon zone. The place feels divorced from any world outside the village; huddled against the coast, with rising fields behind and the containers proscribing the view, even the 'empty expanse' of sea and sky feels 'oppressive and close'.[100] Told in the third person, the chapters alternate between the experiences of Timothy, an incomer who has bought a run-down house overlooking the sea, and Ethan, a local fisherman and friend of Perran who previously lived in Timothy's house, and who has mysteriously died.

The title of *The Lip* refers to a rocky outcrop at Bones Break which overlooks a zawn of black volcanic sand.[101] Teenager Melody Janie Rowe lives alone in a caravan concealed in the woods behind the lip. Her family's 'Cafy', bought by her father for her mother, is now closed and unfrequented by tourists; food putrefies in the freezers in its basement.[102] A loner, isolated from and surveilling the 'emmets' who mill over Bones Break taking in the view, Melody Janey forms a tentative friendship with Richard Brown, a Mancunian, and his rescue dog Archie.[103] Richard is actually Nicholas Cartwright, a landlord questioned over the rape and murder of one of his tenants. Released without charge, he has been relocated to Cornwall under a pseudonym for his own safety. Whilst quietly processing his own trauma, he befriends Melody Janie and helps her to confront her little sister Lucy's suicide at the lip; except that Little Sister Lucy turns out not to be her sibling at all.

Both *The Many* and *The Lip* write against a postcard version of Cornwall and the coast, to the extent that the Cornwall on the page is radically de-romanticized. In *The Lip*, the delineation of a North Cornish littoral retains an aesthetic appreciation of the view with which we are familiar. The north coast's own rugged, craggy beauty draws tourists to the lip to look out and to take photographs from it.[104] This is the only point at which Melody Janie and the visitors align, although Melody Janie feels she looks with indigenous, knowledgeable, and legitimated eyes. However, Melody Janie's first reference to the beauty of Bones Break reveals that it is, for her, inescapably coupled with darker realities of the landscape, aspects which are kept behind rather than included on the postcard. The narrative opens with Melody Janie's memory of witnessing Little Sister Lucy jump off the lip. She tells us, 'I have often wondered what she thought of in those last moments. I like to believe that if she thought of anything, it was of my land, of the overwhelming beauty of it from the lip.'[105] The aesthetic beauty of this place is associated with its antithesis from the first moment that we encounter Melody Janie and 'her' land.

A dichotomy is also present in the picturesqueness of the place versus its name: Bones Break. When Richard mentions that Bones Break is so-called because it is a 'notorious suicide spot', Melody Janie disagrees, despite this aligning exactly with her own traumatic experience. Her interpretation of the place name's origin is less gloomy, and she instead connects it to a wave, or break, named by surfers because the rocks make it 'impossible to surf'. Melody Janie is angered when Richard ups the ante here, surmising that perhaps they meant that 'the wave broke on the bones of suicide victims'.[106] Melody Janie's reaction, and her misinterpretation, is about more than being too close to the subject matter, and to her beloved land. Her suppression of suicide, and its innate connection to this place, demonstrates to us that Melody Janie sees Bones Break differently to others. She is withholding, from herself and from us, characteristics of this place that are of vital import, and this will be crucial as we reach the final twist in the narrative.

The Many goes further in its de-romanticization of the Cornish littoral. Firstly, it replaces a touristic aesthetic of the beach with something harsher. I have discussed above, and in other chapters, how the remnants of the mining industry, particularly engine houses, are co-opted into an aesthetic of the Cornish coast. This is not possible here with the paraphernalia of an active (though barely) fishing industry. In a flashback to his holiday with his partner Lauren, to the very same beach above which he has just bought a house, Timothy observes:

> The beach has an industrial look about it. Grey stones over which lies a thin coating of diesel, dropping steep down towards the sea, which looks unnaturally calm under the same film of oil. There are a few rusting hulls on the hard standing below the road, and bisecting the beach is a chain which runs up into the mouth of a stone building, in which he can see a heavy winch.[107]

This is a beach without sand which has been taken over by the practical apparatus of industry (an industry which, of course, pre-dates tourism) and is polluted with by-products from that industry; it is a long way from the more familiar understanding of the beach as leisurescape, and viewing it jars with Timothy and Lauren's expectations of a seaside getaway.

This anti-touristic delineation extends from the beach to also include the sea. Corbin explains how, culturally, sea bathing comes to be seen as a cure for a whole range of illnesses and disorders from the middle of the eighteenth century.[108] This understanding of the therapeutic benefits of immersion in the sea remains salient today, and is evidenced by the popularity of cold-water swimming for general health, chronic pain, and mental health conditions. However, the characteristics of the sea in *The Many* preclude an affirmative relationship with this natural element. Although the sea within the container-cordoned zone is barren, it is not inert. As a 'green' incomer, as Ethan calls him (and green meaning naive here rather than environmentalist), Timothy takes a dip in the sea shortly after moving into Perran's house. That he slices his feet on the rocks portends Ethan's warning.[109] He tells Timothy that 'if the tide doesn't get you, the chems will. You want to stay healthy past forty, alive past fifty, you'll remember to stay well out of the water.'[110] This is not just Ethan's proclivity; the Department for Fisheries and Aquaculture have warned of '[a] profusion of biological agents and contaminants' which could make you 'sick, or sterile'.[111] Whereas Corbin locates part of the pleasure of sea bathing in the 'aesthetics of the sublime', where there is only the pretence of danger, here the sea poses an existential threat, and in ways beyond the natural threat of the sea.[112] This version of the Cornish beach and sea is at odds with, indeed makes impossible, an experience of the littoral as a leisurescape.

In both novels, we step behind the postcard to be reorientated to a different perspective: one of lived experience of place through inhabitation. Ultimately, this shows us a destabilizing experience of place rooted in the fear of detrimental change. Both novels contain many of the actual concerns (around mass tourism, second homes, and the decline of traditional industries like fishing) of Cornish residents. We see Melody Janie's fear of the impacts of tourism manifest itself in her self-appointed position as owner and custodian of Bones Break and her impulse to surveil those treating *her* land with disrespect. She declares her spying 'an act of revenge', for

> [i]f they knew about Melody Janie down here, [on the rocky shelf below the coast path where she is concealed from view] watching piss dribble down their legs, they might think twice about what they have done, and what they continue to do. They might realise that this is a place that demands respect and nurture in equal measures,

not the grass-straining acid of urine, not the discarded bottles and crisp packets, not the flattening impressions of military-grade hiking boots.[113]

Yet her act of revenge is an impotent one. Hidden as she is on the cliff ledge, they do not know she is there. Her attitude to holidaymakers of 'let them visit, but don't let them stay' is her justification for remaining hidden, and is inherited from her dad, who hated their presence but needed their custom in the Cafy.[114] Yet she has no such grounds now that the Cafy is closed. Melody Janie fashions for herself, through watching visitors to her land, what she sees as the right kind of tourist, those who treat it with respect or who are 'discovering the medicine for their grief here'.[115] While we may wish for the same, we are simultaneously aware that she is powerless to affect who visits, which in turn exposes not these people for their behaviour but the fantasy of her position as custodian.

The stakes are higher for Melody Janie than for her father because she must bear witness to the 'spread' of tourists from Petherick to Bones Break that her father had feared. Petherick is a worrying exemplar of what is to come. It is a place where the 'simmering rage' of locals, priced out of their own town, spills over into violence.[116] There is no suggestion that this is violence born out of some kind of innate, Celtic savagery on which stereotypes of the Cornish have been known to draw. Rather, this is violence born of fear in the face of mass tourism, where enacting punishment on individuals becomes the outlet for a lack of actual agency in the face of detrimental change. Melody Janie sees the kind of future that is possible for Bones Break when she walks through a new estate of holiday lets and 'purpose-built second homes' in Petherick. The modern houses, boxes with huge swathes of glass, are designed to maximize access to a sea view. The marketing boards promote a luxury coastal lifestyle, depicting 'gorgeous people on gorgeous sand'. Yet Melody Janie is there out of season, and instead of a particular type of life, there is a 'complete absence of life'. It is a 'ghost town' which feels 'like an abandoned outpost or an old movie set of one, like some post-apocalyptic wilderness, like hibernation'. Except, of course, permanent residents like Melody Janie are not hibernating. Instead, they are destabilized by their own home becoming 'alien' to them as they are being alienated from it.[117]

In *The Many* we see very similar fears in the local population, which also results in distrust, surveillance, and violence. Here, however, what unfolds is not just destabilizing for the locals, but for the integrity of the narrative itself. Timothy turns up in the middle of ongoing anxieties over the future of fishing, and the hardship that has already been inflicted on the cove by the containership cordon. Timothy's arrival is doubly disruptive to the small fishing community because he is 'the incomer', and because he has bought the house that belonged to Perran, whose loss they are all grieving. Timothy comes to represent all incomers to this community; he is the locus for their fears, and so they are driven to surveil him. Ethan 'hears the stories' that Timothy's presence generates, that

> Timothy has come to resurrect Perran. He has come to destroy Perran's house, to erase his memory. He's come because that's what upcountry folk do, to replace the drudgery of the city with that of the coast. He has come to save them from themselves, or to hold up a mirror to them and they will see themselves reflected back in all their faults and backwardness. He has come to change them, to impose himself on them, to lead them or to fade into their shadows.[118]

Their fears are economic, psychological, and even existential.

Later, Ethan tells Timothy that, eventually, they will 'forget there was a time you weren't here'.[119] Before enough time has passed for this to happen, though, they vandalize his home (to them Perran's home) in the middle of his renovations. He returns one night to find the door forced open. The power is out, and he stumbles around in the pitch-black bumping into upturned furniture (lately purchased for the house). He cannot tell what is wet underfoot or what is causing the 'sharp chemical smell', but in the morning he discovers that paint has been 'poured out over the new carpets' and that '[t]here are tens of pairs of footprints walking through it in every direction'.[120] Ethan had also told Timothy that another way to make the locals forget him would be to leave. Here they try to force his hand through ratcheting up their hostility towards him.

The unrest and violence in both novels is part of a wider destabilizing experience of place caused by environmental disasters, and metaphorically, their relationship to suppressed grief, which threatens the very fabric of the Cornish worlds presented to us as readers. As already discussed above, both novels register environmental damage and contamination of the Cornish coast. Melody Janie is angered by over-tourism at Bones Break, and the harm to the environment inflicted by holidaymakers, who ironically, are there to enjoy its beauty. In *The Many* the results of industrial pollution—mutant fish, oil-slicked beaches, 'plastic shrapnel' at the shoreline—makes the cove impossible to aestheticize and contributes to its strangeness.[121]

In both narratives environmental disasters—a landslide in *The Lip* and flooding in *The Many*—form climactic moments. These events remind us of the liminal nature of the coast and 'the perceived threat posed by this unstable meeting point of land and sea'.[122] Melody Janie feels the vibrations as 'her' land rends. She describes 'a crackling cracking, like long lightening, then the staccato machine-gun fire of splintered rock dispersing, striking water after an excruciating drop'.[123] In *The Many*, on the same morning that Timothy surveys the vandalization of his home, daylight also reveals that 'the sea has risen overnight and the beach has been entirely drowned'. The café 'is now an island floating in the sea [...] unhitched from the land'.[124] While both of these events can be classed as natural disasters, they are also redolent of rising sea levels and more extreme weather events caused by climate change. In *The Lip*, there have been ominous warning signs: other landslides and rockfalls had occurred in the previous year during multiple storms. Melody Janie explains to Richard that '[a] lot of the coast path around Bones Break sits on an overhang'.[125] The ocean's pummelling of the rockface hollows out the cliff face, destabilizing the ground above it where Melody Janie and Richard stand, and where holidaymakers drink in the view.

These ecological events inflict irreversible change on the Cornish littoral, whilst simultaneously calling attention to that space as 'topographically unstable' and so vulnerable to further transformation. As a permanent resident with intimate knowledge of the coastline, Melody Janie both registers, and mourns, its alteration. In contrast, Richard admits that he does not possess the same knowledge or insight. He tells her 'I don't see it all as you see it. That landslide on the eastern headland, I've walked past that a dozen times, but I had no idea it had only just happened. To me it was part of the landscape, part of the coastline.'[126] In *The Many*, as Jimmy Packham identifies, Ethan experiences a sense of loss in the aftermath of the flood. The permanent change is disorientating: 'He feels as though everything has been replaced by someone who knows this place well, but who has had to reconstruct it from memory.'[127] Packham argues that '[w]ith the beach in a state of continual erasure and renewal, it remains for Ethan the *heimlich* and familiar space of home, and, simultaneously, the *unheimlich* space, out of kilter with itself, from which he is gradually being alienated'.[128] Environmental events here heighten the strangeness of place, even for locals, and make it clear that people are destabilized as well as the land.

The protagonists and the coastal landscapes of their novels are deeply interrelated. The environmental disasters which wreak havoc on the Cornish coast in *The Many* and *The Lip* can also be read as an externalization of the emotional turmoil of those protagonists. The personal loss suffered by Timothy and by Melody Janie is suppressed from their own conscious thought, and is concurrently withheld from the reader, until the denouement of the respective narratives. Melody Janie's sister turns out to have been her mother, who committed suicide by jumping from the lip. Timothy has come to Cornwall following the death of his baby son, named Perran it turns out, just like the previous owner of the house he has come to renovate. Therefore, the actual rending of their worlds, the 'fracturing and splitting' of the rock in *The Lip* and the deep fissures that 'run and spread throughout the fabric of the whole place' towards the end of *The Many*, are symbolic of what loss has done to their lives.[129] The unfamiliarity of their environment, after the cliff collapses in *The Lip* and after the storm in *The Many*, the strangeness of this new world to them, is reminiscent of the experience of grief. In *The Many* too, as well as Timothy actually going to sea with Ethan, the sea is used by Timothy to reference an emotional state of being 'at sea'. For instance, at one point Timothy 'has the feeling he is no longer on land and that the village itself is a sea'.[130] Therefore, when the sea overwhelms the land, flooding it, drowning it, we can see this also as a metaphor for Timothy's grief. Environmental damage here then, and pollution, makes a statement about just that, whilst also externalizing through the Cornish coastal landscape an internal experience of loss.

In *The Lie*, another of Helen Dunmore's Cornish novels, and *The Visitor* by Katherine Stansfield (whose Cornish crime fiction we encountered in the previous chapter), the protagonists inhabit coastal locations whilst dealing with illnesses which alter their perception of, and indeed reconstitute, the world around them. In *The Lie*, Daniel Branwell has returned to Cornwall following the First World War, suffering from shell shock and intense grief after the loss of his childhood friend and first love, Frederick, on the battlefield. Due to Daniel's shell-shocked state, Frederick manifests to him as a grim revenant 'clagged in mud from head to foot'.[131] There are a number of lies which could possibly be the one of the novel's title, but the most obvious is his pretence that Mary Pascoe, who took him in upon his return, is still alive, even though he has, in abidance with her last wish, buried her in her garden (following her passing from natural causes).

In *The Visitor*, Pearl has lived her whole life in Morlanow (meaning 'high tide' in Cornish), a fishing village reminiscent of St Ives. She seems to be suffering from dementia and the text is structured through her increasingly mixed-up memories, so that we bounce around in time from 1880 to 1936. Married to childhood friend Jack, Pearl laments choosing him over their mutual friend Nicholas, and so the memories primarily return to that lost relationship. Both Daniel and Pearl, on the edge psychically, go beyond the physical edge at the end of their respective novels. Pearl swims out into the sea believing she is swimming into Nicholas's arms, and Daniel, chased to the cliff edge by his community (because of the lie), steps off to take what he thinks is Frederick's hand. At the denouement of these novels, then, their imagined worlds are more powerful than the physical reality of their environment, and so they both literally and figuratively go over the edge.

For both Daniel and Pearl there is a layering of time so that, whilst they live in one moment, they simultaneously experience other periods from their life. For both of them, this goes beyond remembering to a vivid reliving. For Daniel, his war experience replays in flashbacks which bring on violent shakes, and in the regular appearance of Frederick. Daniel describes how his memory 'cuts into the past, as sharp as a knife, and serves it up glistening'. It seems so real to Daniel in those moments, and he himself recognizes that '[i]t's not the same thing as remembering, because it has colour and smell and taste'. Those smells are of '[r]aw earth, raw iron, meat, explosive'.[132] The aftershocks of his traumatic experience of the war dismantle the geographical and temporal barriers between his two worlds so that his past bleeds into his present, into the environment which he calls home. At the same time, his affinity with the coastal landscape of his home, fostered in childhood, is transmuted in adulthood into something which helps to explain his new existence between these two worlds. After a flashback episode, during which he is reduced to a shivering, sweating wreck on the floor, he explains that '[i]t washes over me like the hundredth wave and I cling to the rock'. He articulates the experience by referring back to a childhood game played with Frederick, where they would wait until the last minute on a rocky promontory in the sea to run away from the hundredth wave (always the one with the biggest swell) before it engulfed them.[133] When he actually revisits that site, the indifference of the sea to his survival makes him realize how hard he is prepared to fight for his life. It is, therefore, a way for him to understand both the attitude of war to human life and his present situation, as well as giving him a sense of something bigger than himself.[134]

Pearl's memories become an increasingly vivid reliving, and the different eras of her life in Morlanow resurface with growing regularity. Her present cannot be separated from her past. She describes it as being as if 'the past was bottled in the cleft Morlanow filled and it continued to reverberate through the soil and the waves, no matter what she did'.[135] As the narrative and the disease progresses, and the present retreats, she begins to experience time differently so that, for Pearl '[t]ime wasn't behaving as it should. Days were ducking past her, shying from their usual order so that as she looked back over the last week there were holes. Clocks didn't seem to be truthful.'[136] Like Daniel, her local environment is an anchor despite the destabilizing experience of her condition. For Pearl it is the sea and swimming in it which, even though it is always changing, and even though it has dangers which she well recognizes, remains a constant in her life from childhood, and throughout her illness. Due to its presence in all eras of her life, it is also where she can most easily connect to the past that she most wants to access, to her girlhood and to Nicholas. We are told that

> [t]he years fell away when she swam, as if the effort of each stroke took her further back in time. Perhaps if she swam for long enough she could find the young girl watching Nicholas launch a model boat with a white handkerchief sail, find the fish salted in the palace [where women had packed the pilchard catch] and her mother singing them to sleep.[137]

It may at first seem as if her relationship to the sea is accentuating her immersion in her past at the expense of her present, but, as will become clear, it is impossible for her to find herself in her present time.

Both Daniel and Pearl are alienated from aspects of their present environment, and this ultimately leads them to be cast off in the world created by their illnesses, which ends in their death. In *The Lie*, acts of deception occur because of the impossibilities of communication for a shell-shocked soldier such as Daniel, in the immediate post-war era. As mentioned above, the most obvious candidate for the falsehood of the novel's title is the fiction Daniel creates around Mary Pascoe's death, telling people that she has gone to stay with her sister, when he has actually buried her in her garden. However, Daniel also lies about Frederick's death, in order to conceal the full horrors of his final moments from his sister Felicia. Felicia gives him the opportunity to tell the truth, and he confesses to her that his letter was a falsehood, yet she recognizes the impossibility of communication even though she is willing to be told. She understands why '[e]veryone had a letter like that one we had'.[138] Therefore, whilst Daniel is burdened with an excess of remembering, his experience of war has created an 'unbridgeable gap' between himself and non-combatants within his community.[139] In the immediate post-war era, there was an unwillingness to confront the awful impacts of the war. Pictures of bodies were banned, but the visibility of shell-shocked soldiers, because they had returned, was problematic. Wyatt Bonikowski explains that

> [p]hotographs of shell-shocked soldiers [...] were printed for public consumption, showing blank faces and twisted limbs, suggesting a haunting excess written on the surface of the body but pointing to a deeper, invisible disturbance.
>
> The shell-shocked soldier was not dead, but he was not quite alive either since he seemed to be inhabited by some alien force encountered at war and brought home with him.[140]

Just like actual shell-shocked soldiers, and other characters from modernist literature (such as Septimus Smith in *Mrs Dalloway*), Daniel is a kind of revenant, stuck between life and death. As Bonikowski explains, 'silence manifests itself most emphatically upon the soldier's return from war, in his encounter with a home that has become strange'.[141] The lies which are Daniel's undoing now seem to have been inevitable, a product of the impossibility of articulating his experience. On a walk with Felicia, he passes an engine house and describes it as 'half ruined now. Crows fly up as we approach. The walls are thick with ivy.'[142] This moment is representative of the death of mining, but it also signals the lack of a possible future for Daniel, and both the decay and the crows foretell of his own death. Ultimately, there is no possible route to reintegration into his previous life. He is cast out from his local community, which is vividly represented when they chase him to the cliff edge. He tries with everything he has to outrun them, and we might think here too of the equally impossible task of outrunning his own demons caused by war. In his final moment, his psychic and physical situation become one, and he goes from being on the edge to the space beyond it, reaching for Frederick's invisible hand, and so to his death.[143]

Pearl's alienation from her home is not due to her illness, but is caused by the encroachment of tourism into Morlanow. Like other locals, Pearl and husband Jack are pushed up the hill into newer houses, while cottages are made over for holidaymakers.[144] The refashioning of this fishing village for a tourist market makes Pearl's home strange to her. There are many instances of this, but her reaction to a poster on the door of the ticket office encapsulates how she is disorientated within her own home:

> The poster showed the seafront with several new-looking fishing boats moored up. Two people stood admiring it: a fisherman and a little girl in a pretty cream dress. The rest of the seafront was empty. The sea filled most of the poster. It was beautiful: rich blue with purple to show the gentle swell. The hills that flanked it were gold and though the sun itself wasn't in the picture she could feel it in every drop of the paint. It was as if heat was seeping from the paper. It looked such a wonderful place, so still and quiet, so many lovely new boats, that she found herself wishing she could go, but then she saw 'Morlanow' written underneath. She was already here.[145]

Tourism also imposes a different concept of time onto Morlanow, so that it is not just Pearl's dementia which affects how time is experienced by her. While Pearl has, like Daniel, an excess of time, simultaneously living in the present moment and reliving past eras of her life, the railway company looking to entice holidaymakers to Morlanow promotes it as 'timeless Cornwall'. Though the poster with this slogan features a fisherman with a bussa jar of pilchards, he is alongside mermaids and King Arthur. This is not Pearl's past reflected back at her.[146] In presenting Morlanow as a place that differs from Pearl's lived experience, it erases her past as we might also expect her illness to do. Yet, crucially, this is part of a collective forgetting, precipitated by external forces, rather than the kind of memory loss we would associate with dementia. In this new era, 'there were no seine boats and no great nets to shoot, no maids to tend the fish and no palace to keep them safe and salted. There was nothing but forgetfulness in Morlanow'.[147] Morlanow has lost touch with its original purpose, with the reason why a settlement was first created on the very edge of the land. Therefore, '[t]he past, parcelled together by fish, by catches, by stories shared then shared again—is fading'.[148] Pearl and her fellow inhabitants have been displaced physically from their home, and from their own history, which is inextricably connected to that home, and which is being erased because of the different priorities of tourism.

It is Pearl's experience of Morlanow in an era of tourism, then, which destabilizes her sense of self, cutting her off from her own history and physically removing her from the village. Rebecca Bitenc identifies 'the dominant discourse of dementia [narratives] as "loss of self" and argues that 'the core element of [...] dehumanisation [of those suffering from dementia] lies in the fact that dementia is commonly understood to be synonymous with "losing one's self"'.[149] Pearl's experience is exactly the opposite—it is her excess of time, and of remembering, that reconnects her in the most vivid way possible with her own history, and with Morlanow's past as it was experienced, and not as it is packaged for a tourist market. It is how she accesses what she sees as her true self, the one she had lost in marrying Jack instead of Nicholas. This is why Pearl's past becomes more real than her present. When she swims out into the sea for the final time, she does so because '[t]here was nothing left on land'. The sea, the one constant in her life, and the place where she can most easily access that past, merges with Nicholas and satisfies her one desire to be reunited with him.[150]

All the novels under examination in this chapter go beyond an aesthetic rendering of the Cornish littoral. The Cornish coast functions here both as a point of connection out towards other territories, positioning it globally, and as a stopping point where emotional and psychological edges must also be dealt with. In this context, the coastal aesthetic is either irrelevant, or it is tied to something darker and less certain. All of the characters encountered in this chapter have an intense relationship with the coastal site, both positive and negative, through which they are formed and changed, at the same time as the landscape itself is reimagined for us as readers.

Chapter Four

Urban Cornwall

Mr Simons's dream is to live inland. That's where I'd like to live, Muster Lee, 'mong the trees, where nothin'd meet my sight but trees. Out o' sight o' the say [sea] for ever.

The Cornish Journal of Charles Lee (22 November 1892)[1]

We are leaving this village, with its face turned to the water, and people say constantly: 'you will miss the sea.' And my instinct is to resist. I won't miss it. But how can I know? If I haven't been able to understand the presence of the sea, what chance is there of understanding its absence?

Philip Marsden, *The Levelling Sea* (2011)[2]

In this and the next chapter we too are turning away from the sea to inland locations: Truro in this chapter, and the clay area and Bodmin Moor in Chapter Five. In the most recent BBC adaptation of *Poldark*, which first aired in 2015, Truro is relocated to the coast, with the port scenes filmed at Charlestown.[3] Truro is actually an inland port, sitting around ten miles from the coast at the head of the Fal estuary. Such is the dominance of the aesthetic of the coast in this adaptation of Winston Graham's novels, and in the construction of Cornwall more widely, that this inaccuracy is permissible, even necessary, to keep the sea in view. It is a very different attitude to that expressed by Mr Simons above, as recorded in the journal of the novelist Charles Lee, who wants to get away from the sight of the sea. It is a desire not often aired today, as we can see from the reaction to Philip Marsden's plans above, because of the dominance of the coastal site, the sea view, as the premium site: aesthetically and commercially. Truro does not possess an aesthetic value for the 'sun, sea, sand' promotion of Cornwall. Unless transformed to fit, Truro sits outside a tourist narrative because it occupies an inland space often completely absent from the cultural production of Cornwall.

Truro also does not fit because it is an urban space. *Dan Daddow's Cornish Comicalities* (2016), one of the novels discussed in this chapter, refers to 'the urban sprawl of Truro'.[4] This chapter is provocatively titled 'Urban Cornwall' because it is not a term often used, or which seems to have a basis for existence in connection with Cornwall. There is very little sense, in terms of how Cornwall is portrayed, of it having urban sites. Of course, the extent of its urbanity is limited and, though a city, Truro is no bigger than many other towns in Britain—yet, at the same time, city status is inextricable from a concurrent urban designation. The positive and negative (and often stereotypical and problematic) connotations of urban sites as worldly, progressive, and connected on the one hand, and noisy, crowded, and chaotic on the other are relevant to, but also modified by, Truro. Truro's urbanity holds it in tension with a common perception of Cornwall as remote and rural. Truro is both connected and remote. It defies stereotypical ways of seeing Cornwall, as well as being defined or confined by those same versions of place. Truro is therefore a perfect case study for exploring a different kind of space within Cornwall, and within fiction of Cornwall.

It is not surprising, therefore, that there are few fictional renderings of Truro. At the same time, though, Truro is not a hidden space within Cornwall, as places such as Camborne and Redruth are absent from a tourist view today. Truro's interior location is also a central one so that, as David Mudd points out, '[i]t just isn't possible to find a map of Cornwall without Truro appearing on it. All roads, it seems, lead there or else pass so close as to make no difference.'[5] It is not that Truro is omitted from histories, or from consideration by travellers (although Wilkie Collins does miss it out completely from his *Rambles Beyond Railways* of 1851), but it is often only mentioned in passing, because it is a place through which people pass. This reflects its function, but does not focus on it as a place in its own right. In novels too Truro, if mentioned, is most often a place through which people pass (rather than stay or experience in any meaningful way) either en route to West Cornwall or headed east for England. For example, in Thomas Hardy's short story 'A Mere Interlude', two of the characters stay for a night in Truro, but for readers it remains distant: we get to hear about it, but we do not get to experience it with them.

This chapter focuses on a book series and two other novels which significantly feature Truro, and they are among only a small number of texts to do so: Winston Graham's *Poldark* series (twelve books written between 1945 and 2002), Alan M. Kent's *Dan Daddow's Cornish Comicalities* (2016), and Jack Clemo's *Wilding Graft* (1948). Spanning the late eighteenth to mid-twentieth centuries in their settings, these texts all resist an aesthetic rendering of Truro. In *Poldark*, Truro of the late eighteenth and early nineteenth century is a place for business and dissipation, where money, status, and power is accessed and performed. In *Dan Daddow*, mid-nineteenth-century Truro reeks of fish from the quay, essential for commerce, but also symbolic of the moral decay of the town. In *Wilding Graft*, Truro during the Second World War is a place where people come to escape the war and be safe, but it is not a place to hide—it is where people are seen or found, tracked and accosted.[6] There is an interplay in these novels between performance, visibility, and invisibility within the Cornish urban space, which forms the focus of this chapter.

Truro's award of city status in 1877 was something of a fluke. Firstly, it won out over Bodmin, St Columb and St Germans to be the location for the cathedral of the new Cornish diocese. All of the sites in the running had something to offer, but Truro's central location, its rail and road links, and the potential of the site of St Mary's Church as the location for the new cathedral was to its advantage. Yet no one really knew what happened next. Did Truro automatically become a new city? Truro had to grasp the nettle so as not to miss the significant opportunity of becoming the only city in Cornwall. An application was made and city status conferred by Queen Victoria. It was the first city to be confirmed as such that did not yet have a cathedral (which would take the next thirty years to build). For future towns, application for city status was separated from the creation of an episcopal see; Truro had sneaked in while the procedure was still unclear.[7]

This is not to say that Truro did not deserve its city status. Looking back, it is difficult to think that anywhere else in Cornwall was in the running for the status that Truro has enjoyed since 1877, because it already felt at the centre of things: commerce, industry, fashion, and social life. In 1809 the Reverend Richard Warner finds that in Truro 'all the modes of polished life are visible, in genteel houses, elegant hospitality, fashionable apparel, and courteous manners'.[8] In 1824 F.W.L. Stockdale, like Warner, journeys through Cornwall and remarks that '[t]he town of Truro, may not improperly be denominated the metropolis of the county'.[9] John Passmore Edwards, born just outside Truro at Blackwater, generously used his acquired fortune to erect public buildings in the area. In 1896, at the opening of the library which he had financed, he remarked that his chief reason for doing so was that 'Truro is the centre of Cornwall'.[10]

This characterization of Truro is reflected in Winston Graham's series of twelve *Poldark* novels. Truro is first seen in the opening pages of book one when the saga's protagonist, Ross Poldark, returns to Cornwall from fighting in the American War of Independence. Exiting the coach at Truro in the year 1783, Ross looks around at the town for the first time in a decade, and we are told that

> Truro in the old days had been the centre of 'life' for him and his family. A port and a coinage town, *the* shopping centre and a meeting place of fashion, the town had grown rapidly in the last few years, new and stately houses having sprung up among the disorderly huddle of old ones to mark its adoption as a winter and town residency by some of the oldest and most powerful families in Cornwall. The new aristocracy too were leaving their mark: the Lemons, the Treworthys, the Warleggans, families which had pushed their way up from humble beginnings on the crest of new industries.
>
> A strange town. He felt it more on his return. A secretive, important little town, clustering in the fold of the hills astride and about its many streams, almost surrounded by running water and linked to the rest of the world by fords, by bridges, and by stepping-stones.[11]

Truro's first of many appearances in the *Poldark* series gives a sense of its importance and grandeur, its development and growth, but also of the performative way in which it presents itself to the world outside the rivers that almost encircle it. Here too, though, is a suggestion of the reverse: of the town's secretive nature, and therefore its duality as separate, isolated, couched inside its flowing rivers, whilst simultaneously connected by them and across them.

Truro, then, occupied quasi-metropolitan status, over and above other Cornish towns, as early as the eighteenth century. This is not to say, though, that some of those other sites did not rival Truro at various points in history. Located just ten miles down the River Fal, Falmouth (and before Falmouth, Penryn) was its closest competitor. Truro and

Falmouth are often paired together in guidebooks of Cornwall, just as they are linked by the River Fal, but they are quite different. A burgeoning maritime port from the seventeenth century onwards, Falmouth is coastal and has a more exotic feel than Truro, not just because of the palm trees lining the streets, but because it also enjoyed an international mix of people coming off the boats into port, and goods such as spices and cloth coming in from around the world.[12] In Alan M. Kent's *Dan Daddow's Cornish Comicalities*, Dan is very aware of the differences between Truro and Falmouth. He says,

> Falmouth, I knew, was more multi-cultural; its position as a deep-water harbour brought the larger ships in: the tall-masted brigantines and schooners, that all had too deep drafts and could not make their way up the Fal to the port of Truro. Falmouth brought peoples from all over the empire. There, could be found on its streets, Africans and Indians, Poles and Russians, South Americans—and even souls who had made it over the seven seas from China. Truro was feeling very provincial when compared to all that wonder.[13]

Here, as discussed in Chapter Three, the port of Falmouth is a locus of connection to the rest of the world, which is a less prominent way of characterizing Cornwall compared to the more salient version of the Duchy as rural and remote. As a busy coastal port, Falmouth is more immediately connected to the outside world, and to a global network of exchange of goods. Falmouth, therefore, had a lot to recommend it. It also had the upper hand in certain respects. Ships headed for the port of Truro had first to come through Falmouth's coastal entrance to the Fal, as its name suggests. The road connecting Falmouth to Truro was a 'vital' route, not only for the transportation of goods, but also for information.[14] Therefore, Truro's connectedness and its timely access to up-to-date news (aspects very important to its metropolis status) was partly reliant upon a nearby town, which it could also class as an economic rival. Consequently, there were battles over things which might impact the status of either, including the location of Truro's water boundary, which had once reached all the way to Falmouth harbour. By 1709 the Borough of Truro had no choice but to accept that Falmouth now had control of the land and river closest to the sea.[15] This also meant that Truro, although less vulnerable in its inland position, now had to rely on Falmouth's coastal defences to protect it from any potential attack.[16] If rivals, they were also unavoidably connected: geographically, economically, and defensively.

Across its history, Truro had experienced highs and lows of prosperity, and would do so again in the nineteenth and twentieth centuries whilst riding the fortunes of the metal mining industry. Daniel Defoe, in his tour of Great Britain in the early eighteenth century (published 1724–27), did not hold out much hope for Truro's chances against Falmouth. 'The town is well built', he declares, 'but shows that it has been fuller, both of houses and inhabitants than it is now; nor will it probably ever rise while the town of Falmouth stands where it does, and while trade is settled in it as it is'. Celia Fiennes visited Truro shortly before Defoe and found it to have 'become a ruinated disregarded place', a sad deterioration from its former status as 'a great trading town'.[17] The period of the late eighteenth and early nineteenth centuries, when the *Poldark* novels are set, is a high point for Truro, during which it can be described as a 'rich and confident town'.[18] In this moment, and indeed for 'hundreds of years' it was prospering on the back of the profits from Cornwall's primary industry, so much so that 'the streets of the town could be said to be paved with tin and copper'. It also then suffered due to the disastrous collapse of that industry in the nineteenth century, and from the gradual decline of its port, partly due to the loss of mineral exports across the century.[19]

In the 1920s when the River Kenwyn between Lemon Quay and Back Quay was concreted over, it seemed to sound a death knell for Truro's industry, and its identity.[20] Yet it was done with a specific purpose: to provide adequate parking for those who would come to Truro to buy goods.[21] Truro had always been a locus for the purveying and procuring of goods; its desire to capitalize further on its commercial potential is an example of Truro's staying power. So too is its mammoth building effort to erect a cathedral in the aftermath of mining's collapse. Whilst Truro experienced significant dips in prosperity over the course of the nineteenth and early twentieth centuries, it gradually succeeded in wrenching away the assizes and administrative powers from Bodmin, which had a long history as a centre of power in Cornwall, so that by the early twentieth century it could claim to have also taken the title of county town, as well as that of the only city in Cornwall.[22] How Truro managed this in the face of significant economic challenges has something to do with the awareness of the importance of performance from those working in its interests.

Performing Truro

The effectiveness of Truro's performance as an important county town depended largely on its ability to control the optics by crafting the aesthetics of its space. This had much more to do with its built environment than with its natural features, such as its three rivers which, as they became increasingly less navigable, were bridged and built over.[23] The demolition of Middle Row in the 1790s had the biggest visual impact on the heart of the town.[24] The *Poldark* books span across this period of change, and in *The Four Swans* (book six) Ross witnesses Middle Row's demolition. Middle Row would have been a costume drama's dream filming location. A row of higgledy-piggledy shops and stalls, also containing the market house and the prison, it would have been a cramped and busy locus for the bustling life of the town. Either side of Middle Row were narrow streets covered in dirt and muck which added to the difficulty of squeezing past travellers coming towards you. Ross Poldark's anticipation of 'a large new street' which would bring 'space and air' is certainly realized.[25] The result of Middle Row's demolition was the epitome of what Truro was trying to achieve in its reinvention of itself. Boscawen Street is 'a very wide and spacious street with an air of importance'. The concurrent rechristening of surrounding streets as King Street, Princes Street, and Duke Street also gives some indication of the distinction Truro was aiming for.[26] Middle Row's demise had produced an almost overindulgently wide main street, one fit for its county town pretensions, and for its rise in status later in the century.

Truro's benefactors, patrons, and governors, from the late eighteenth century onwards, seemed, from our perspective at least, to have had a clear idea about the direction in which Truro was heading. They were remodelling Truro into a spa town (minus the actual spa) of the far southwest. According to S.P.B. Mais, they succeeded. When he visited Truro in the 1920s he called it 'decidedly a town with an atmosphere, [...] [that] might not be displeased at being termed the Bath of the Duchy'.[27] He would have gained that sense not only from the wide cobbled street at the centre of town, but from the style and look of the buildings. Several key sites within Truro are built with Bath stone, including parts of the cathedral, the Assembly Rooms, and the majestic row of Georgian Houses on Lemon Street. The prevalence of Bath stone is at first surprising, given the availability of and local connection to granite. Yet local man made

Figure 5: Engraving of Boscawen Street (c.1830) (Courtesy of Kresen Kernow)

good Ralph Allen owned Bath stone mines and facilitated its use in Truro, at a time when visiting Bath was very fashionable for local aristocrats, as it was across the country. Bath stone gave Truro gravitas, conveyed not only through the style into which such stone could be cut, but in the warmth of the yellow stone that was very different to the harsh greyness of granite.[28]

Even when building in granite, there was an acute eye for style, and for the statement that a building could make about itself and the town more widely. For the Town Hall, rebuilt in 1847 (now the Hall for Cornwall), the architect Christopher Eales produced an impressive frontage in the Charles Barry style, looking out across the wide expanse of Boscawen Street, and to the rear Back Quay and the River Kenwyn.[29] The grand arches and detailed window mouldings recall Barry's Italianate design of the Pall Mall Reform Club, and can be seen as part of Truro's claim upon a metropolitan identity.[30] Alongside the Bath-esque grandeur of other parts of the town, such architectural choices during the late eighteenth and nineteenth centuries can be seen as resulting from a self-conscious aim to perform a metropolitan status via the built environment of the town. Such stylistic choices connect it to London and other cities by projecting Truro as the fashionable town of Cornwall and the south-west.

Underperforming Truro

Dan Daddow's Cornish Comicalities undermines the performative aspect of Truro's status through the attitude of its eponymous protagonist, who bitingly cuts down and exposes spectacle as pretention. 'The town', he affirms, 'still wanted to be grander than it was'. Looking up Lemon Street he declares that it 'so wanted to be Bath, but failed miserably'. To Dan, Boscawen Street's eminence is just fakery. He tells us that '[a]ll around were the façades of dwellings that gave the deceit of being some bustling city, but actually were just false fronts to otherwise dowdy brick dwellings'.[31] A seasoned theatre manager, he is attuned to the performative aspects of Truro's built environment and unmasks them by revealing what lies behind the scenes.

As our narrator, though, Dan is our only access to this world, which lives and breathes through his attitudes and prejudices. His account is written in 1900, fifty years after the events it recounts. He claims his mind 'is still razor sharp', his memory infallible, and that we the reader have complete access.[32] Yet we see his taste for performance too; we see him dissemble, we witness drug taking, we hear him confess his unreliability and indulge his imagination, and we are left to wonder, therefore, about the access we are getting to this world. Truro through Dan's eyes, then, is always unstable. His unglossed version of Truro, and Cornwall as a whole, is arresting, though, partly because in our age of mass tourism, it sets a challenge to a romanticized version of Cornwall to which we may have become inured.

Dan Daddow's Cornish Comicalities dismantles Truro's aesthetic, not only through ridiculing the pretensions of Truro's built environment, but also by forcing the reader to pay attention to smell. The space is olfactorily intrusive. It smells so noxiously of fish, sailed inland to be salted, gutted, cooked, or sold, that 'you would barely believe humanity could stand to live there'. 'Fish', Dan laments,

> belched from old men's guts, it was farted from children, it fused in the damp vaginas of middle-aged women. Fish spewed from the quayside onto the tidal muds where crabs gnawed and sucked down the remains [...]. The smell of fish exuded from every drain, every orifice in the ground, every sewer, every leat, every chute, every well (holy or unholy), every granite kennel, every gully and every launder. It heaved itself into every barrel and bottle, every pocket and handbag, under each nail, in each crevice.[33]

In the *Poldark* novels our attention is occasionally brought to the stench of the narrow streets which are clogged with waste, but in *Dan Daddow* we are made to continually experience it.[34] Smell, in this version of Truro, undermines any performance of power, wealth, or status that the town is attempting to enact through the aesthetic of its streets and buildings.

The ubiquity and inescapability of foul smells in Truro acts as a democratizing element, regardless of the desires of those in the upper echelons of society to distinguish themselves. At the same time, it prevents the performance of wealth from being disconnected from the industries (in this case fishing) from which it is often derived. As John Urry argues, 'smell is a subversive sense since it cannot be wholly banished'.[35] In Truro, '[t]he scales and stench could be lightly found on clothes too—on bussles and towsers, bonnets and ribbons, frocks and top hats, spats and silks, boots and petticoats, hats and caps, fans and gloves, feathers and furs. Posh or poor—it mattered not. It was still there.'[36] As well as the direct comment here that it infiltrates the fabric of 'posh or poor', the length of the list of clothing and the range of items, from towsers (an apron worn by balmaidens) to the feathers and furs of the upper classes, reinforces the uniformity with which smell is encountered within this urban environment.

Smell, then, 'demarcated the unnaturalness of the city' so that 'the modern project to create a pure, rational order of things is undermined'.[37] This impacts the built environment and its symbolism, but, significantly, also the social structures and relations within urban spaces. Stallybrass and White point out that 'the city [...] still continued to invade the privatised body and household of the bourgeoisie as smell', exactly as we see happening within homes in Truro.[38] This is even more problematic for class divisions when we recognize a social need to hierarchize smell. As Constance Classen, David Howes, and Anthony Synnott argue, 'manipulating odour values is a common and effective means of generating and maintaining social hierarchies. This may explain why smell is enlisted not only to create and enforce class boundaries, but also ethnic and gender boundaries.' They go on to say that '[a]s the upper and middle classes, at first reluctantly, began to purify their bodies, their homes and their streets of dirt, they grew more conscious of the malodours of the working classes which did not'.[39] In Truro, though, smell overpowers these attempts at distinction, making a mockery of them. Those who had thought themselves in control of the social hierarchy of smell, those whose distinction derived from an absence of smell, or from being sweet-smelling, have no way to avoid smelling the same as those at the bottom of that social scale, those whom they had positioned outside acceptable society because of their foul odour. This has implications for how the different classes exist alongside each other within the Cornish urban space, and for the performance of wealth and status that Truro is engaged in.

Looking, Seeing, and Being Visible

Try to forget the overpowering smell for a moment and return to the image we had of Truro at the beginning of the last section, as an environment constructed to exude wealth and status. This is a very different aesthetic to that of the coastal site which, while access to it can be connected to wealth and status, is primarily based on its natural features. Truro's style, the experience of its space, is created by its human-made environment which emulates an English style of spa town, or at least an English (and the continental styles which have influenced English cities) metropolitanism in style rather than the individuality, the particular Cornishness, which is a key feature of promotion of the coast as a destination. Truro is performing an aesthetic, but not one that is tied to natural beauty—rather one that is allied with status, power, wealth, and governance.

The expansive view accorded at the coast is actually precluded by Truro's built environment and its inland location. As discussed in the next chapter, there are inland sites (in the clay area and on Bodmin Moor) which afford a view of both coasts at the same time, reminding us of the proximity of the coast and the conditional nature of being inland when it comes to a peninsula like Cornwall. In Sarah Moss's *Signs for Lost Children*, the asylum sits atop one of the hills overlooking the city.[40] Ally, a doctor who works at the asylum, appreciates its location as another one of the spots from which it is possible to see both coasts. Yet at the same time that this possibility is touted, it is also jeopardized by 'the way the mizzle veils this thin slip of land between two coasts', suggesting that, on the morning she pauses to enjoy the micro-scale view of settling rain droplets, the mizzle has taken away access to Cornwall's edges.[41] In *Dan Daddow's Cornish Comicalities*, ironically, the haze from the stench of fish brought inland from the sea prevents any possibility of a view because it 'seemed to leak from the sky' so that 'the sea and sky often melted and fused together'. As a result, 'the town never had a horizon'.[42] The prospect view is drastically occluded in *Dan Daddow*, and so the experience of

Truro's inland location is intensified by a cocooning of its buildings and inhabitants inside a world where that kind of view, that kind of looking and seeing, is prevented.

Whilst this urban space prevents one kind of looking, it opens up possibilities for viewing of another kind. This is particularly the case at the heart of Truro, in the wide expanse of Boscawen Street (since the demolition of Middle Row), which acts as a stage overlooked by grand buildings. Within this human-made site, instead of looking taking place across an expansive landscape, it becomes about looking at buildings, objects, and people within the enclosed site, which intensifies the effect of display, of performance, and of visibility. The built environment, created to impress and to foster looking at it, is also shaped to bring the eye to people and objects that exist within it. It is the experience and effects of looking and seeing, performing and being seen in these novels that I want to consider now, followed by an examination of how looking and seeing is both classed and gendered, and how it is also problematized and undermined by these same texts, and by other aspects of the physical environment.

Both the *Poldark* series and *Dan Daddow's Cornish Comicalities* feature the same example of this kind of viewing at the heart of their fictional Truros. Boscawen Street acts as a space for viewing which has a visual and symbolic effect similar to the performance of power and status of the buildings themselves. From 1305 until 1838 (*Dan Daddow* stretches the historical boundaries to its setting in the 1850s) Truro acted as one of the coinage towns: this was the process by which tin was assayed for quality before being sold. Heavy ingots of smelted tin were brought to Truro for a corner (termed *coin* in French, hence 'coinage') to be cut off and weighed.[43] It was a very public display of wealth, and of the important role Truro played within this industry. The ingots were transported into the centre of Truro, through its streets and past grand houses (many of which had been built on the very same proceeds of mining), and stacked outside the Coinage Hall, initially overlooking Middle Row and later the wide cobbled sweep of Boscawen Street. The commercial heart of the town, it could not have been a more apposite location at which to visibly and tangibly display wealth. This was particularly so in the expanded version of the space. Without Middle Row, the Coinage Hall forms the head and focal point of the eastern end of Boscawen Street, the gaze channelled down the newly aggrandized thoroughfare to where the ingots were exhibited.

On this Boscawen Street stage, the ingots are unmissable and are gazed at by characters in both the *Poldark* series and *Dan Daddow's Cornish Comicalities*, with similar elements foremost in the description of the scene. In *The Loving Cup* (book ten), George Warleggan, from his upper chamber in the bank which overlooks Boscawen Street, avariciously observes 'several glistening blocks of tin for the coinage'.[44] It is the lustre of the blocks of tin, piled in the open air, that is often noticed. In *Ross Poldark* (book one), Demelza observes that they 'glittered darkly in the sun'. When Ross sees them in *The Four Swans* (book six) they 'glistened unattended'. Dan Daddow, in very different weather, observes '[a] slight fall of sleet onto the shimmering blocks of tin' while the stamps on the ingots, imprinted to confirm their purity, 'sparkle like mackerel scales'.[45] Their visibility is emphasized by their luminosity, which in turn reifies wealth; as does their immovability, which *Poldark* registers. Although very valuable, the blocks of tin can be left on display without security, as they are too heavy to be removed clandestinely.[46] Thus, this al fresco, public display of Cornwall's mineral wealth simultaneously reinforces the tin's quality and worth, and the control of the town over the coinage process.

The glittering ingots, assayed and stamped with proof of their quality, their purity, is also tangible proof that Cornish mining's 'industrial prowess' reputation (discussed in Chapter One) is befitting.[47] As is also the case with how this reputation operates, the end product of the mining process, transplanted into the urban theatre, remains connected to the figure of the miner whose work and skill has brought the ore to grass. Both the *Poldark* series and *Dan Daddow's Cornish Comicalities* inscribe the miners into the coinage scene; indeed, it is the miners who deliver the ingots onto the Boscawen Street stage. In *Ross Poldark* (book one):

> A long mule train was coming down the street with the heavy panniers of tin slung on each side of the animals and with a number of travel-stained miners plodding slowly along by their side. They had walked miles since dawn from some outlying district with this tin for the coinage hall, and would ride home on the backs of the weary mules.[48]

Such a scene connects the ingots to their origins and to the labour that produced them, which is also emphasized here by the labour of the weary mules. In *Dan Daddow*, the 'Cassiterite glowing' in the sunlight is accompanied by '[t]he low dialect grumble and cussing of miners, and the yelps of their dogs over the ever increasing coinage rates'.[49] This performance of wealth within the urban space cannot, therefore, be divorced from the material processes of its creation, even if the miners are only in the end spectators, and not recipients, of the wealth their labour has produced.

That is not to say that this space is one which always renders visible the working class or the urban underclass, either to the reader, or to other characters who inhabit their world. Theirs is a very different issue of visibility than that of their middle- and upper-class counterparts. Whereas the upper echelons of society may encounter problems by being too visible and too known, as we will see later, for the lower orders this space is where they need to be seen to survive, and in some respects Truro's built environment enables this, while in others it pushes them away from the central spaces in a manner reminiscent of other, larger cities.

The separation between classes is not as acute in Truro as Friedrich Engels observes in Manchester, but there are still some similarities. Of Manchester he believes that 'a person may live in it for years, and go in and out daily without coming into contact with a working-people's quarter or even with workers'. The layout of the city screens the working-class areas behind thoroughfares lined with shops. Middle- and upper-class residents can travel from homes in the suburbs to the city centre through these streets, traversing the working quarters 'stretching like a girdle' around the commercial centre, without having to see them.[50] In *Dan Daddow's Cornish Comicalities*, Michael, one of Dan's working-class theatre recruits, lives away from the centre of Truro in a poor part of town that Dan realizes few people visit or even know about. Due to regular flooding of this part of town, Michael's makeshift abode, part of what is described as a 'wooden shantytown', is on stilts in the middle of the River Allen, one of the rivers that engirdle Truro. His route to the centre of town is similarly make-do and consequently difficult to traverse, very different to the permanency and style of the centre of town. Dan is taken by Michael 'around a maze of planks and wharves' and across '[w]obbly bridges of wood and rope'.[51] The unsuitability of the land, the impermanency of the built environment, and its unacknowledged presence speak to the status of those living there, and of their difficulty in being seen within the urban space of Truro.

However, the screening of the working class as occurs in Engels' description of Manchester is not so absolute in fictions of Truro. Characters of different classes occupy the central spaces of Truro, though, of course, not on equal terms. Their experiences of that space are very different, as are the problems that the Cornish urban space creates for them. In *Dan Daddow's Cornish Comicalities* and in the *Poldark* books, working-class characters, on particular occasions, find their way onto either the literal stage of the Assembly Rooms (most of Dan's troupe, including Michael above, are drawn from various working-class backgrounds) or onto the effective stage of Boscawen Street, and surrounding streets. These are intentional moments of display by the working class and the narrative eye is sustained on their action—very different to simply being present as the least noticed part of the public space. Their visibility within that space, to people of their own and other classes, is due to their own agency, not simply due to them being spotlighted by the narrative eye of the text.

The corn riot we witness in *Poldark* and the guizing on the winter solstice in *Dan Daddow's Cornish Comicalities* make the working classes visible within the Cornish urban space, but in that visibility they are also a potential threat, both to the personal safety of persons of other classes, and to the very structure of society itself. In *Demelza* (book two), the miners stage a riot in Truro because of the prohibitive price of corn. We can contextualize this uprising with the striking millworkers in *North and South* (1854–55) and the striking miners in *Germinal* (1885), both fighting against their exploitative pay and conditions, and, like the Cornish, the very real possibility of starvation, and both similarly a threat to life and to the capitalist system. There is also a specifically Cornish context which heightens the threat of the rioting miners as perceived by outsiders. As already discussed in previous chapters, even into the eighteenth and nineteenth centuries, 'West Barbary' remains an available characterization of the Cornish. It was a reputation that was particularly identifiable with tinners, who were central to the frequent food riots in Cornwall during this time.[52]

In this moment, then, the rioting miners are the spectacle, deliberately making themselves visible to the town. This is very different to their previous appearance in *Ross Poldark* (book one), as escorts to the tin their labour has raised from underground, and seemingly compliant servants of the capitalist system. The intended stage for their protest is again Coinage Hall, the very centre point of the town and the site where the tin ingots are exhibited. Initially, as the rioters pour into the town en masse, they get lost within the smaller streets, demonstrating that they are outside their natural environment.[53] Eventually, they find the corn warehouses, and forcibly seize the corn when their proffered price is refused. This is not their space, yet it is the necessary space within which to protest their suffering, and not just because the corn and corn factor are located here. The urban stage is where they have most chance of their protest being noticed by other classes; it is a central meeting point on which they can converge to form a mass movement. It is also the appropriate site upon which to protest inequality because, as Raymond Williams notes, it is where the gulf between rich and poor is 'more intense' and 'more evidently problematic'.[54] The urban site is the crucible where these contrasts are most starkly realized. The desperation of the working poor publicly plays out in Truro, an environment built to display wealth, and wealth often acquired from the miners' labour.

The narrator recognizes the plight of the miners to be 'a fair grievance' whilst simultaneously acknowledging the very real potential for uncontrollable violence and destruction.[55] That potential is conveyed through the way in which the miners are depicted as one unstoppable body. The contradictory nature of Truro's streets means that the overly wide expanse of Boscawen Street is surrounded by a network of narrow streets and passages. When the tinners get lost en route to the Coinage Hall they become bottlenecked in these streets which act 'like a collar about them'. At first, it seems as if the built environment actualizes the yoke of labouring men and women. Yet, while bystanders are forcibly dragged along in the crush, the rioters instead become moulded into a 'great crowd animal' which, as one body, whilst temporarily losing direction, is inexorable in its objective to reach the Coinage Hall and the corn warehouses nearby.[56]

Fittingly, then, the 'crowd animal' is continually likened to water: they are a 'stream', a 'flood', a 'wave' which sweeps up all in its wake. At a choke point on a bridge, the crowd must slow 'as rushing water will slacken and fill up a narrow channel' until the '[p]ressure eased, [and] the crowd ebbed, at first slowly, then more quickly towards the centre of town'.[57] Water is a suitable metaphor to describe the danger of the miners pouring into town as one. It also suggests the porous nature of Truro's built environment. Such people are not securely screened from the public and commercial centre of the town, but find a way in as water would. Water is a particularly apt description in relation to Truro's streets because it has been built surrounded by and over the top of three rivers. Like the miners, these rivers make their way into the centre of town through leats that were harnessed to drive water wheels for industry, just as the miners' labour is harnessed within the mines.[58]

The torrent of miners flooding into the central spaces of Truro overrides the usual separation between the different classes operating within the urban space, and makes impossible the usual social etiquette regarding physical contact between people. Demelza fights hard not to be 'pushed into the river' but '[m]en and women were squeezed upon her from all sides, elbows and staves poking and pressing, and jerking'. She is in physical danger from the pressure of the flood, which prevents her from breathing at one point. Yet her concerns are also class-based and, with the anger of the 'horde' increasing, she is aware that '[h]er good clothes were too conspicuous'.[59] Demelza is a miner's daughter, these are her people, but her marriage to Ross, and into the ancient land- and mine-owning Poldark family, has raised her out of her class. While both her and Ross's politics, and actions, are always on the side of the poor, in this moment she understands the primacy of the visual: her clothes signal her as someone who deserves their ire.

In less fraught circumstances, Margaret Hale in *North and South* similarly stands out to the factory workers as someone of a higher rank because of her clothes. The overfamiliarity of the factory girls, to the point of touching her clothing without permission, is initially strange to her and contravenes the 'rules of street politeness' which she understands.[60] It is her family's fall in station which means that they now live on the thoroughfare by which these working-class men and women walk to work and not, as Engels above points out, in a quarter where the lower classes are screened from view. Margaret, then, is out of place, and this is the reason for the close contact with the factory women. As mentioned above, in Truro no such division of space on class lines is possible. In the riot, though, by taking up all the available space, the miners dissolve the usually observed distances between classes that exist within the shared space of the town. They stand twenty men abreast, filling the width of the streets down which they flow.[61] In that moment, not only do they replace those above them on the social hierarchy as the class with primacy in that space, but they literally ram their protest against the bodies of those observing.

In *Dan Daddow*, the perceived threat posed by the working classes within the Cornish urban space is less direct. However, couched within the traditions of an annual festival celebrating the winter solstice, where the working classes dress up to mock their 'masters', the act of disguise and comedic performance heightens the sense of danger to those against whom the satire is directed. On Dan's first night back in Truro, poised to assume his new role as manager of the Assembly Rooms Theatre, Boscawen Street and other nearby streets literally become a stage for its working-class inhabitants (the male ones at least). Men such as Pentecost Langdon, who later becomes part of Dan's theatre troupe, celebrate the winter solstice as guizers, blackening their faces with coal for disguise (hence the moniker 'guizers') so that their actual identity cannot be discerned. It is an old custom of which the lower classes have ownership. Dan describes it as a 'freakish world' playing out before his eyes, but we also know that he has taken part in such events before and so can see his desire to remain aloof as a snobbish compulsion to disguise his working-class roots in the face of this specifically working-class cultural expression. For that evening, and as with the miners' riot above, the social hierarchy of visibility is inverted. The lower orders are on display, marching, singing, and mumming, occupying the town's central spaces and watched by '[a] good proportion of the town', but they are also protected by the act of guizing which hides their true identity in the very moment of their assumption of visibility.[62]

The town's authorities, Dan notes, wish to end guizing, fearful of its anarchic potential. Most subversive, although ostensibly in jest, is the mummers' mimicry of those in authority, including a mock Vice-Warden who pronounces that beer will be free, parsnips and turnips taxed, and apprentices will only have to work one day a year. The proclamation clearly addresses a working-class audience, while portending an overthrow of the current structure of society by that group. The revelling here does indeed end in fighting, despite the town corporation's Victorian bouncers. In this moment, the traditional structures of power within the urban space have been upset, by the violence but also by the occupation of the town's central spaces by those more usually peripheral. The event exposes the fragility of the 'veneer of civilization', the volatility below the surface and, crucially, that the social structure of society survives through co-operation and not just control.[63] Remember too that this is Truro in 1850, and, as in the Falmouth description above, this is a Cornwall very much connected to other countries. So we can assume that such riots as we see here are taking place within the context of the 1848 revolution in France and the wave of uprisings elsewhere in Europe, and thus the resurfacing in Britain of fears, first emerging with the 1789 revolution, that anarchy could spread across the channel from France.

The built environment of Truro facilitates moments of visibility for the underclass of Truro too. While in Manchester the thoroughfares act as a barrier, blocking the destitute from sight, in Truro the network of opes (narrow alleyways), many leading off Boscawen Street, connect the principal streets to each other. The opes are a sudden and striking contrast to the expansiveness of Boscawen Street. Their nature and the experience of traversing them is perfectly described by one such ope off Boscawen Street known as Squeeze Guts Alley: so-called because it is so narrow you have to squeeze your guts past someone coming in the other direction. The kind of places where plenty of dirt and detritus would accumulate, these are not however the 'forced labyrinths and alleys of the poor' that Williams talks of existing in overcrowded cities, and which Engels identifies in poor quarters in Manchester.[64] Truro's opes are passages enabling transit around the town for all classes. They are, therefore, also pinch-points where the underclass can get the attention of those passing through.

In *Bella Poldark* (book twelve), Clowance (Ross and Demelza's daughter) is in Church Lane (today Cathedral Lane), a cut-through from Boscawen Street to High Cross, when she sees Philip Prideaux coming towards her. Wanting to avoid him, she contemplates a retreat into Boscawen Street, but realizes that 'there was no escape'. Such are the confines of the narrow lane that he spots her immediately. As they converse, a beggar also utilizes the geography of the ope to solicit for money and is rewarded with a shilling from Philip. Even then, it is difficult to escape his 'overwhelming' gestures of thanks, Philip telling him to '[g]o away', but both having to witness his joyful antics as he exits the ope. Although Philip confesses the act is self-indulgence (getting a kick out of being called 'milord'), rather than altruism, the beggar has benefitted from a space in which he cannot be so easily overlooked or dismissed.[65]

While action is needed for the working classes to make themselves visible, those from the upper echelons of society already stand out. Philip looks like a suitable person to importune for money, and Demelza's awareness of the signification of her dress during the riot has been discussed above. For Dan Daddow, and for Osborne Whitworth in the *Poldark* series, visibility on Truro's streets poses a much greater danger due to their transgressions within that space. Truro is a place where they can indulge in dissipation: both procure prostitutes within the town. Dan Daddow's first liaison takes place in Squeeze Guts Alley, adding another layer of meaning to its nomenclature.[66] Not only does he run the risk of discovery in a known location for prostitution, but the narrowness of the opeway means it is very difficult to escape detection should someone come the other way. The ope requires intimacy, not just of the illicit kind, but simply to cross the path of someone else utilizing the thoroughfare. Dan, then, runs a huge risk, but his alcohol-fuelled bravado prevents him from worrying about discovery in the moment.

In the *Poldark* novels, Osborne Whitworth is the vile and self-serving vicar whom Morwenna Chynoweth is forced to marry. Despite his hauteur, Osborne is far more concerned than Dan that his illicit business in Truro will be discovered. When frequenting places down by the river, he removes his clerical collar, dons a heavy cloak, and walks quickly through the night-time streets, but he is ever-fearful of being recognized. He worries too that he might be blackmailed by the woman he is visiting. On another occasion, he thinks the pot-boy from the Seven Stars Tavern has recognized him, and that he might report him to the churchwardens. He is very aware that to be found hanging around the area by the quay at night would be difficult to explain away (he does not seem to consider that he could legitimately be there to minister to the prostitutes in his role as a religious man). His anxiety is heightened by his self-image as 'a prominent citizen of Truro', so that he expects to be recognized by anyone he encounters. Truro for Osborne is a place where he can satisfy his carnal cravings, but, while not accompanied by guilt, his sorties are always accompanied by fear of discovery, and as it turns out, rightly so.[67] Despite Osborne's conceited exaggeration of his status (there are many more prominent citizens), his awareness does also speak to the actuality of class-based visibility within the Cornish urban space.

For Osborne, this discoverability is in the end deadly. When his wife, supported by Dr Enys, refuses to resume marital relations after the birth of their child, Osborne resumes an affair with Morwenna's sister Rowella, sneaking along to her home every Thursday, while her husband Arthur Solway visits his parents elsewhere in town. He convinces himself that to be discovered leaving the home of a former parishioner and family member is more excusable than to be seen at the dockside cottages, where it would be obvious that he was there to procure sex. He soothes himself with thinking that 'there were few people about in the cobbled streets' as he makes his way, as soon as darkness has fallen, to Rowella's home. Even then, as the arrangement continues, he remains cognisant that 'his visits carried their continuing risk'.[68] His fear is realized when Arthur returns home early due to his sister being ill. Osborne's presence is imprinted on the hail covering the ground outside his house. Arthur discerns that 'there were other footprints, larger than his, heavier than his, part obscured by the hail, part outlined by it [...]. And the footprints appeared to go up to the door but not to return from it.'[69] He climbs up to the bedroom window and discovers his wife's lover. Osborne's corpulence has prevented his footprints from being fully obscured. Even after he has seemingly retreated from view, the hail holds an echo of his presence there. Consequently, on his way home after his next visit to Rowella, Osborne is murdered by Arthur. His fears over visibility within the urban space were merited and are ultimately the moments which foreshadow his end.

Unlike the working-class characters above, visibility in Truro for other classes is fraught with danger because of the difficulty of remaining anonymous. To be seen is heightened because it makes it much more likely that one will also be known. This is quite different to the possibility of anonymity touted by other urban spaces, where one can become lost as just another face in the crowd. Truro, though, is the opposite. It is the place where the upper classes are on display to each other and where people such as Ross Poldark are most often recognized and known. It is where the 'everyone knows everyone' maxim of Cornish society is most intensely, even uncomfortably felt. People are met with at exhausting regularity, people are surveilled by others who already know their history, and gossip abounds.

Truro, then, is the most public of spaces in the Cornwall of the *Poldark* novels, and there are a few reasons for this. Truro becomes a central point, a gathering place, for the great and the good. It offers many things to draw people in; it is where people come to buy goods and to access information (from London and elsewhere). It is the place where you will first hear the latest news or learn about the latest fashions. Many social occasions take place across the country houses of Cornwall too, but Truro is the most public space where these kinds of performances of wealth and status take place—in the streets, at balls at the Assembly Rooms, and at the town houses of the wealthiest aristocrats. Truro attracts people because it is known as the place where 'the élite of Cornish society' will be seen.[70] As discussed above, this is reflective of Truro's actual position as a significant, fashionable county town within Cornwall during the late eighteenth and early nineteenth centuries, which has been identified as '[t]he heyday of society in the small country town'.[71] For instance, the *West Briton* reports on 8 March 1811 that the Assembly Rooms at Truro 'attracted almost all the fashionables of the neighbourhood, the dancing being kept up with great spirit to a late hour'.[72] This is very much reflective of what is also happening in other towns and cities in this period and what we also see in novels of the period, such as the representation of Bath in Jane Austen's *Northanger Abbey*. Truro has the feel and reputation of a city long before that status is conferred.

Yet the intensity of being observed and known in Truro is specific to that environment. Conveniently and centrally located within Cornwall, and an urban space within a predominantly rural setting, there is unsurprisingly a funnelling of people into this space to socialize on a larger scale. Ultimately it is still a relatively small town. It is not, then, a sprawling metropolis, but rather a compact and knowable space with social 'stages', like the Assembly Rooms and Boscawen Street, coupled with narrow alleys from which people can observe, but within which it is impossible to be safely ensconced out of sight. The lived experience of the space, its ambiguity as a social space—its liminal status between town and city—means that middle- and upper-class protagonists are always at risk of being seen and known when they do not wish to be.

George Warleggan, Ross Poldark's enemy in the *Poldark* books, is very aware of the importance of spectacle, and puts on a show of wealth in Truro. Earlier we saw him enviously looking down upon the blocks of tin glistening in the street, and his is a similar kind of display of wealth. He owns a town house in Truro, where he puts on lavish parties; a carriage and four, and many servants sumptuously clothed in Warleggan liveries, declares the extent of his wealth. He achieves the level of spectacle he desires because '[p]assers-by stopped to stare'. In *Demelza* (book two), Ross rides past George's town house and, while 'not a man who would have gone in for display had he been able to afford it' is astounded at the depth of George's pockets during an economic downturn, and while he cannot even afford a second horse.[73]

The excessiveness of George's show of wealth, though, is where the performance falters, because he overacts the part of the rich aristocrat in a bid to conceal his humble origins. He tries to make a boon of his lack of lineage when proposing marriage to Elizabeth Poldark, saying, 'I can't bring you breeding, my dear. But I can bring you a certain kind of gentility which is the more punctilious because it is only one generation deep.' In a way he is right, and Elizabeth appreciates his version of gentility, enacted in public and private, but it is exactly his over-refinement in manner and behaviour which sets him apart from the people whom he wishes to be like.[74] George's enmity towards Ross is fuelled by his sense of his own inferiority, which Ross kindles more than any other.[75] Ross is a man who does not abide by the rules of his class, rules which George works so hard to live up to. George thinks that '[m]oney would soon talk before breeding' but it is clear it never will; the rules are for a game that he can never fully play.[76] This is most noticeable as he enacts his persona in Truro for, despite the extravagant spectacle of wealth, his origins are encoded into his body. Despite George being one of the most powerful men in Truro, richly clothed in the latest London fashions, 'there was yet something about his stance [...] which was reminiscent of his grandfather, the blacksmith'.[77] Gary Bridge and Sophie Watson recall Pierre Bourdieu's argument that 'different types of gait and inclination of the head can express class position [...]. So much is communicated before a word is spoken and this has consequences for thinking about the public in terms of social interaction in the "public" spaces of the city.'[78] It is in the public space of Truro that the flaw in George's performance is most noticeable. Ross assesses him as they cross what will become Boscawen Street. He assumes that George's financial success has given him confidence to embrace, rather than endeavour to hide, physical markers of his working-class roots, such as his bullneck, when in fact they show through despite his performance of wealth. Within this crucible of scrutiny, to perform breeding proves impossible, no matter how hard George tries to perfect it and how much money he has.[79]

Ross does not enact a public persona, or pay any attention to the implications of being seen and known in the public space. Shortly after his return to Cornwall he walks openly in Truro with the prostitute Margaret, something Osborne Whitworth or Dan Daddow would never dream of doing.[80] He brawls in the Red Lion public house with George.[81] Going against the class beliefs of his peers, Ross openly defends his servant Jim Carter, on trial in Truro for poaching.[82] Ross, therefore, has not considered, but also does not seem to understand, how the public space of Truro operates. For example, he mistakenly thinks that he will be able to keep the shareholders of the Carnmore Copper Company, who meet in Truro, secret, and he is surprised when his friend and banker Harris Pascoe knows the details of his refusal to stand for parliament.[83] Ross has not given due consideration to the impossibility of secrecy in Truro, a hub of gossip and surveillance, or, though later he is to become Member of Parliament for Truro, the politics of the transactions, decisions, and relationships in which he is involved. There are often significant consequences felt by Ross to his openness in the public space, such as the failure of Carnmore, which almost bankrupts him—yet despite some very close calls, nothing is permanently damaging, partly due to his class position. There are others for whom there is far more at stake in the public space.

Women of Truro

There is a photograph of Truro that looks down Lower Lemon Street to Boscawen Street. The city is heavily decorated with garlands and flags, potentially for the coronation of King George V in 1911. In the foreground is a man, Henry Hodge, sleeves rolled up, pulling a cart towards the photographer.[84] Another man in a suit and hat is cycling towards the opening to Boscawen Street. A postman looks towards the camera. A horse and trap waits at the junction of the two streets. All these details and more are included in the superscript for the photograph, yet a nun with her back to camera is not mentioned. Closest to the camera, she is the largest figure in the shot. Swathed from head to toe in deep folds of black material, we can tell very little about her or her features as she draws level with Henry Hodge, and is about to pass the postman, bound for Boscawen Street. We know Henry's full name, but we know nothing about the woman in shot. She is at once the most noticeable feature of the photograph and the most hidden from our gaze. It is as if this heavily covered woman does not want to be seen, or is not allowed to be seen, and this speaks to the problems for women around negotiating the public space within towns and cities, and for the implications of gender within Truro's public spaces.

It is necessary to understand the streets and buildings of Truro not as blank or neutral spaces into which people travel but, as we have already seen in relation to class, as produced through social relations. The Red Lion Hotel, a gathering place in Truro since 1769, and regularly appearing in the *Poldark* novels, advertised in the early twentieth century a 'handsome and commodious Ladies' Drawing Room' as one of its selling points.[85] Such female-only spaces are not uncommon in department stores, restaurants, meeting places, and train stations once women become more mobile, without chaperones, within the public spaces of towns and cities towards the end of the nineteenth century. The presence of such

Figure 6: An unidentified nun walks down Lower Lemon Street towards Boscawen Street (c.1911) (Courtesy of Royal Cornwall Museum)

spaces makes economic sense, making it easier for women to come into city centres to shop and socialize. They may speak to a genuine concern for women's safety, but that such spaces are created at all also indicates that women's presence within the public space is highly problematic.[86]

We will come to the issue of traversing the Truro of the twentieth century for Irma in *Wilding Graft* shortly, but I first want to return to the late-eighteenth-century Truro of *Poldark*, and Demelza Poldark, Ross Poldark's wife. Demelza's daily life plays out on the North Cornish coast, not more than a few hours on horseback from Truro, but the coast is a very different space in terms of how codes of behaviour in relation to gender impinge on daily life. There is a sense in which, at home on the coast, especially on Poldark land, when working the fields, in the garden, or walking, Demelza is not so tightly bound by social expectations of femininity.[87] Everything is a little looser, less strictly controlled or observed.

Truro, though, for Demelza, is a very different space with very different rules and consequences. On her first journey into Truro with Verity, following her marriage, she is glad to be wearing Verity's grey riding habit because 'it helped her to see herself as a lady and behave with the dignity of one'.[88]

Demelza is already aware, then, of the part she must play whilst shopping in Truro. This is emphasized by the items they buy, and the reasoning Verity gives: morning dress, riding habit, gloves, a hat, stockings, all at Verity's instruction as to material and style, are referred to as 'furnishings' because, as Verity exclaims, '[d]o you think the house should be decorated without its mistress?'. Verity's dressing up of Demelza is to enable her to play the part of Mistress Poldark of Nampara. Her specific requests as to style—genteel but not ostentatious—show a concern to craft Demelza's public image to suit expectations of femininity, whilst not drawing undue attention.[89]

At social occasions in Truro, though, Demelza is very much a spectacle who draws significant male attention and, later, the same is true when she attends events in London and Paris. Her first foray into Truro society is at a party held by George Warleggan at his town house, followed by a ball at the Assembly Rooms, to celebrate the restoration to health of King George III. Demelza is always both uncomfortable about and taking a childlike enjoyment in the painting and preening for such occasions, mostly because she was not born to it. This also means that she has an eye for the falsity, ridiculousness, and excessiveness of such occasions, and of expensive dresses which expose her body and have 'a lot of beautiful lace hanging [...] where she didn't need it'. Similarly, she is acutely aware of being stared at, and of the import of such looks by men such as Sir Hugh Bodrugan, who finds her 'a pridey morsel to look at', and she finds this both flattering and inconvenient.[90] Later, at the public ball, glasses of port give her the courage to act as 'lion tamer' of those men clustered around her while Ross, who gives little thought to what she must negotiate, is off playing cards.[91] There is a lot at stake here for Demelza at such social occasions: she must be appropriately feminine, and must also successfully perform the part of Mistress Poldark of Nampara. Her behaviour, comportment, and dress must belie, rather than exude, her social origins, even though most people present are already aware of her low birth, because her behaviour in response to her suitors will be judged all the more harshly because of it.

It is in the urban, public space of the streets of Truro where most is at stake for Demelza as someone performing as an upper-class woman. Not only is this where her performance of both acceptable femininity and class can be most closely scrutinized, but it is also where she is least in control of how others read that performance.[92] As discussed earlier, she is most obviously in danger during the miners' riot in Truro, when she is caught up in the crush caused by them pouring into the narrow streets. During the riot is when Demelza has least control over her body, and how other people touch her body. Both being identified as an upper-class woman and failing in this performance during the melee are dangerous for Demelza. As Patricia Ingham identifies, the very act of walking unaccompanied in public leaves women not only open to interpretation beyond their control, but open to interpretation literally as streetwalkers, as prostitutes.[93] For Demelza, this is the danger of any slippage in her performance of both gender and class, yet at the same time, being identified as an upper-class woman makes her more visible, and so potentially more of a target for the miners' ire. In this chaotic moment, there is a danger of both literally falling, and being trampled by the crowd, and a more figurative fall which would be disastrous for her reputation.

Truro Encounters

Jack Clemo's novel *Wilding Graft* follows the trials and tribulations of a cast of characters living tough lives in the china clay mining district of mid-Cornwall on the eve of the Second World War. Central to the narrative are Garth Joslin and Irma Stribley, who, years before the novel begins, had fallen in love in the clay area whilst she was visiting family. A scandalous kiss, Irma being only fifteen and Garth being in a relationship, ends her visit and permanently marks both their lives, yet their love endures during their separation. Truro is the location of their story's denouement when they finally meet again. Many of the issues discussed so far of visibility and performance, and their relationship to gender and class, are also relevant to this twentieth-century fictional version of Truro. Yet it is also a text which offers, for Irma, an experience of the public, urban Cornish space that is defined by her agency.

As the Second World War continues, Cornwall is designated a safe harbour for those who need to be evacuated from London. While a city too, Truro is thought to be an unlikely target. In this context, Truro is homologous with Cornwall as a peripheral, rural, and therefore safe space in wartime Britain, rather than with other cities, such as London, Cardiff, and Coventry, deemed potential targets for attack. Truro seems set to become overpopulated though, and Mrs Rundle, a Truronian landlady, thinks '[t]hese Londoners will turn the county into Bedlam [...] if they swarm down like the billet committees is preparing for'.[94] Truro looks likely to get a lot busier, more recognizably urban, through the influx of evacuees from other cities, yet the fact that it is a suitable place for them seek sanctuary attests to its ambiguous urban status in a national context.

In *Wilding Graft* Truro both epitomizes and asks us to rethink urban spaces, and how they operate through the specificity of the Cornish context. Truro can be a quiet place, a backwater where little happens, and a more recognizably crowded urban space. It may be classed as a safe place for evacuated Londoners, but there is simultaneously a suggestion that this is an environment which corrupts its inhabitants. Mrs Rundle is thought 'a homely soul, not yet corrupted by city standards of mercenary, as opposed to human, values', having only moved to Truro five years previously, and bringing with her a more benign and friendly way of interacting with people from her village origins.[95] Garth thinks that towns are places that enable people to corrupt themselves if they do not have guidance.[96] Garth goes to Truro (and St Austell and Plymouth) after his relationship with Edith Spragg ends, and his neighbours note that he returns late at night. There is a suggestion here that these cities and towns are places of dissipation but, in reality, he just walks the streets, brooding. Yet he still has to seek out these urban places, 'all tensed up like a fellow in purgatory'.[97] There is no simple binary here, however, between the urban and the rural in terms of the familiar dichotomy of bucolic innocence versus urban amorality. The primary environment of the novel is the china clay mining area of mid-Cornwall (which will also be the focus of the next chapter). A human-made landscape scarred by open-cast pits for mining clay and boroughs of waste sand, this is also not straightforwardly a rural enclave that can be set up in opposition to Truro.

In *Wilding Graft*, we experience Truro from the perspective of working-class characters. Coming from around twelve miles away, they are familiar with Truro's streets, but not at home there. Akin to the Truro of the *Poldark* novels, this fictional Truro is a place where people are seen, often when they do not wish to be. People bump into each other with disconcerting regularity, are approached by people whom they do not know, and are tracked and surveilled beyond their control. It is rarely a place of escape, much more so a place of exposure, often to others of their own class and also from the clay area, who seem to need to know everything about each other's history. Minnie Lagor, a young girl of the clay area known for her 'slip' with Ted Blewett, which led to the birth of her illegitimate child Shirley, looks beyond the car park at Lemon Quay (the river by this point has been concreted over) to 'the crowds jostling through Lemon Street' and finds it 'all somehow tense, threatening'. No wonder, given that for Minnie there is no hope of being lost in the crowd. In unnervingly quick succession, she is confronted by Ted Blewett's mother, Sal, whom she has never met but knows by sight, then her own mother, from whom she wishes to hide her tryst with Mervyn Griffiths (who might also show at any moment), and then Garth, who is equally unsettled by Minnie's approach to him. Not deterred by Sal Blewett's directness with her, which makes her wince, she confronts Garth with all her knowledge of his past until he 'felt emotionally bare'.[98] He escapes into Boscawen Street, only to be accosted by Griffiths, who knows of Garth from Minnie, but whom he too has never met. Ironically, it is Garth's isolation, as he broods upon his lost love Irma on the streets of Truro, which makes him more visible to others. He 'hugged his suffering' yet 'there was also a grandeur, a quiet strength about him which [...] was forcing several people to stare long and curiously at him'.[99] Not only is anonymity impossible here, but people act on their recognition of others, to confront them, catching them off guard. The networks of knowledge and knowing established in the clay area are transplanted into Truro where people are more likely to be seen and encountered, and where people feel more able to confront others with their knowledge of their lives, as if they know them better than they can know themselves. The streets of Truro, then, are where people like Garth and Minnie are most exposed.

It is Irma Stribley's story, which plays out in Truro's streets, its museum, and its cathedral, that turns on its head the constrictions of that urban space experienced by other female protagonists. Whilst initially happenstance that Irma and Garth are both in Truro at the same time, their reunion is made possible by her agency. Her actions invert the system of surveillance of women in the public space, and the bind of being known which has already been discussed. In the Royal Cornwall Museum, positioned on the mezzanine encircling the ground floor, Irma has the advantage of stealth to listen in on Griffiths and Mr Rundle's conversation about Garth. Griffiths is exposed in his central position within the hall. While he does discover her lurking above, and while the sunbeams radiating down illuminate her, they also put her face into shadow, delaying the moment of his recognition of her—and, even then, she refuses Griffiths her name so that he cannot confirm her identity. Whilst Griffiths gazes up at her, she has control over when she can be seen by them and, looking down upon them with 'an intent watchfulness', reverses their awkward crick-necked gaze up at her with a steely one of her own.[100] It is Griffiths and Mr Rundle whose cheeks colour upon learning their conversation has been overhead.

With the knowledge she has gleaned, Irma sets out to track Garth through the streets of Truro, a surveillance for the purpose of a joyful and meaningful reunion, rather than the portentous gazing we have encountered elsewhere. The denouement happens in Truro Cathedral, which is 'like a stage purposely set for her and Garth'. Yet crucially, unlike the Assembly Rooms or Boscawen Street, this is a stage with no audience, '[n]o vergers in view, no casual sightseers!'; they are alone. Irma approaches Garth in the knowledge that the scene is set for her and with 'the knowledge of her power over him and of a higher Power claiming them both'. In this moment the cathedral is a sanctuary from the public space of the streets. There is no watching and interpreting by others, and no social prescriptions determining their communion as 'eye to eye, they read each other's souls'.[101] In this moment they have both cheated the demands and consequences of the urban space of Truro.

Truro sits apart from many of the other spaces in Cornwall as the most developed town, then as its only city, but even then it is never straightforwardly urban. This chapter has endeavoured to explore the complexities of its position within Cornwall, and the nuances of Truro as a space within some of the small number of literary texts in which it features. There are times when its streets familiarly resemble other urban spaces, and others when the idiosyncrasies of Truro enable us to reassess urban and rural spaces, and the relationship between them. As an internal space within Cornwall, with no view of the coast, Truro has received very little attention within literature of Cornwall, or analysis of that literature, and does not usually feature in the most familiar and prevalent versions of place to which we have access. It is clear, though, that while offering no view of the kind that is most familiar in touristic promotion of Cornwall, performing, viewing, seeing, and knowing are key to how Truro has been created, and how it is experienced.

Chapter Five

Moor and Clay

> *My room is a bright glass cabin,*
> *All Cornwall thunders at my door,*
> *And the white ships of winter lie*
> *In the sea-roads of the moor.*
> Charles Causley, 'The Seasons in North Cornwall' (1951)[1]

To-day this part of Cornwall might well be called a 'white country'. For everything here is white. The dumps are white, the streams look like milk, there are pools and tanks of white water, and great stacks of white clay. The men themselves, as you see them coming home from their work, look as if they had been rubbing powdered chalk over their faces and hands.
A.K. Hamilton Jenkin, *The Story of Cornwall* (1934)[2]

As discussed in previous chapters, this book is interested in casting light onto versions of Cornwall that have not received enough attention. Chapter Three of this book examined the case of the coast in fiction and non-fiction. As discussed, there are aesthetic and economic factors, tied to tourism, which encourage an obsession with the Cornish coast. Chapter Four has explored the literary portrayal of Truro as an urban, inland site within Cornwall. This chapter remains inland and focuses on literature located in the china clay mining region of mid-Cornwall, and on Bodmin Moor, a granite moorland in north-east Cornwall. Given the predominance of the coast, a specific effort needs to be made to go in search of 'all Cornwall', and to write back into the imaginary of Cornwall, work which inhabits its interior spaces.

Cornwall's interior is unique due to the narrowness of the peninsula and the topography of the sites that form the focus of this chapter. Only around twenty miles apart, these industrial and moorland locales have specific and unique visual identities. At the same time, it should be recognized that any interior location within Cornwall is at most eleven miles from either the north or south coast. This is perhaps partly why the sense of Cornwall having an interior at all is regularly overlooked. While villages from within the clay mining region are truly interior locations, to the south the area also opens out into St Austell Bay, with clay still being exported via Fowey and Par harbours, and popular tourist attractions such as Charlestown having a history as clay ports. From interior vantage points within 'the clay', and by climbing tors on Bodmin Moor, it is possible, weather permitting, to see both coasts, and these days to reach either coast by car in a maximum of around twenty minutes from the very centre of Cornwall. At the same time, those same vantage points also operate to make the coast feel further away. If unclimbed, clay tips (human-made mountains of sand, the waste product from the processing of clay) interrupt sightlines to the coast in a similar way to the tors and rocky outcrops of the moor. At ground level on the biggest expanse of moorland in Cornwall, it can stretch as far as the horizon, thus making it seem as if there is no coast.

The fiction of Daphne du Maurier and Jack Clemo are the best-known literary works to fully locate themselves within these two interior sites. Jack Clemo wrote three novels, all of which have the clay area as their primary site.[3] From the early 1990s onwards, there has been increasing interest in Clemo from within Cornish Studies. Du Maurier stands out as one of the most famous authors to have links with Cornwall, and to have imagined it in her work. Her early novel of 1936, *Jamaica Inn* (based on a real inn located on Bodmin Moor), makes good use of the Gothic potential of the moor as a horrorscape. This chapter, therefore, coalesces around these authors' works, while also bringing in other works where these locations appear, including Rumer Godden's *China Court* (1961), a country house family saga, and Katherine Stansfield's retelling of the Charlotte Dymond mystery, *Falling Creatures* (2017), which was also discussed in Chapter Three.[4]

Clemo and du Maurier are two very different writers of Cornwall from strikingly different backgrounds. They lived and wrote within fifteen miles of each other in mid-Cornwall, yet the landscapes which they inhabited and wrote about were entirely disparate. Du Maurier settled in a sea-view mansion near Fowey, while Clemo was born, lived, and wrote in a small cottage embedded within the human-made landscape of the china clay mining industry. In many ways, this chapter is an exploration of two distinct Cornish literary 'countries': 'du Maurier country', which was born out of the Cornwall of du Maurier's novels, and 'clay country', a landscape shaped by the industrial necessities of open-cast china clay mining, which was the inspiration for Clemo's writing for much of his life. Whilst this chapter establishes and recognizes the significant differences in their literary Cornwalls, crucially, their works also signpost points of connection which lead to a more nuanced understanding of the worlds at the centre of their texts.

Clay Blindness

In Rumer Godden's *China Court*, mine and moor are of the same landscape. The house of the novel's title is situated near the fictional village of St Probus.[5] Godden seems to have merged the two interior locations of the clay area and Bodmin Moor: the house is 'built on the edge of the Cornish moors that have a strange foreign flavour as they roll to the skyline, with their tors and the pale-coloured Chinese coolie-hat shapes of the sand dumps at the different china-clay works breaking the dark landscape'.[6] Foreignness here covers both the human-made, alien landscape of clay country and the tors of the moor, one the result of extracting kaolinized granite, the other a granite landscape feature caused by erosion and weathering.

China clay extraction is crucial to China Court, the country house of the novel, and to the maintenance of the generations of families that live in the property. No secret is made of the fact that the family own clay mining concerns—indeed, this is the 'China' of both the house and the novel's name, but significantly, that mining process is always located offstage. Like many of 'the brood' (Eustace and Adza Quin's children), the first generation born at the house between 1841 and 1853, we only hear about the family's clay mining concerns second-hand. Eliza has been to the nearby quarry that the family also own, but only Little Eustace, the eldest boy, has seen the clay works. Eustace senior teaches the other children about the china clay world that is out of sight. For Eliza, it consequently takes on a magical quality. She chants '[p]igments, ceramics and pigments', taking delight in the unusual words. She is proud of 'our china clay' which 'is the best in the world'. When she is not taken to see the clay works like her brother, 'the first buffets of being only a girl begin to be felt'.[7] Eliza's gender-based exclusion is mirrored by the excision of the labour of working-class Cornishmen in the extraction of minerals, an economy which is central to the wealth of the Quin family, but which is debarred from the pages of the text.

As I have said elsewhere, by putting the clay country at the centre of the text, Jack Clemo's literary work demands that we look at the clayscape and the lives of its people. It is a direct look, an inhabiting of the clay world which texts such as *China Court* do not allow.[8] It is also a gaze which is still not required from the tourist, who can either pass by the clay tips next to the A30, on their way further west, or enter this part of Cornwall for specifically demarcated tourist activity. Even the old-style conical tips, referred to above as being like a 'coolie-hat', are today naturalized, the verdure helping to hold the piled white sand in place, and to camouflage them.[9] I have previously argued that visitors who venture off the A30 into 'the clay' are often destined for sites such as the Eden Project which, even though it has been built in a disused clay pit, does not require a looking at or an understanding of the clayscape or its history.[10] Not much has changed in that respect since I last wrote on this topic, other than an increased intensity in tourist traffic to sites within the clay, such as Charlestown. Historically, Charlestown was a port used for the global export of clay, but its enhanced status, in recent years, as one of the most visited tourist destinations in Cornwall is connected to its use in the BBC *Poldark* series reboot that aired from 2015 to 2019. While Charlestown's history and connection to the clay industry is accessible (at Wheal Martyn China Clay Museum, for example), its picturesqueness not its past function is its draw, along with its connection to *Poldark* which is increasingly drawn on and referenced within the location itself.[11] In this context, the sustained looking at the clay that Clemo's novels require of us is all the more important. *Wilding Graft* (1949), *The Shadowed Bed* (1986), and *The Clay Kiln* (2000) are all set within the clay works and clay villages of this area and are intensely immersed in this environment.[12]

Many of the discussions in this book thus far have been about understanding a particular aesthetic of Cornwall, while also looking for alternative ways to read it and to read versions of Cornwall that do not fit that mould. It is easier to understand the clayscape as the antithesis of a Cornwall that works within a touristic narrative. Sites like the coastal engine houses, or like Charlestown, have an industrial history, but can be incorporated into that aesthetic because they fulfil a particular kind of Cornish beauty. However, to understand that the clayscape has an aesthetic of its own is to begin to complicate how the different versions of Cornwall can be understood, and to flesh out a Cornwall beyond tourist-friendly versions.

Laura Knight's two paintings *Men Working in a China Clay Pit* (1912) and *The China Clay Pit* (1914) challenge an understanding that Cornish beauty is post- (or pre-) industrial.[13] Both paintings depict men labouring within clay pits. At the upper border of each is a sliver of green indicating the edge where the natural environment and the pit meet. While it is obvious that the extraction process has required the destruction of the green environment, these artworks are not a lament for that loss. Knight carefully observes the light as it falls onto, and is reflected by, the white clay. Both paintings depict simultaneously industrious activity within the pit and an idiosyncratic beauty that is present whilst the extractive work is still in process, indeed that is created by it. The variations in whiteness of the exposed rock face, becoming blues and browns in places where other mineral deposits show through, gives the earlier painting in particular a brilliant luminosity. In this same painting the flow of the clay water (water is used to wash the clay out of the rock face) cascades over the pit edge and the rocky terrain within the pit, catching the light before merging with the rock face.

Horrorscape

In his non-fiction book *Rising Ground*, which documents his search for the 'spirit of place', Philip Marsden climbs a tor on Bodmin Moor and can see the sea at sunset as 'a strip of gold'.[14] Similarly, in Stansfield's novel *Falling Creatures*, set on Bodmin Moor, Shilly and Charlotte Dymond climb Roughtor to see the whole vista of the moor laid out before them and the sea as a 'line of light on the horizon'.[15] The coast is visible, but only just, as a small slither in the distance. This is all the coast that is available. In du Maurier's *Jamaica Inn*, not even that is available; the moor is 'like a desert land to some unseen horizon'.[16] As Marsden comments, the sea seems 'a world away' when one inhabits the granite moorland occupying the centre of Cornwall, which can be overwhelming in its sense of 'too much space'.[17]

It seems a suitable space, therefore, for fictional drama, but one which is not realized as often as cliff edges and crashing seas. Like the clay area, Bodmin Moor is more often side scenery for tourist traffic which travels through it on the A30 (which cuts a path through the moor right next to

Jamaica Inn) en route to coastal destinations. In *Picturing Cornwall* Rachel Moseley discusses Cornish production company o-region's 2016 film *Brown Willy*. Set entirely on Bodmin Moor and filmed in black and white, the film sees two friends attempt to climb Cornwall's highest peak on a stag do. As she notes, this film is highly unusual in being set in Cornwall without a single view of the sea, so that it 'insists relentlessly on place beyond the bright, coastal edge'.[18]

The comedy of *Brown Willy* is based on the two protagonists getting lost on Bodmin Moor, which the filmmakers point out is difficult to do these days, a fact that forms part of the comedic undercutting of the characters for audiences who are aware.[19] The drama of *Jamaica Inn* and *Falling Creatures*, both set on nineteenth-century versions of the moor, is based on the opposite. Minus a major road cutting through its heart, and our modern-day mapping and technology, getting lost on the moor is a moment of utmost peril for any character. In *Falling Creatures* local knowledge of the moor is therefore vital. Shilly says, 'I knew where a marsh started but that was because I was born on the moor. Charlotte was born by the sea. It made a difference, something like that.' This plays out when Charlotte's misstep traps her in the marsh and Shilly must perform a rescue as the 'black water seeped from the earth at her [Charlotte's] feet'.[20] In *Jamaica Inn* even the knowledge of those born on the moor is not enough to escape its clutches. Joss recounts to Mary his brother Matthew's death by drowning in Trewartha Marsh. No one knew what had happened to him until the waters receded in the summer and his body appeared 'sticking up in the bog, with his hands above his head, and the curlews flying round him'. The moor is always waiting to suck you into its marshes. This story sets up the jeopardy for when Mary must traverse the moors and, losing sight of her uncle and the path he chooses through the bog, must find her own way.[21]

The danger inherent in traversing the moor is heightened by certain features used in both novels. Mist often cloaks the moors, so thick, Shilly relates, that her lantern casts light no further than her own feet. Even to the knowledgeable moor-born Shilly it feels as if the topography of the moor changes as you pick a path through it: tors seemingly appear and disappear, 'hiding in plain sight'.[22] In *Jamaica Inn* Mary is told on the journey to her new home that the moor is a 'wild, rough place' where '[t]hey don't like strangers', and this seems to stand not only for its inhabitants but for the moor itself.[23] In both novels, then, the moor is personified. It seems to possess evil intent towards those who venture onto it. After

Charlotte's body has been discovered on the moor, Shilly has a flashback of the marsh. The place returns to her, the smell, the power of the land to 'pull bodies into its depths' and a creeping sensation that '[t]here was something beneath the cold, clogging surface. It was waiting for me.'[24] The moor is a horrorscape.

The World on the Horizon

Jack Clemo's novel *The Clay Kiln* is important to the discussion which unfolds throughout this chapter. It is a novel I have discussed previously in *Cornish Studies*, and I refer to that discussion briefly in this section as an important corollary to the argument about *Jamaica Inn* that follows, and for the further exploration of Clemo's novel later in this chapter.[25] Like *Wilding Graft*, discussed in the previous chapter, *The Clay Kiln* has a large cast of characters, all of whom are eking out their existence within the challenging environment of the clay. Most of those characters intersect in some way with the protagonist Joel Kruse, who likens the clay world that he inhabits to being in a kiln that is suffocating him, confining him. The kiln of the title, and which Joel refers to here, is where the extracted clay is dried. By the end of the novel he has met Lorraine, and Gwen, Joel's sister, has met Euan. The central tenet of the novel is that these couples are able to realize what is divinely predestined for them by God's will. Joel, through Lorraine, is now outside his kiln, but accessing these truths, and his destiny, was only possible within the environment in which he had previously felt so trapped.[26]

As I have argued elsewhere, Clemo sets up the clayscape as a contrast to more straightforwardly beautiful sites, and as a location overlooked by tourists, whilst advocating for its idiosyncratic beauty. In *The Clay Kiln*, this contrast is achieved through the depiction of Falmouth and the Isles of Scilly.[27] Laura Knight's viewpoint above, which sees beauty in a working clay pit, is echoed by Euan in *The Clay Kiln*. I have quoted this section before, but it is useful here as a starting point for understanding the complexity of Clemo's clayscape aesthetic. For Euan and Gwen, the clayscape possesses its own particular, industrial beauty, which speaks to him and draws him into communion with it. Whilst Euan is walking with Gwen, we are told that

> [h]is eyes narrowed with a sort of yearning, a strange fixedness of recognition and communion. They had passed over the woodland with indifference, but were held by the claywork fantasy. He knew

the idiom of his countryside, the bleak lyricism of the flowing sand. There was poignant beauty now in the scene as the gravel poured out over the ridge, groping blindly down among the folds and ruts of the dune's face, settling into the furrows like grain, yet hostile to the mood of fertility. It fascinated Euan, the sight of the outcast soil flung nakedly out under the arc-lights, moving softly and gently with its quiet menace to the rhythms of the breeding earth.[28]

Such a recognition of beauty both challenges our previous assumptions based on an aesthetic of the Cornish coast, and requires us to look more closely at the different literary world which now gets the opportunity to take up the centre of the text.

Crucially, Clemo's characters, including Joel, Lorraine, Euan, and Gwen, ultimately reject a more familiar 'domestic exotic' Cornwall, one that is more straightforwardly beautiful, one that they could access on the edges of the clay landscape and beyond.[29] This is not an easy choice; the clayscape can be ugly, menacing, and horrific too, just as much as Bodmin Moor, because this industrial location provides an idiosyncratic beauty and simultaneously its antithesis.[30] It is this paradox, located in the 'quiet menace' that the environment provides to the natural world, which makes its beauty both complex and individual.[31]

Jamaica Inn contrasts the moorland at the centre of the text with Helford. Events take place entirely on Bodmin Moor and surrounding villages or on the north coast, but the novel begins with Mary Yellan travelling from Helford, her home in West Cornwall, to live with her Aunt Patience and Uncle Joss, following the death of her mother. This move throws her into a dangerous and wholly disparate world of drinking and smuggling at her uncle's hostelry on Bodmin Moor. As Avril Horner and Sue Zlosnik state, '[i]n this novel, Cornwall is constructed as two starkly contrasted landscapes: it is made clear from the very start that Bodmin Moor, although only forty miles or so away, is "a different world" from Helford'.[32] Throughout *Jamaica Inn*, these two Cornish worlds are defined through contrast with each other. The descriptions of Helford could be used in holiday brochures; it has 'shining waters', 'green hills', 'sloping valleys', and 'lush grass', while the moors are 'barren', 'bleak', 'rough', and 'sodden'.[33] Through this contrast the danger of the environment surrounding Jamaica Inn is heightened and, as events unfold there, Helford becomes increasingly desirable as a place of refuge.

Helford, however, as I have said previously, 'is the Atlantis of this novel, always imagined but never realized'.[34] From the first page, Mary is travelling away from her homeland and, while a return is desired, in the end it is refused, even when the obstacles of return are removed. Instead, at the close of *Jamaica Inn*, Mary chooses Joss's brother Jem over her beloved home, and leaves Cornwall at his side.[35] In never allowing the reader to inhabit Helford alongside Mary, the novel ensures it remains a distant Eden, yet one with which they are likely to be more familiar than the rough moorland in which the action plays out. Helford retains an important function in the text as an imaginative construct to which Mary continually returns. For instance, when out on the moors at Christmas time, while Joss lies insensibly drunk at Jamaica Inn, Mary's mind turns to Helford. She remembers that 'home at Helford people would be decorating with holly and evergreen and mistletoe. There would be a great baking of pastry and cakes, and a fattening of turkeys and geese.'[36] Here is the safety, community, and sense of enjoyment that is missing at Jamaica Inn, and which Mary can only access through memory. In contrasting these two environments—one in which the harsh reality of the story is played out, the other a rosy memory—the bleakness of Jamaica Inn and the moors is emphasized.

Connecting Worlds

Whilst Clemo was continuing to explore industrial Cornwall in the twentieth century, just as many writers had done in the nineteenth century, du Maurier was accessing a pre-nineteenth-century Cornwall as her literary inspiration. *Frenchman's Creek* (1941), *The King's General* (1946), *Castle Dor* (1962), and *The House on the Strand* (1969) all draw the reader back to a Cornwall of the more distant past. We can position Clemo as an inheritor of the mining literature of the nineteenth century and, on the surface at least, du Maurier as creating a fictional Cornwall that is more palatable to a tourist market. However, this does not mean that their fictional worlds are walled off from each other. Rather, there is a dialectic here that this chapter intends to explore.

In 1971, du Maurier was interviewed by Wilfred De'Ath for the BBC.[37] In that interview, there is a moment which exemplifies what I have argued elsewhere is the reductive categorizing of du Maurier's fiction as simply romantic, something that is tied up with a concomitant romanticization of the Cornish landscape.[38] De'Ath comes to visit du Maurier at Kilmarth, located on the same estate as her previous home Menabilly (which is widely accepted as the inspiration for Manderley in *Rebecca* (1938)). They walk and talk, dog in tow, through the fields towards the coast. Unprompted, as if in anticipation, du Maurier pushes against a labelling of her work as romantic, pointing out that *Frenchman's Creek* (1941) is the only romantic novel she ever wrote. Du Maurier's statement is followed by De'Ath in voiceover declaring that 'this is the sort of romantic landscape where you would almost expect to find Daphne du Maurier—it's remote, beautiful, even lush'. What is revealed when they reach the coast, though, is Par docks, an industrial site for the export of china clay located near Fowey. This is one of the locations where Clemo's clay world is connected to the coast. Rather than remote, the harbour is a point of connection, as we have seen in previous chapters, and here it is where china clay is shipped to a global market. For De'Ath, though, it is an interruption to the typically beautiful view of the coast he had clearly anticipated. 'Doesn't that spoil the…' he begins. 'Oh, no,' du Maurier exclaims, 'that's part of our industry, part of our livelihood'. 'So you don't mind that,' he tries again. 'Oh no,' she repeats. What is telling, though, is that despite a repudiation by du Maurier of both the romantic labelling of her fiction and of the Cornish coast before them, and despite this industrial site visually appearing on the screen, the voiceover added later still holds onto these very assumptions. De'Ath at the coastal edge near Fowey is met with a sight which subverts his expectations because the picturesque coast is shared with the necessities of an extractive industry, one that is still active. His, and the programme's, inability to engage with this view speaks to the power of the Cornish coastal aesthetic and the importance of repositioning less familiar landscapes to the centre of the text or screen.

The transportation of clay, from the point of extraction and refinement to a global market, is what connects the china clay mining region of mid-Cornwall to the rest of the world. On a micro scale, it also connects the various locations within the clay area to each other, from the inland pits, through the town of St Austell, to the harbours of Pentewan, Charlestown, Par, and Fowey, which are positioned along the southern coastal edge of the clay area, dotted around or near St Austell Bay.[39] With his characteristic prejudice about his home and its people, in his autobiography, *A Cornish Childhood*, A.L. Rowse divides the town from the clay villages situated on the 'western escarpment behind St Austell' or the 'Higher Quarter' as he calls it, which

> conveyed to our minds the sense of a civilization altogether rough and raw and rude compared with ourselves—or rather of an absence of civilization as we understood it, living next to the town, three-quarters of a mile away. The men of the Higher Quarter, the china-clay villages that clustered in the high bleak uplands, were known to be fierce, fearsome creatures; there was no taking liberties with them: they were much more likely to take liberties with you. The best policy was to give them no cause of offence, avoid their company, give them a wide berth, especially if, as was usually the case, they were travelling the road in groups.[40]

Rowse's characterization of these Cornishmen from the clay uplands is reminiscent of outsider viewpoints of the Cornish from the likes of D.H. Lawrence and Henry Havelock Ellis, who register an alienness that is often connected to Celticity. Robert Louis Stevenson, in *Across the Plains*, describes a group of Cornish miners on a train in America as a 'mysterious race'. Stevenson muses 'that some of the strangest races dwell next door to you at home' yet Rowse makes this distinction with men living less than a mile away from his childhood home.[41] Despite Rowse's effort to carve up the clay area into distinct locations, what actually connects through all these clay country locations is the transportation of clay from pit to port, from inland territory to the coast. In Rowse's time, the horse-drawn clay wagons carve out paths across the clay area, marking their routes to the coast with the scattered remnants of china clay powder that they leave in their wake.[42] Therefore, the necessities of the industry, the reason why any of these villages exists in the first place, is the common thread. Rowse likens the 'narrow grooves' of people's lives in this area during his childhood (he was born in 1903) to this process. He observes that '[l]ife proceeded therefore along very well-worn ruts, as deep as the tracks the heavily-laden clay-wagons wore in our road on the way to the station or down Slades to the little port of Charlestown'.[43] This procession of clay, extracted from within the ground, connects the interior of Cornwall's clay area with its coast, and with the world beyond.

The clay area appears in du Maurier's 1952 novel *Castle Dor* where she makes use of the strangeness of the clay landscape, and its proximity to the coast. The novel is a joint venture, the last and unfinished novel of Cornish writer Arthur Quiller-Couch, which was passed to du Maurier by his daughter after his death.[44] It was the perfect project for du Maurier, a story rooted in both Fowey's and Cornwall's distant mythic past. Set in the nineteenth century, the plot centres on Linnet Lewarne's affair with Amyot Trestane, both of whose lives are doomed to repeat that of Tristan and Yseult because they are at the mercy of ancient forces around the earthwork of Castle Dor. The clay area is only briefly mentioned in the novel, but it becomes important to the resolution of the plot.

In the literary worlds of both Clemo and du Maurier, we are made aware that the coast is also connected to the inland clay area through rivers which have been turned a milky white by the waste from the clay refining process. Today, measures are in place to limit pollution of the natural environment by the clay industry. However, although this was a problematic side effect of china clay mining it has, perhaps quite oddly, become a positive identifier for the area. When a new shopping centre and cinema complex was built in St Austell ten years ago, as part of a major regeneration of the town centre, it was named White River Place. In *Wilding Graft*, the River Fal is 'clay-clogged'.[45] In *Castle Dor* there is a more straightforward observation that 'the River Par; even the Fal itself [is] chalky white these days'.[46] The River Par empties into St Austell Bay at Par, right next to Fowey, and the River Fal flows into the English Channel at Falmouth. Including this observation in a novel where the forces of a distant past are predominant also makes evident the inescapable nature of the more recent connection between the inland clay area and the coast, at Fowey and beyond. This watery connection of the clay-polluted water literally seeps into the primary environment in which the novel is played out.

That connection, though, is not a menacing one in *Castle Dor*. The novel registers the ugliness of the clay region, much like Clemo sometimes does, while at the same time casting it as a potential place of sanctuary for the protagonists, into which they have the opportunity to retreat. For the denouement in *Castle Dor*, the characters are taken out of their primary environment and pass through the china clay region en route inland to Castle-an-Dinas, where the novel ends with Amyot's death. Doctor Carfax, a scholar who recognizes that Amyot and Linnet's love story is mirroring that of Tristan and Yseult, sees the clay country for the first time in many years, despite its proximity to his home, on his journey to Castle-an-Dinas to try to prevent the ensuing tragedy. The visual jarring of the clay area, its oddness after Fowey, is heightened by the length of time that has elapsed since Carfax has seen it, and the constantly changing nature of the clayscape due to the extractive process. Carfax is surprised at the change in this landscape since he was last there: 'Hamlets that had barely existed save for a cottage or two were now ugly villages linked together; and topping them everywhere were the great white clay peaks themselves, turning the moorland landscape into an unlikely range of mountains.'[47] Despite the proximity of his home to the clay area, it remains an unknown landscape. The ugliness he perceives in the clayscape (very different to the complexity of Euan's engagement with it above) contrasts it with the picturesqueness of the primary setting of Fowey.

While this alternative clay landscape remains on the periphery of the text's geography, connected to the world at the centre of the text by the clay water, and alien to both Carfax and the reader, it has an important role to play. At breakfast, shortly before his walk through the clayscape, Carfax ponders his research: certain puzzles in the Tristan legend which suggest that Tristan did not leave Cornwall, but rather 'passed into another Cornish kingdom'. Significantly, the text suggests the clayscape as 'Tristan's "Blanche Lande"'.[48] There are several references within Arthurian texts to the 'Blanche Lande', and in Béroul, which du Maurier consulted as part of her research for the novel, it is a region within Cornwall where Tristan and Yseult seek refuge once banished from the court of King Mark. Given the hills of white sand which dominate the clay area, it is a fitting corollary. In making the clayscape the white land mentioned in Béroul for the nineteenth-century re-enactment of the Tristan and Yseult tale, du Maurier weaves the clayscape into the underlying mythos of the story and, while it remains on the periphery, connects this landscape to the primary one of Fowey. Crucially, the symbolism employed by du Maurier suggests that this 'ugly' and inhospitable industrial landscape, so different from Fowey and which the characters only pass through en route to the novel's tragic denouement at Castle-an-Dinas, is actually a safe haven in disguise: one which is tragically overlooked by Linnet and Amyot.

Worlds Within Worlds

A notion of Cornwall as an ancient place where it is possible to feel the presence of the past has long been a preoccupation of writers. For example, the poet Wallace Nichols notes that

Cornwall's aura of the past certainly stimulates the writer's imagination. If you go through Madron Village towards the open moor beyond you are on the edge of prehistoric country, filled with the memories and memorials of a lost race ... one feels near the beginning of things on a Cornish moor.[49]

D.H. Lawrence characterizes Cornwall's ancient past as Arthurian; for him, Cornwall 'is not England. It is bare and dark and elemental. Tristan's land [...]. It is old, Celtic, pre-Christian.'[50] For Virginia Woolf too, the experience of Cornwall throws her back into an ancient past, so that when in Cornwall she 'often think[s] about the Phoenicians and the Druids'.[51] We can imagine that notions of this past as somehow still alive and particularly accessible in Cornwall are handed down through literature about the region until new artists to Cornwall arrive with this concept already formed in their mind. Towards the end of the nineteenth century, ancient Cornwall becomes relevant to the emerging tourist industry and the production of images to attract a metropolitan visitor. It is equally relevant, from the beginning of the twentieth century, to the Cornish-Celtic Revival, which sought to restore aspects of Cornwall's ancient past.

Du Maurier inherits from previous writers of Cornwall a preoccupation with its ancient past. Many of du Maurier's Cornish novels make this past accessible, enabling the reader to enter the world that Nichols, Lawrence, and Woolf look to experience above. The concept of a brooding, ancient past present within the Cornish landscape is central to the plots of *Jamaica Inn* and *Castle Dor*. As we have seen, in *Castle Dor* mysterious forces at work around the ancient earthworks of the same name set Amyot and Linnet on a doomed path that echoes the fate of Tristan and Yseult. The Virago book cover describes the novel as 'a spellbinding love story and a superb evocation of Cornwall's mythic past'.

In *Jamaica Inn*, the ancient past seeps into the present through the treacherous landscape of Bodmin Moor. The palimpsestic nature of the moor is key to the concept of ancient Cornwall put forward in *Jamaica Inn*; du Maurier uses it to create an atmosphere of mystery and foreboding in her Gothic novel. As Horner and Zlosnik argue, '[h]er sense of identification with the peripheral culture of Cornwall may be seen as deriving from her attraction to its strangeness, the "otherness" of a landscape permeated by relics of the past and hints of beliefs alien to the seemingly rational world of the twentieth century'.[52] This past is therefore alien and unknowable, thus heightening its impact and the Gothicness of the narrative, but, at the same time, its eternal presence is suggested by the emphasis du Maurier places on the timeless quality of the landscape. When Mary begins to explore the moorland surrounding Jamaica Inn, she is aware not only that the landscape 'belonged to another age' when 'pagan footsteps trod upon the hills', but that it is a landscape 'untouched by human hand'.[53] Thus, by standing on the moor, Mary is in a space that provides an accessible link to a pagan past, a connection made all the more tangible because the landscape is unchanged from that ancient time.

It is Francis Davey, vicar of Altarnun, who is most keenly aware of the past in *Jamaica Inn*. His Christian garb disguises a pagan believer, just as 'beneath the foundation-stone [of Altarnun church] lie the bones of [...] pagan ancestors, and the old granite altars where sacrifice was held long before Christ died upon His cross'.[54] Only when Mary is kidnapped by the vicar, and taken onto Bodmin Moor, is the presence of ancient forces in the landscape fully revealed to her. While she has roamed here many times before, and while there has always been a sense of the brooding potential beneath the surface, much as Shilly has felt in *Falling Creatures*, it is now, in the presence of Francis Davey, that the true nature of this landscape is realized, and Mary is made to face the 'monsters of antiquity'.[55] The final scenes of *Jamaica Inn* show du Maurier's descriptive powers at their best. She takes an established trope of Cornwall and weaves it into a less familiar literary landscape, to create a powerful sense of place for her reader. She writes:

> Here on the summit the wind fretted and wept, whispering of fear, sobbing old memories of bloodshed and despair, and there was a wild, lost note that echoed in the granite high above Mary's head, on the very peak of Roughtor, as though the gods themselves stood there with their great heads lifted to the sky. In her fancy she could hear the whisper of a thousand voices and the tramping of a thousand feet, and she could see the stones turning to men beside her. Their faces were inhuman, older than time, carved and rugged like the granite; and they spoke in a tongue she could not understand, and their hands and feet were curved like the claws of a bird.[56]

At the climax of the novel, the past which has pervaded the whole novel most strongly suggests its presence so that, through Mary's imagination, it takes a physical form.

Perhaps surprisingly, there is also an ancient presence within the modern industrial environment of Clemo's clayscape. The relationship to ancient Cornwall here, though, is more complex because it is mediated by the modern environment, which has overwritten the original landscape. There is a tangible Celtic presence in *The Clay Kiln*, but the past is not as directly accessible here as it is in *Jamaica Inn*. While in du Maurier's novel the form of the landscape is immutable, in the clay it undergoes constant change. Here the landscape has a new form and purpose. The necessities of the clay mining process create a landscape which smothers and destroys the natural environment, replacing it with an unnatural, human-made landscape. This landscape is constantly evolving as pits are expanded and new tipping sites for the waste sand must be found. At times, the tips even encroach onto the villages built to house the clay workers. Houses are knocked down and families relocated, as happens to the Kruse family in *The Clay Kiln*. Therefore, in Clemo's landscape the ancient past, still latent within the original landscape, must negotiate with its industrial successor, creating a more complicated mix and power dynamic.

In the opening scene of *The Clay Kiln*, Joel Kruse is inside the land, at the bottom of a clay pit that, later in the novel, will subsume his home. Even here there are subtle indications of the continued presence of something older. Clemo writes, '[h]e crossed the pit bed, picking his way among the blasted stone and scraps of timber, the network of rails, the unloaded wagons; stolidly he moved between the huge masses of granite, gnarled and twisted shapes like pillars of some temple'.[57] Here, the newer elements of the rails and wagons are in proximity to the granite, which is older and more mysterious. There are similarities here to the way in which du Maurier describes the granite on Bodmin Moor in *Jamaica Inn*. She writes, 'on the high tors the slabs of stone leant against one another in strange shapes and forms, massive sentinels who had stood there since the hands of God first fashioned them'. She calls them granite 'altar-stones', while Clemo likens the clay pit granite to the pillars of a temple.[58] The significant difference is that in the clayscape the ancient granite is mixed up with newer elements, while on Bodmin Moor it is undisturbed; the ancient past within the clayscape is not as accessible as it is on the moor.

Roche Rock, located close to Joel's home, is a pre-Christian landscape located within the clay area. A rocky outcrop with the ruins of a monk's cell built into the rock, it dominates the local skyline. Clemo describes it as follows: 'Despite the ruined mediaeval oratory on the massive central rock, the atmosphere of the place at nightfall was entirely pagan. The ancient Celtic gloom lapped powerfully upon the black stone, gripped and submerged the surrounding soil in a harsh drowse of barbarism.'[59] This small area of land is encircled by, and sits in absolute contrast to, pit and tip: a landscape harnessed for industrial exploitation. This small but significant space has survived intact, impervious to smothering by the encroaching industry, and serves as a reminder of a previous existence of this landscape prior to industrialization.

As in *Jamaica Inn*, this ancient presence, while tied to the physical environment of the rock, is felt by the local inhabitants through a perceptible change in atmosphere. Roche Rock's effect permeates the nearby village. Although one of many clay villages, Roche is described by Clemo as 'particularly grim and inhospitable', and the inhabitants as 'a tribe apart'.[60] The reason is the influence of the rock:

> [T]he place itself [Roche village] had a depressing aspect, as if it were a mere remnant of a lost pagan world. Its chilly gloom was pagan, despite the church tower on the hilltop. It was the atmosphere of the Rock seeping down among the dwellings and becoming void of significance in its transformation from the natural to the civilized form.[61]

An ancient force seeps down into the village. At the same time, however, such power is potentially impotent when it meets the built environment.

While Roche Rock has some influence on the nearby Roche village, in many places in Clemo's clay world, ancient Cornwall has been overwritten. Marvran Creba is Joel's first girlfriend before he meets Lorraine. En route to the Kruses' home, and passing through the vicinity of Roche Rock, she is fully aware of the pagan atmosphere enveloping her, that '[t]he ancient Celtic gloom lapped powerfully upon the black stone' of the rock. Here, directly around the rock, the mysterious ancient force is strongest, unbridled even. Significantly, however, its power 'dwindled only when it reached the clay dumps'. At the point at which modern and ancient meet, there is a smothering of ancient power. The reader is made to feel that as Marvran travels away from the ancient influence of Roche Rock and into the clayscape, she once again enters a realm of safety. Here there is only a 'faint rasp of the wind and the plash of water in the micas nearby', sounds which seem comforting rather than confrontational.[62] Across the clayscape, therefore, there are points, such as Roche Rock, where an ancient past breaks through into the industrial present. However, this past has in many places been overwritten, literally built on top of, by the comparatively new industrial usage of the landscape, which has forced that land into new forms.

As in *Jamaica Inn*, characters in *The Clay Kiln* are influenced by their environment. Some characters exhibit affinity with the modern industrial landscape, while others are still drawn towards the brooding, ancient presence. Joel is entirely a product of the clay. In the opening chapter, when we meet Joel at the bottom of a clay pit, the reader is informed that '[t]he atmosphere was natural to the place; it was natural to Joel. His character had been moulded by these surroundings.' For Joel, the human-made environment is his natural habitat, to the point that he 'unquestioningly accepted the sand-dunes and clay-beds as natural features'.[63] This unnatural environment is natural to him, and it is his home.

There are other characters within *The Clay Kiln*, however, who exhibit affinity with Roche Rock, rather than the altered clay landscape which surrounds it. For instance, Cal Mannell and Lela Skiddy, standing in the vicinity of the rock, are seen 'to belong to it, to be part of the pagan dereliction that brooded here'.[64] This is described as a particularly squalid area, made so because of the pagan influence, and yet it is fitting for these inhabitants. It is Olive Buzza, of all the characters in the novel, who is most closely allied with the pre-Christian element of Roche Rock. Olive, the local prostitute, is sympathetically drawn by Clemo. She is not crushed by the difficult circumstances of her life, but rather forges her own path. She sets out to win Joel, believing that they have similar natures. Olive is Joel's fate. Succumbing to her will maroon him in his kiln world. He eventually rejects this path and Olive marries Charlie Crago who, near the end of the novel, murders her in the woods near Barrakellis farm. Significantly, Olive's Spanish blood, inherited from her father, is described as an 'ancient streak [...] common in the inhabitants of the coastal regions of West Cornwall'.[65] It is this inheritance that draws Olive to Roche Rock, rather than to the clayscape in which she lives. We are told that 'Olive felt its savage power and released herself into it, letting the pre-Christian magnetism pull upon her blood'.[66] Olive is elemental; she has no kinship with the human-made landscape but, just like the ancient power of the rock, in the end her vitality is smothered.

Olive's nature in *The Clay Kiln* is wholly tied to her ancient inheritance, and this is given as an explanation for her behaviour. She is seen to represent 'primitive values', but this does not just refer to what is perceived by others in her community as her loose morals.⁶⁷ Olive's primitiveness means that she lacks artifice in her social interactions. It is clear that her emotions are not checked in any way, but can be read from her facial expressions. We are told that 'fear marked her face, a shrinking, physical and mental, from an expected reality; fear at issue with craving and impatience'. Similarly, when Olive tries to persuade Joel to become her lover, there is no guile in her approach. Joel is taken aback by her directness when she announces, '[y]ou're a real man, and that's what I want'. At the same time, however, he is drawn to her 'rude female power exposed and vulnerable to him'. Olive is fully aware that her method of courting is very different from other village girls who 'drop all sorts of subtle hints', but she feels they do not 'make it clear […] the way they put out their feelers'. For someone of Olive's nature, such play-acting is unthinkable.⁶⁸

Olive's nature can be contrasted with Marvran's. Marvran bears the name of a character in the medieval Cornish play *Origo Mundi* and so, like Olive, she is connected to an ancient past. Joel certainly associates her with Roche Rock: for him that location is 'always charged […] with the presence of Marvran'.⁶⁹ However, Marvran recoils from any such inheritance. It is explained that '[s]he could never have turned to the old Celtic superstitions, or felt anything but repulsion towards the gods of blood-intimacy whose influence still brooded about the Rock'. This is the fundamental difference between Marvran and Olive. In rejecting the ancient past, Marvran is the antithesis of Olive. Marvran does not possess Olive's primitiveness, or her openness, but is contrived. It is explained to the reader that 'Marvran was not by nature a primitive. She had always possessed something of the artificial dignity that belongs to the more refined strata of village life.'⁷⁰ Whereas Olive's face communicates her feelings, it is on Marvran's face that her artificiality is registered, which is something that Joel notices:

> He turned again to study her face, now visible to him for the first time in the glare of electric light. It appeared quite different from the face he had seen in the faint lamplight of his home […]. Its features had been subdued then, with a hint of mystery. But now they were too sharp, even theatrical. She had more lipstick on her mouth than when he last saw her, and it gave her an almost garish artificiality. Her bright, pitiful mouth had appealed to him on the downs,

moved him to tenderness, but the present scarlet blob in the pale, flat-cheeked face merely marked her as a creature not of this world.[71]

This is a ghastly description of Marvran which sees her mysterious features as further falsified and brutalized by the application of make-up. Significantly, it is her appearance here which ends Joel's obsession with her and enables him to find his true love Lorraine. However, until the point where Lorraine arrives to release him from his kiln world, his future is represented by Olive and Marvran and 'the necessity of choosing between these alternatives—Olive's lure or the resistance of the subtly guarded, subtly challenging virginity of Marvran'.[72] Joel had previously believed that with Marvran 'the true fire burned behind that mask', while Olive's 'potent freedom was but a counterfeit'.[73] While in the end, neither extreme is his fate, and no choice must be made between the two, the text informs the reader that with regards to Marvran and Olive, the exact opposite is in fact true.

Given Marvran's artificiality, and her rejection of the primitive ancient spirit associated with Roche Rock, it is conceivable that she would relate instead to the artificial environment of the clayscape. However, it is clear that this is not the case. As I have discussed previously, upon returning to the clay area from Falmouth, Marvran yearns for the latter's exoticism, now lost to her.[74] Marvran has bought into the lure of the 'domestic exotic' which other characters in the novel have rejected for the paradoxical ugly-beautiful dynamic of the clayscape.[75] While at Falmouth, 'the squalid clay-pit cottage', her family home near Roche, had 'grown somewhat repugnant'.[76] She had never intended to return, but a failed love affair draws her back into the clay world. Once there, Marvran is unable to fit back into her old life; she is 'unreconciled to it'.[77]

Marvran sees herself, and is seen by others, as modern, but the text shows the reader that in her naiveté, she misunderstands the full implications of this identification. Gwen Kruse comments, in reference to another village girl, that '[s]he's got the modern streak worse than Marvran'.[78] Marvran's 'modern streak' is a given; she is the mark against which other girls' modernity is measured. Marvran identifies herself as such, when she mentions a collective of 'us moderns' to her cousin Joan.[79] The text demonstrates that, while rejecting both 'the old Celtic superstitions' and her original environment of the clay, Marvran embraces instead what she believes to be modernity. However, within the text the dichotomy of ancient and modern is presented as 'the gods of blood-intimacy whose influence still brooded about the Rock' versus 'the civilised gods of intellectual advancement'. This is the actual choice open to Marvran yet, crucially, she does not understand modernity's import. We are told that

> [s]he had not, indeed, worshipped these modern gods, for she was still comparatively uneducated; but she approved of them, unthinkingly, moving within the progressive elements of working-class society which she felt to be superior to the earthy, primitive values represented by Joel and Olive.[80]

Marvran's ignorance is exposed by the narrator here. She harbours only pretentions of superiority over everyone else around her because of her 'modern streak'.

Significantly, Marvran's misunderstanding of modernism prompts her to reject the Cornish-Celtic Revival through her disavowal of the Gorsedh ceremony—a Celtic tradition, introduced to Cornwall by Henry Jenner in 1928. Marvran witnesses a Gorsedh ceremony at Roche Rock, a fitting site, but it is an event which further highlights the rock's incongruity with its industrial surroundings. Bards recite in the Cornish tongue with industrial landmarks as backdrop. Marvran is thoroughly unimpressed and uninspired. She tells Joan that '[t]he ceremony was boring, just jabber in Cornish, a foreign language to us moderns'. Having made this statement, however, Marvran still recognizes the ceremony as a modern event and the people taking place as modern. She comments, '[a]ll those modern bourgeoisie—pretending they're Druids or Bards. We just laughed.'[81] This reaction is perhaps not surprising given Marvran's rejection of ancient Cornwall, but her ridicule of the modern bourgeoisie is again representative of her misguided positioning of herself as modern in relation to both ancient and industrial Cornwall.

The episode in which Marvran recounts the Gorsedh ceremony to Joan is significant because it demonstrates the clash of Cornish cultures present within the clay world. The visual dichotomy of Roche Rock and the clay tip symbolizes deeper cultural divisions between the clay country audience and the bards. Clay culture is represented in this scene by Marvran's father, Eli Creba. Marvran notes that he 'didn't care much for the Gorsedd', yet Eli's rejection is for different reasons than Marvran's own. Joan observes that 'his idea of Heaven is your annual Band Festival here at Bugle [...]. A score of brass bands blaring all day long.' This aligns Eli's tastes with the centre ground of Cornish, working-class, industrial culture and so explains his removal, culturally, from Cornish revivalism. Within this scene the rock, representative of Cornwall's ancient past, has drawn the bards of the Gorsedh, the 'modern bourgeoisie' as Marvran calls them, into the clay country as they seek communion with that past through ceremony.[82] Ultimately, though, the revival is culturally removed from many of the clay world audience, such as Marvran's father. The clay land locals and the bards of the Gorsedh are also separated by class; the bourgeoisie revivalists and the working-class clay worker are here brought together, but they embody different cultural futures.[83]

Joan, Marvran's cousin, to whom the Gorsedh episode is being related, is a reminder of the developing tourist culture at Falmouth that exists on the very edge of the novel's world. It is with Joan that Marvran resided when there, and her visit to the clay country is to impart news of events since Marvran returned home. At this point in the narrative, we are aware that Marvran has rejected the clay world of her father, the ancient sympathies of Olive, and the modern-ancient tradition of the Gorsedh. She is most closely allied with Falmouth due to her assumed modernism, yet her life there was cut short; Falmouth has already rejected her.[84] Therefore, while all other characters in this novel have a place, either within the clay world or without, it is Marvran who remains culturally displaced.

As the above discussion has concluded, therefore, within the clay world, even though the clayscape dominates, there is a cultural multiplicity at work. It is clear, however, that because of the presence of the industrial landscape, access to an ancient past must negotiate this new landscape. At times, that past is overwritten by the new, whereas in du Maurier's novels that past is more directly accessible. Significantly, Cornwall's ancient past is a literary trope which both writers are concerned to explore within their work. In this respect, these two writers, who in other ways are so far apart in their approach to Cornwall as literary subject matter, have a common concern. Whilst recognizing this similarity, the unique characteristics of the primary Cornish world at the centre of each of their texts ultimately determines the contrasting ways in which their work relates to an ancient Cornish past. Yet in putting interior locations of Cornwall, the clayscape and the moor, at the centre of their texts, they both push more common versions of Cornwall off-centre, providing alternative versions of place. The more familiar Cornwalls exist on the horizon, and there remains recognition and connection between these Cornish worlds. Ultimately, though, these fictions are unavoidable journeys into territories that in other texts are so easy to pass by.

Conclusion

Looking and Seeing

You cannot say Cornwall is this, or that. You cannot describe it in a word or visualise it in a second. You may know the country from east to west and from sea to sea, but if you close your eyes and think about it no clear-cut image rises before you.

C.C. Vyvyan[1]

C.C. Vyvyan's comments touch upon two key elements of this book. Firstly, in arguing that Cornwall is not easily captured or conceptualized, that it cannot be described 'in a word', she suggests the complexity of place which has been articulated in this book as multiple and alternative Cornwalls. Crucially, though, when Vyvyan thinks of Cornwall 'no clear-cut image' comes to mind. It has been my contention that, in fact, the opposite is the case in the cultural construction of Cornwall. There are particular and pervasive ways, within specific historical eras, which have dominated how Cornwall is imagined. These stereotypes become entrenched and are enfolded into the cultural make-up of place until accepted and internalized by cultural consumers, rather than questioned or deconstructed. The versions of place which dominate are also those which are economically advantageous, giving impetus to their salience and their perpetuation. Cornwall's experience of industrialism in the nineteenth century, followed by its reinvention as a tourist site from the end of that century, crystallized in each of these cultural eras two dominant versions of place.

An awareness of multiple versions of place operating simultaneously is therefore the starting point for unlocking alternative Cornwalls. Their existence beneath the surface requires that they are discovered or unearthed like Cornwall's mineral wealth, closeted below ground and brought to 'grass' by the miner. The ability to identify alternative Cornwalls is crucially dependent on discarding the 'cultural baggage' which predetermines, as well as fixes, understanding of place, whilst simultaneously understanding place as culturally created.² A viewpoint is necessary, therefore, that can look past dominant versions of place to access what lies beyond, or below.

There are a number of ways in which those alternative Cornwalls have been accessed in this book, all of which involve looking and seeing differently. To return to where we began this journey, and the poetry of A.L. Rowse, in the poem 'Home-Coming to Cornwall: December 1942', another of his poetic protagonists is, this time, travelling back into rather than away from Cornwall. Suffused with Rowse's own anxieties and frustrations about his homeland, this is not by any means a joyous return, but there is still excitement as the Cornish landmarks appear from the train window, at the same time as a strong desire to '[p]ull down the blind / Over the lovely landscape'.³ There is both a consuming of and a rejection of the Cornwall available from the train window. We are told, too, of the kind of viewing available here because '[i]t is night and we are entering Cornwall strangely'. The train's route through the poem passes through Launceston, Egloskerry, Tremeer, and Otterham, and then 'out upon the shaven moonlit moor'.⁴ This is both an atypical route, and a physical journey into Cornwall that is no longer possible. The perspectives in this book have sought to open up new routes into Cornish literary worlds, through introducing lesser-known texts, exploring less familiar locations, and producing readings of texts which go against the grain.

A feminist viewpoint, as adopted in Chapter One, provides access to subsumed or hidden worlds, and enables interpretation of these worlds. The discovery of a female counter-narrative of Cornish mining is only possible if the predominant narrative of mining is understood to be gendered, and therefore exclusionary of a female perspective and identity. Consideration of balmaiden narratives defamiliarizes the dominant narrative by providing a point of view that has not previously been taken into account. The experiences of balmaidens, previously invisible, becomes one of painful visibility for the society in which they exist. Ultimately, Cornwall's experience of industrialization and collapse cannot be fully understood without incorporating their alternative perspectives.

Chapter Two's exploration of the nature of Cornwall's positioning as beyond England has hopefully given a sense of the complexities of that relationship, as well as the ways in which Cornwall as a place of escape can be both rejected and manipulated, for dramatic potential. Noel O' Reilly's *Wrecker* and Daphne du Maurier's *Rule Britannia* are examples of how stereotypes of people and place can be twisted into a writing back against that positioning. In our post-Brexit world, du Maurier's novel resonates in new ways, as it points to underlying tensions and instabilities inherent within Cornwall's England-but-not-England identity, at a time when new imaginations of place rethinking Cornwall's relationship to England, Britain, Europe, and the rest of the world might be possible. Where are and what are the Cornwalls of a global identity, something which has always been available through Cornwall's connectedness, and through its history of emigration?

Chapter Three makes a case for going beyond an aesthetic appreciation of Cornish place, at a time when the place-image of Cornwall based on an aesthetic of the sea and coast is more dominant than ever. Cornwall as Instagrammable place has saliency.[5] Rachel Moseley has elucidated how 'Cornwall becomes one with the nation' during the Second World War, its otherness minimized during this time of crisis.[6] During the pandemic, too, we have seen Cornwall function as comfort television, reassuring viewers, through an explosion of Cornish travel shows, and with the help of those by now familiar drone shots along the cliffs and coast, that Cornwall was still there, even if they could not reach it in person. The same aesthetic of the coast was employed when Cornwall was chosen as the location for the 2021 G7 summit. Its function was as backdrop: an image of brilliant blue sea and white sand against which world leaders shook hands and socialized. The collaborative artistic response to the G7 in the form of the *Behind the Postcard* short film is telling in its choice of title and its content, which gave voice to the multiple and complex realities of place, as well as a joyful expression of culture, from inside Cornwall. The postcard image of Cornwall is a one-dimensional aesthetic, behind which a host of other Cornwalls exist. Some of the overlooked issues, of poverty, illness, and hardship, which are so often hidden behind the postcard, are experienced at the cliff edge in Chapter Three, which also mirrors the psychic edge of many of the characters in the novels explored. We can, then, open up our understanding of the Cornish coast to a wider range of possibilities, even if they do not complement picturesqueness. Indeed, there is an imperative to look behind the postcard. At the coastal edge, this other kind of looking has to include confronting the realities of coastal erosion and biodiversity loss, which threaten the very aesthetic with which we are so taken. We are all on the edge when we understand, as Raynor Winn puts it, that the 'ribbons of life' of the coastline, 'this last strip of wild between the land and the sea', are 'becoming, for much of our biodiversity, the last hope'.⁷

To turn our faces from the view and head inland is to contemplate further the possibilities of Cornish literary space. Chapters Four and Five inhabit interior locations where familiarities of place are left behind, and indeed are challenged, by places not usually included within a touristic narrative of Cornwall. The performativity of Truro is very different to the 'false backs', as Erik Cohen calls them, which tourist locations can create for visitors, to satisfy their expectations of place.⁸ Truro's built environment is a confident assertion of wealth and status which anticipates, and makes plausible, the granting of city status in 1877. Crucially, though, evidence of the dirty and smelly industries on which Truro has been built can undercut that status through their pervasive presence. Truro's grandiosity, particularly the central, stage-like expanse of Boscowan Street, makes visibility something to be negotiated. It is Truro's presence as a quasi-urban site within Cornwall which prompts us to reconsider rurality and the ways in which a Cornu-centric lens can interrogate this positioning.

Situated on the granite backbone running down the centre of Cornwall, Bodmin Moor in north-east Cornwall and the china clay mining region of mid-Cornwall are locations that challenge the most dominant stereotypes of Cornish place through their heterogeneity. These are Cornish worlds just as much as the coastal realms which are so much more familiar, and they offer further literary versions of Cornish place. A writer such as Jack Clemo swings the lens onto what for outsiders might initially seem an alien and alienating world, but it is central in his literary vision of Cornwall.⁹ Ultimately, it is the river, turned milky white with clay, that flows through Clemo's literary world to du Maurier's, which suggests the possibility of connection between multiple Cornwalls, and that the dominant versions of place cannot escape their alternates. Alternative Cornwalls are there to be discovered and, once uncovered, they enhance our understanding of place. There are, of course, other texts, voices, and perspectives to be considered beyond the bounds of this book, offering to further enrich our understanding of Cornish place, and Cornish literary worlds.

To conclude, I would like to return to the image of the engine house, the touchstone in this book upon which we have mapped the transition from mining to tourism, the primary cultural and economic context within which the texts we have explored are enmeshed. For those living in Cornwall, engine houses remain part of a quotidian experience of place.

The poet John Wedgwood Clarke refers to the engine house as 'a ruined memory palace whose granite walls are weirs of ivy'.[10] This description recognizes these granite remnants of industry as a memorial to mining's collapse, whilst also lamenting that collapse. The ivy emphasizes the long inactivity of this once vital component of mining's endeavour; and 'weirs' recalls the water that would once have been pumped out of the ground within such a building. In referring to the engine house as a memory palace, a relationship is declared to the engine house's—and Cornwall's—past. However, a memory palace is also an imaginative space within the mind, which we might populate by recalling images—at once familiar, easily visualized, and disparate—that provide a connection between the present-day, physical world we inhabit, and how we interpret and make meaning of that world through individual imagination and experience. The engine house within the Cornish landscape, then, offers both a prompt for and container of remembrance, and a symbol of the multiple and diverse Cornish worlds that we might uncover.

Notes

Introduction: Cornwalls

1. Rowse, 'Passing by the Coast of Cornwall', pp. 51–52.
2. Ibid., p. 52.
3. With regard to the English novel Showalter explains that 'women's territory is usually depicted as desert bounded by mountains on four sides: the Austen peaks, the Brontë cliffs, the Eliot range, and the Woolf hills'. She goes on to describe her work, *A Literature of Their Own*, as 'an attempt to fill in the terrain between these literary landmarks and to construct a more reliable map from which to explore the achievements of English women novelists' (*A Literature of Their* Own, p. ix).
4. Showalter, *A Literature of Their Own*, p. xvii.
5. Kent, *The Literature of Cornwall*, pp. 17–18.
6. Payton, 'Introduction', p. 2.
7. Williams, 'On Ideology, Identity and Integrity', p. 68.
8. Deacon, 'In Search of the Missing "Turn"', pp. 214, 218, 226.
9. Deacon, 'From "Cornish Studies" to "Critical Cornish Studies"', p. 15.
10. Mitchell, *Cultural Geography*, p. xv. Emphasis in the original.
11. Showalter, *A Literature of Their Own*, p. xvii.
12. Deacon, 'From "Cornish Studies" to "Critical Cornish Studies"', p. 15; Mitchell, *Cultural Geography*, p. xv.
13. Mitchell, *Cultural Geography*, pp. 5–6.
14. Deacon, 'From "Cornish Studies" to "Critical Cornish Studies"', p. 17.
15. Bender, 'Why Move the Lighthouse?', pp. 60, 66.
16. Tuan, *Space and Place*, p. 54.
17. Rodman, 'Empowering Place', p. 205.
18. Thacker, *Moving Through Modernity*, p. 3.
19. See Goodman, 'Rural Geographies'. It is also in 'Rural Geographies' that I begin to consider Deacon's notion of multiple Cornwalls and how the work of feminist

geographers provide a route into uncovering those different versions of place which exist simultaneously (pp. 148–51).

20   Massey, *Space, Place and Gender*, p. 2.
21   McDowell, *Gender, Identity and Place*, pp. 40, 68.
22   Ibid., p. 4.
23   Moseley, *Picturing Cornwall*, p. 3.
24   McDowell, *Gender, Identity and Place*, p. 4.
25   Harris, 'Christian Heroism', pp. 42–43.
26   Ibid., p. 43.
27   Kent, *The Literature of Cornwall*, p. 111.
28   Collins, *Rambles Beyond Railways*, p. 102.
29   Deacon, *Cornwall*, p. 165.
30   Payton, *Cornwall*, p. 215.
31   Ibid., p. 209.
32   Ibid., p. 198.
33   Ibid., p. 199.
34   Deacon, '"The Hollow Jarring of the Distant Steam Engines"', pp. 11–12.
35   Ibid., pp. 10–11.
36   Payton, *Cornwall*, p. 209; Deacon, '"The Hollow Jarring of the Distant Steam Engines"', p. 11.
37   Ibid., p. 18.
38   I also briefly discuss Deacon's and Payton's work on 'West Barbary' and 'industrial prowess' in Goodman, 'At Work and at Play', p. 43.
39   Mitchell, *Overrated Cornwall*.
40   Waters, 'Cornwall Local Turns One Star TripAdvisor Reviews About Mevagissey into Art', para. 4 of 7.
41   Goodman and Mathieson, 'Introduction: Gender and Space in Rural Britain', p. 7.
42   Westland, 'The Passionate Periphery', p. 158. I also discuss this in Goodman, 'Women at Sea', pp. 174–75.
43. Thomas, p. 108.
44   Qtd in Payton, *Cornwall*, p. 198. I also briefly discuss Berg's characterisation of nineteenth-century Cornwall in Goodman, 'At Work and at Play', p. 43.
45   Qtd in Deacon, *Cornwall*, pp. 182.
46. Payton, *Cornwall*, p. 263.
47. Deacon, *Cornwall*, p. 182.
48. Payton, 'Paralysis and Revival', p. 28.
49. Showalter, *A Literature of Their Own*, p. xvii.
50. Payton, *Cornwall*, p. 209.

Chapter One: Mining Class and Gender

1   Harris, 'The Mine', p. 56.
2   Orchard, 'Wheal Coates', p. 61.

Notes

3   Daldorph, 'King Tin', p. 190.
4   Harris, 'The Mine', p. 56; Orchard, 'Wheal Coates', p. 61.
5   Orchard, 'Wheal Coates', p. 61; Daldorph, 'King Tin', p. 190.
6   Payton, *Cornwall*, pp. 215, 194.
7   Danahay, *Gender at Work*, pp. 1–5.
8   'Bal' is the word for mine in Cornish (*Gerlyver Kernewek / Cornish Dictionary*).
9   Rebel Brewing Company is no longer trading. This was the description used to describe the beer when it was being sold.
10 Lakeman, 'Balmaiden', 026–055.
11 Dalla, 'Balmaidens' Chant', 004–021; This song is based on a surviving contemporaneous snippet of a folk song. For more information see Mayers, *Balmaidens*, p. 223. There are a number of slightly different versions of this chant, sometimes using 'walk' instead of 'work' and 'looby' instead of 'lobby'. The lyrics refer to buddling (buddy), spalling (rocky) and treloobing (lobby) which are all names for different processes balmaidens carried out on the ore at the mine's surface (Buckley, *Cornish Bal Maidens*, p. 3).
12 'Hireth' is a Cornish word which means a longing or yearning for home (*Gerlyver Kernewek / Cornish Dictionary*).
13 Gads and boryers (also called borers) are metal implements used with a hammer to create holes in the rock (for more information see Orchard, *A Glossary of Mining Terms*, pp. 8, 21).
14 Darke, *Ting Tang Mine & Other Plays*, p. 7.
15 Mayers, *Balmaidens*, p. 23.
16 Ibid., p. 2.
17 Ibid., p. vii.
18 I first discussed Victorian anxieties around balmaidens' and their role in Goodman, *Salome Hocking: A Cornish Woman Writer*; this chapter builds on and significantly develops the discussion of balmaidens and their position within Victorian society (pp. 15–23).
19 Danahay, *Gender at Work*, p. 1.
20 Roper and Tosh, 'Introduction', p. 3.
21 Danahay, *Gender at Work*, p. 24.
22 Clarke, 'Strenuous Idleness', p. 37.
23 Ibid., p. 28.
24 Qtd in Clarke, 'Strenuous Idleness', p. 37. Emphasis in the original.
25 Danahay, *Gender at Work*, p. 127.
26 Ibid., p. 134.
27 Ibid., p. 29.
28 Deacon, '"The Hollow Jarring of the Distant Steam Engines"', p. 11.
29 Payton, *Cornwall*, p. 209.
30 Kent, *The Literature of Cornwall*, pp. 131–33.
31 Payton, *Cornwall*, p. 209.
32 Ballantyne, *Deep Down*, p. 37.

33 Kent, *The Literature of Cornwall*, p. 134.
34 Ballantyne, *Deep Down*, pp. 29, 24.
35 Ibid., p. 49.
36 Danahay, *Gender at Work*, p. 139.
37 Ballantyne, *Deep Down*, p. 24.
38 Ibid., p. 27.
39 Ibid., p. 49.
40 Zola, *Germinal*, p. 27.
41 Ibid., p. 21.
42 Ballantyne, *Deep Down*, p. 39.
43 Ibid., pp. 25–26.
44 Ibid., p. 61.
45 Danahay, *Gender at Work*, p. 45.
46. Payton, *Cornwall*, p. 209.
47. Ibid., p. 209.
48 Roper and Tosh, 'Introduction', p. 18.
49 Payton, *Cornwall*, p. 209.
50 Ibid., pp. 254–55.
51 This extension was not possible indefinitely, however. Payton comments that '[b]y the period between the First and Second World Wars, however, the myth of Cousin Jack which underwrote such behaviour was no longer sustained by the reality of Cornish prowess, the huge structural changes that had overcome Cornwall since the latter part of the century making claims of Cornish superiority seem increasingly hollow. The widespread deployment overseas of an assertive Cornish identity was only credible for as long as Cornwall itself was credible as the root source of that identity' (*Cornish Overseas*, p. 25).
52 Mallett, 'Masculinity, Imperialism and the Novel', p. 155.
53 Roper and Tosh, 'Introduction', p. 13.
54 Payton, 'Paralysis and Revival', pp. 30–31.
55 Payton, *Cornwall*, p. 209.
56 For example, *Deep Down* was researched by Ballantyne in the 1860s, the very decade where the fallibility of Cornish mining was beginning to show. Copper prices fell from 1861 onward until, by 1867, they were so low that mines could no longer be profitable, leading to inevitable closures on a mass scale (Payton, *Cornwall*, p. 239).
57 Ibid.
58 Ballantyne, *Deep Down*, pp. 38–39.
59 Bosanketh, *Tin*, pp. 34–35.
60 Ibid., p. 39.
61 Ibid., p. 142.
62 Dawson Scott, 'Foreword'.
63 Lowry and Dawson Scott, *Wheal Darkness*, p. 34.

64 Ibid., pp. 126–27.
65 Ibid., p. 264.
66 Ibid., p. 269.
67 Dialect changes significantly throughout Cornwall, with some words even being local to individual villages. I grew up in Treviscoe in mid-Cornwall and my family used this dialect term. It does not appear in K.C. Phillipps's *A Glossary of the Cornish Dialect*.
68 Atwood, *The Handmaid's Tale*, p. 18.
69. Payton, *Cornwall*, p. 209.
70 Goodman, 'Rural Geographies', pp. 153–54. The discussion here about the problematics of balmaidens' visibility builds upon my brief discussion of this in 'Rural Geographies'. Mayers informs us that '[a]llmost no personal writings or diaries survive' that have been written by balmaidens and Gill Burke concurs with this viewpoint (Mayers, *Balmaidens*, p. 217; Burke, 'The Decline of the Independent Bâl Maiden', p. 181). It is difficult to know if writing has been lost, or if they did not write about their own lives. Literacy did improve within the time period that balmaidens were working, but there are obviously other factors, such as time, materials, and inclination.
71 Women in Cornwall never worked below ground, even though they did in mines elsewhere in Britain and in Europe. In Cornwall it was believed to be bad luck for women to enter the mine and thus balmaidens remained at grass (above ground). See Mayers, *Balmaiden*, p. 3; Schwartz, 'In Defence of Customary Rights', p. 14.
72 Schwartz, '"No Place for a Woman"', p. 89.
73 Danahay, *Gender at Work*, p. 7.
74 Qtd in Mayers, *Balmaidens*, 219.
75 See Smith, 'In Her Hands'.
76 John, *By the Sweat of Their Brow*, p. 15.
77 Ballantyne, *Deep Down*, pp. 114–15.
78 Ibid., p. 49.
79 Ibid., pp. 114–15.
80 Ibid., p. 117.
81 Payton, *Cornwall*, p. 209.
82 Ballantyne, *Deep Down* p. 38. Emphasis in the original.
83 Qtd in Schwartz, 'In Defence of Customary Rights', p. 16.
84 Schwartz, 'In Defence of Customary Rights', p. 16.
85 Lowry and Dawson Scott, *Wheal Darkness*, p. 12.
86 Mayers, *Balmaidens*, p. 172.
87 My discussion of *Norah Lang* in this chapter builds upon my initial discussion of the book in *Salome Hocking: A Cornish Woman Writer*, where I argue that Hocking redraws balmaidens through Norah, and by placing her at the centre of the text (p. 18). I also briefly discuss the nature of Norah's visibility in 'Rural Geographies', pp. 153–54.

88 Hocking, *Norah Lang*, p. 10.
89 Ibid., p. 13. See also, Goodman, *Salome Hocking*, p. 23.
90 Hocking, *Norah* Lang, p. 76.
91 Qtd in Mayers, *Balmaidens*, p. 220.
92 Qtd in John, *By the Sweat of Their Brow*, p. 31.
93 Zola, *Germinal*, p. 129.
94 Davis, *Life in the Iron Mills*, p. 48.
95 Ibid., pp. 52–53.
96 Ibid., p. 47.
97 Goodman, *Salome Hocking*, pp. 18–19.
98 Hocking, *Norah Lang*, p. 9.
99 John, *By the Sweat of Their Brow*, p. 11.
100 Hocking, *Norah Lang*, p. 14.
101 Ibid., p. 13.
102 Ibid., p. 16.
103 Stanley, 'Introduction', p. 4.
104 Fox, *Class Fictions*, p. 102.
105 Payton, *Cornwall*, p. 209.
106 Ballantyne, *Deep Down*, p. 24.
107. Payton, *Cornwall*, p. 209.

Chapter Two: Beyond England

1 Braddon, *Wyllard's Weird*, p. 8252.
2 Anon., 'On the Way to the Lizard', p. 208.
3 Vernon, 'Border Crossing', p. 153. See also my discussion of Vernon's positioning of Cornwall in relation to the work of Daphne du Maurier in Goodman, 'Women at Sea', p. 181. As discussed further below, as well as Vernon, Rachel Moseley, Joan Passey, Shelley Trower and I are all interested in Cornwall's ambiguous status in relation to England. I often use the term 'England-but-not-England' to describe this status and in all cases it echoes Vernon's conceptual work referenced here.
4 Payton, *Cornwall*, p. 1.
5 Ibid., pp. 76–77.
6 Payton, *Cornwall*, pp. 92–93; Deacon, *Cornwall*, p. 82.
7 Payton, *Cornwall*, p. 117.
8 Moseley, *Picturing Cornwall*, p. 3.
9 Cornwall Council, *Census 2021*.
10 Cornwall Council, *Cornish National Minority*.
11 Kernow King, 'Proper Job!', para. 8 of 14.
12 Williams, 'On Ideology, Identity and Integrity', p. 69.
13 Payton and Thornton, 'The Great Western Railway', pp. 85–86.

Notes

14 Kent, *The Literature of Cornwall*, pp. 14–15.
15 Lowerson, 'Celtic Tourism', p. 128.
16 Payton and Thornton, 'The Great Western Railway', p. 92.
17 Thomas, 'See Your Own Country First', p. 111.
18 Robbins, *Nineteenth Century Britain*, p. 25.
19 Thomas, 'See Your Own Country First', pp. 107, 114–15.
20 Ibid., p. 120. I also briefly discuss Thomas's work on the domestic exotic in Goodman, 'Seeing the Clay Country', pp. 34–36.
21 Ibid., p. 108.
22 Qtd in Payton and Thornton, 'The Great Western Railway', p. 93.
23 Payton and Thornton, 'The Great Western Railway', p. 85.
24 My understanding in this chapter of the complexity of Cornwall's England-but-not-England status and its relationship to literary constructions of place builds upon my work on Daphne du Maurier's novels *The Loving Spirit* and *Frenchman's Creek* in Goodman, 'Women at Sea', pp. 181–82.
25 Westland's chapter on Cornwall and romance fiction is entitled 'The Passionate Periphery'; I discuss this further in Goodman, 'Women at Sea', pp. 175–76.
26 Westland, 'The Passionate Periphery', p. 154.
27 Qtd in Gunne, 'World Literature', p. 247.
28 Goodman, *Salome Hocking*, p. 34.
29 As I have argued elsewhere, in the case of du Maurier's Cornish novels the epithet of 'romance fiction' has often been reductive of the complexity and subversiveness of her work (Goodman, 'Women at Sea', p. 171). I hope that the discussion within this book about Winston Graham's *Poldark* series makes a similar case for his work.
30 Oltermann, 'Escapist Dreams', paras 9 of 15, 15 of 15, 4 of 15; Jakat, 'The Rosamunde Pilcher Trail', para. 12 of 13.
31 Heath-Stubbs, 'To the Mermaid at Zennor', p. 46.
32 Passey, 'Corpses, Coasts and Carriages', p. 6.
33 O'Byrne, 'The Spectator and the Rise of the Modern Metropole', p. 57.
34 Messent, *The Crime Fiction Handbook*, p. 5; Priestman, 'Post-war British Crime Fiction', p. 184.
35 Fletcher, 'Introduction', p. 5.
36 Priestman, 'Post-war British Crime Fiction', p. 185.
37 Knight, 'Regional Crime Squads', pp. 29–30, 28.
38 Kilday, *Crime in Scotland*, pp. 1–3.
39 Arnold, *Celtic Literature*, Ch. 3.
40 Ibid., Ch. 6.
41 Ibid., Introduction.
42 Ellis, 'The Men of Cornwall', II, p. 415.
43 Ibid., I, p. 330.
44 Ibid., I, pp. 332–33.

45 Payton, *Cornwall*, p. 187.
46 For example: Stonex, *The Lamplighters*, pp. 102, 224.
47 Trip Fiction, 'Talking Location with Emma Stonex', para. 1 of 5.
48 Stonex, *The Lamplighters*, p. 10.
49 Ibid., p. 28.
50 Ibid., pp. 10, 148.
51 Ibid., p. 26.
52 Ibid., p. 70.
53 Ibid., pp. 280, 202, 341.
54 Trip Fiction, 'Talking Location with Emma Stonex', para. 1 of 5.
55 Priestman, 'Post-war British Crime Fiction', p. 184.
56 Collins, *The Dead Secret*, p. 259.
57 Ibid., pp. 329–30.
58 For example: Ibid., pp. 97, 280.
59 Ibid., pp. 264, 241, 186.
60 Ibid., p. 263.
61 le Carré, *The Night Manager*, pp. 95–99. Emphasis in the original.
62 For example: Ibid., pp. 123–24.
63 Ibid., p. 101.
64 Ibid., pp. 110, 128.
65 Ibid., p. 127.
66 Ibid., p. 103.
67 Ibid., pp. 110–11.
68 Messent, *The Crime Fiction Handbook*, p. 7.
69 Ibid., pp. 11–12.
70 Mukherjee, *Crime and Empire*, pp. 2, 185.
71 Leane, 'Unstable Places and Generic Spaces', pp. 25–26.
72 Christie, *Peril at End House*, pp. 1–3.
73 Ibid., p. 153.
74 Ibid., pp. 27, 25.
75 Ibid., pp. 27, 96.
76 Ibid., p. 237.
77 Upson, *Angel with Two Faces*, pp. 19–22.
78 Baraniuk, 'Negotiating Borders', p. 76.
79 Upson, *Angel with Two Faces*, pp. 22, 57, 5.
80 Ibid., p. 66.
81 Ibid., p. 40.
82 Ibid., p. 51.
83 Ibid., p. 277.
84 Ibid., p. 209.
85 Ibid., p. 30.
86 Marcus, 'Detection and Literary Fiction', p. 247.

Notes

87 Upson, *Angel with Two Faces*, p. 275.
88 Ibid., p. 337.
89 Ibid., pp. 250–51, 285–86, 380–82.
90 Ibid., pp. 392, 402–03.
91 Ibid., p. 369.
92 Ibid., p. 403. Emphasis in the original.
93 Passey, 'Corpses, Coasts and Carriages', p. 123.
94 Conan Doyle, 'The Adventure of the Devil's Foot', p. 347.
95 Passey, 'Corpses, Coasts and Carriages', p. 124.
96 Conan Doyle, 'The Adventure of the Devil's Foot', p. 354.
97 Passey, 'Corpses, Coasts and Carriages', pp. 122–23.
98 Trower, *Rocks of Nation*, pp. 121–22.
99 Ibid., p. 124.
100 Passey recognizes the contrast in the story between Cornwall's clean air and the deadly poison that they inhale. It is only by Watson getting himself and Holmes out into the Cornish air after breathing in the poison that their lives are saved ('Corpses, Coasts and Carriages', p. 123).
101 Conan Doyle, 'The Adventure of the Devil's Foot', pp. 333–34.
102 Ibid., p. 337.
103 Ibid., p. 332.
104 Ibid., pp. 337, 358.
105 On Cornwall's peninsularity in the story, see also: Trower, *Rocks of Nation*, p. 121.
106 Trower, *Rocks of Nation*, p. 123.
107 Conan Doyle, 'The Adventure of the Devil's Foot', p. 354.
108 Trower, *Rocks of Nation*, p. 123.
109 Conan Doyle, 'The Adventure of the Devil's Foot', p. 357.
110 Ibid., p. 360.
111 Ibid., pp. 360–61.
112 Mukherjee, *Crime and Empire*, pp. 4–5.
113 Conan Doyle, 'The Adventure of the Devil's Foot', p. 359.
114 Stansfield, *The Mermaid's Call*, p. 214.
115 Ibid., p. 43.
116 Stansfield, *The Mermaid's Call*, pp. 16, 103.
117 Stansfield, *The Magpie Tree*, pp. 16–17.
118 Stansfield, *The Mermaid's Call*, p. 43. Emphasis in the original.
119 Stansfield, *The Magpie Tree*, p. 140.
120 Ibid., p. 310; Stansfield, *The Mermaid's Call*, p. 63.
121 Stansfield, *The Mermaid's Call*, p. 30.
122 Stansfield, *Falling Creatures*, pp. 334–35.
123 Linton qtd in Knight, 'The Postcolonial Crime Novel', p. 176.
124 Stansfield, *The Magpie Tree*, pp. 45, 196.
125 Ibid., pp. 125, 239.

126 Ibid., pp. 167–68.
127 Ibid., pp. 248, 253–54.
128 Ibid., pp. 280–81.
129 We see this play out most straightforwardly in terms of the failure of the state's duty to bring about justice in *Falling Creatures*, where only Shilly uncovers Daniel Carwitham's guilt, whilst the state wrongly hangs Matthew Weeks for Charlotte Dymond's murder.
130 O'Reilly, *Wrecker*, pp. 183, 139.
131 Ibid., p. 137.
132 Ibid., pp. 9–10.
133 Ibid., pp. 31–32.
134 Pearce, *Cornish Wrecking*, p. 2.
135 Ibid., pp. 20, 26.
136 Ibid., pp. 2, 108, 121.
137 Ibid., pp. 5, 103.
138 Ibid., pp. 98, 103, 108–09.
139 Ibid., p. 103.
140 Ibid., p. 94.
141 Ibid., pp. 110, 83–84.
142 Ibid., p. 103.
143 Ibid.
144 Ibid., pp. 83–84, 39–40.
145 Ibid., pp. 118–22.
146 O'Reilly, *Wrecker*, p. 183.
147 Ibid., pp. 154, 139.
148 Ibid., pp. 54–55.
149 Ibid., pp. 136–40.
150 Ibid., p. 183.
151 Ibid., pp. 5–8.
152 Ibid., p. 85.
153 Ibid., pp. 30–31.
154 Ibid., pp. 299–300.
155 Ibid., pp. 9–11.
156 Ibid., pp. 105–06.
157 Ibid., p. 64.
158 Ibid., p. 155.
159 Ibid., p. 180.
160 Ibid., pp. 87, 270.
161 Ibid., p. 183. Emphasis in the original.
162 Ibid., p. 99.
163 Ibid., p. 83.
164 Ibid., p. 191.

165 Ibid., pp. 260–61.
166 Ibid., pp. 301–04.
167 Ibid., p. 183.
168 Ibid., p. 135.
169 Ibid., pp. 155–57.
170 Ibid., p. 79.
171 Westland, 'Introduction', p. vii.
172 du Maurier, *Rule Britannia*, pp. 37–38.
173 Ibid., p. 37–38.
174 Ibid., p. 47.
175 Ibid., p. 177.
176 Ibid., p. 114.
177 Ibid., p. 188.
178 Ibid., pp. 45, 48, 43, 180, 12.
179 Ibid., p. 268.
180 Ibid., pp. 200, 176.
181 Ibid., pp. 176–77.
182 Kennedy and Kingcome, 'Disneyfication of Cornwall', p. 45. Emphasis in the original.
183 du Maurier, *Rule Britannia*, p. 142.
184 Ibid., p. 53.
185 Ibid., pp. 319–22.
186 Kennedy and Kingcome, 'Disneyfication of Cornwall', p. 45.

Chapter Three: On the Edge

1 Murray, ed., *Journal of Katherine Mansfield*, p. 81.
2 Historic Cornwall, 'How Many Miles Long is Cornwall?'.
3 Moseley, *Picturing Cornwall*, p. 33.
4 Ibid.
5 See for example Woodbridge, 'Why Are There So Many Mentally Ill Drug Addicts in Cornwall?'.
6 'Glas', *Gerlyver Kernewek / Cornish Dictionary*.
7 Upson, *The Dead of Winter*, p. 153.
8 For example: Church, 'Cornwall Beaches and Their Sand "Twins" on the Other Side of the Planet'; Roberts, '10 of the Best Beaches You Wouldn't Believe Are in Cornwall'.
9 Thomas, 'See Your Own Country First', p. 108. Such is the dominance of vivid blue renditions of the Cornish coast in various mediums that a film such as the BAFTA-winning *Bait* (2019) by Mark Jenkin is notable for its desaturation of colour, in this case filmed in black and white. Locating a narrative about poverty, hardship, and issues of tourism, second homes and gentrification at the coast in

this form defamiliarizes the Cornish littoral, diminishes the power of the exotic-aesthetic and refocuses the viewer onto the lived experience of that same place.

10 Ibid., p. 120.
11 Williams, *The Country and the City*, p. 173.
12 The engine house remains that sit above Wheal Owles mine on the coast in St Just (and which featured, with the help of CGI, as both Wheal Leisure and Wheal Grace mines in the latest *Poldark* adaptation) is also a marker of the tomb of nineteen men and one boy who died in a mining disaster there in 1893. The mine flooded when inaccurate plans led workers to blast through into a neighbouring mine by mistake. It never reopened.
13 Corbin, *The Lure of the Sea*, p. 140.
14 Moseley, *Picturing Cornwall*, p. 1.
15 Corbin, *The Lure of the Sea*, p. 141.
16 Ibid., pp. 60–62.
17 Ibid., p. 127.
18 Ibid., p. 71.
19 Thomas, 'See Your Own Country First', p. 120.
20 Corbin, *The Lure of the Sea*, p. 73.
21 Moseley, 'Women at the Edge', p. 644.
22 Marsden, *The Levelling Sea*, p. 107.
23 Ibid., p. 20.
24 Pearce, *Cornish Wrecking*, p. 18.
25 Ibid., p. 27.
26 Kneehigh Theatre, *Tristan and Yseult, The Bacchae, The Wooden Frock, The Red Shoes*, pp. 25–26.
27 Trower, *Rocks of Nation*, p. 100.
28 Trower, 'On the Cliff Edge of England', p. 113.
29 Ibid., p. 211.
30 Passey, 'Corpses, Coasts and Carriages', pp. 6–7.
31 Ibid., pp. 61, 68.
32 Ibid., pp. 72, 98, 107.
33 Ibid., pp. 111–12.
34 Shields, *Places on the Margin*, pp. 74–75. I have briefly discussed Shields' work on the liminality of the coast in Goodman, 'Women at Sea', p. 180. This chapter builds upon my discussion of Cornish liminality in that previous work.
35 McCormick, *Living on the Edge*, p. 2.
36 I have previously discussed Moseley's work on Cornish liminality and Laura Knight's paintings in Goodman, 'Women at Sea', pp. 179–80. This chapter builds upon the discussion of the coastal site in the above chapter and in Goodman, 'At Work and at Play', pp. 45–53.
37 Moseley, 'Women at the Edge', pp. 649, 644.
38 Ibid., p. 652.

Notes

39. Ibid., p. 648. I have previously discussed Moseley's work in relation to the Cornish coastal site in Goodman, 'At Work and at Play', pp. 45–46 and Goodman, 'Women at Sea', pp. 179–80.
40. Moseley, 'Women at the Edge', pp. 656–57.
41. Goodman, 'At Work and at Play', p. 50.
42. Ibid., pp. 50–53.
43. Goodman, 'Women at Sea', pp. 171–72, 181.
44. Ibid., p. 172.
45. Tomalin, *Thomas Hardy*, p. 99.
46. Hardy, *Tess of the D'Urbervilles*.
47. On the 1902 map, 'The Wessex of Thomas Hardy's Novels and Poems', the edge of the page vertically transects Cornwall so that only enough of it is included to map the North Cornwall coastal locations of *A Pair of Blue Eyes*.
48. Gatrell, *Thomas Hardy's Vision of Wessex*, pp. 112–13. This map is the first to be published with Hardy's work. According to Richard L. Purdy it was 'drawn by Hardy himself' (Qtd in Manford, 'The "Texts" of Thomas Hardy's Map of Wessex', p. 297). From this drawing the map for publication was created by Stanford of London (Manford, 'The "Texts of Thomas Hardy's Map of Wessex', p. 297). The Osgood, McIlvaine volumes were the first collected edition of Hardy's oeuvre. This map first appeared in volume one, which was *Tess of the D'Urbervilles* and was published in 1895. For more information on the volumes published see Greenland, 'Hardy in the Osgood, McIlvaine and Harper (London) Editions', pp. 57–60. For more on the evolution of Wessex and how Hardy shaped Wessex through revisions to his texts, including for the above collected edition, see Gatrell, *Thomas Hardy's Vision of Wessex*.
49. Manford, 'The "Texts" of Thomas Hardy's Map of Wessex', pp. 298–301.
50. Manford, 'The "Texts" of Thomas Hardy's Map of Wessex, p. 301
51. Gatrell, *Thomas Hardy's Vision of Wessex*, p. 161
52. Dalziel, 'A Note on the History of the Text', p. xl.
53. Hardy, 'front matter', in *A Pair of Blue Eyes*, p. 6. Apart from the 1899 Preface in reference 54 below, all page references for *A Pair of Blue Eyes* are taken from the Penguin edition of the novel. This edition uses the 1873 version of the text. For more information see Dalziel, 'A Note on the History of the Text', p. xxxix.
54. Hardy, '1899 Preface', 'The Persons', 'The Scene', in *A Pair of Blue Eyes*, p. 9; pp. 6–7.
55. Hardy, *A Pair of Blue Eyes*, p. 21. All page references for *A Pair of Blue Eyes* are taken from the Penguin edition of the novel.
56. Westland, *Reading Daphne*, p. 23. See also, Goodman, 'Women at Sea', p. 178.
57. Moseley, *Picturing Cornwall*, p. 33.
58. Hardy, *A Pair of Blue Eyes*, p. 50. For more on the Gothic and *A Pair of Blue Eyes* see Passey, '"A Delightful Place to be Buried In"'.
59. Ibid., p. 323.
60. Ibid., pp. 58–62.

61 Ibid., pp. 308–12.
62 Ibid., p. 209.
63 Diniejko, 'A *Pair of Blue Eyes* as a Cliffhanger', para. 9 of 11.
64 Hardy, *A Pair of Blue Eyes*, pp. 207–10.
65 Ibid., p. 211.
66 Ibid., pp. 220, 218.
67 Ibid., pp. 219–21.
68 Ibid., pp. 308–12, 330–31.
69 Ibid., pp. 335–37.
70 Westland, *Reading Daphne*, p. 23; Hardy, *A Pair of Blue Eyes*, p. 103.
71 Parr, Philo, and Burns, '"Not a Display of Emotions"', p. 88; Bondi, Davidson, and Smith, 'Geography's "Emotional Turn"', p. 3.
72 Bondi, Davidson, and Smith, 'Geography's "Emotional Turn"', p. 3. Emphasis in the original.
73 Davidson and Milligan, 'Embodying Emotion Sensing Space', p. 526.
74 Urry, 'The Place of Emotions Within Place', p. 82.
75 Woolf, *To the Lighthouse*, pp. 68–70.
76 Winn, *The Salt Path*, p. 132.
77 Ibid., p. 56.
78 Ibid., p. 133.
79 Ibid., p. 67.
80 Ibid., p. 185.
81 Ibid., p. 125.
82 Ibid., pp. 176–77.
83 Ibid., p. 162.
84 Dunmore, *Talking to the Dead*, p. 36.
85 Ibid., p. 86.
86 Dunmore, *Mourning Ruby*, p. 94.
87 Dunmore, *Talking to the Dead*, pp. 30–31.
88 Ibid., p. 3.
89 Parr, Philo, and Burns, '"Not a Display of Emotions"', p. 88.
90 Dunmore, *Mourning Ruby*, pp. 94–96.
91 Ibid., pp. 99–102.
92 Ibid., p. 96.
93 Ibid., p. 94.
94 Ibid., p. 95.
95 Ibid., p. 96.
96 Dunmore, *Talking to the Dead*, p. 91.
97 Dunmore, *Mourning Ruby*, p. 95.
98 *The Many* does not state a location and is more abstract in terms of its relationship to actual place, but can be said to be inspired by Cornwall's north coast.
99 See for example Stephanie Cross and Catherine Taylor, '*The Many* by Wyl Menmuir Review', para. 5 of 5.

100 Menmuir, *The Many*, p. 48.
101 Carroll, *The Lip*, p. 5. 'Zawn' derives from the Cornish word *sawn* or *sawen* and means 'a fissure or cave in a coastal cliff' ('zawn, n.', OED).
102 Melody Janie mentions that many people would note the unusual spelling of 'Cafy' and that her father 'would remark that he had chosen the Cornish rather than the French' (Carroll, *The Lip*, p. 31). In the Cornish language the word for café is *koffiji*, but his Cornish version is spelt in a way reminiscent of how the word sounds when spoken with a Cornish accent ('koffiji', *Gerlyver Kernewek / Cornish Dictionary*).
103 'Emmet' is a Cornish dialect word meaning 'ant', which is used to refer to tourists to the region. It is increasingly understood as an offensive term. It is often mistakenly thought to derive from the Cornish word for ant but this is not so (ant is *moryonen* in Cornish)—it actually has the same Germanic origin as the English word 'ant'. In Old English that word is *aemaette* ('ant, n.1', OED; 'moryonen', *Gerlyver Kernewek / Cornish Dictionary*).
104 Carroll, *The Lip*, p. 238.
105 Ibid., p. 1.
106 Ibid., p. 176.
107 Menmuir, *The Many*, pp. 15–16.
108 Corbin, *The Lure of the Sea*, p. 69.
109 Menmuir, *The Many*, pp. 42, 15.
110 Ibid., p. 43.
111 Ibid., p. 23.
112 Corbin, *The Lure of the Sea*, p. 73.
113 Carroll, *The Lip*, p. 18.
114 Ibid., p. 24.
115 Ibid., p. 15.
116 Ibid., pp. 72, 85.
117 Ibid., pp. 281–82.
118 Ibid., p. 21.
119 Ibid., p. 40.
120 Ibid., pp. 110–12.
121 Menmuir, *The Many*, p. 41.
122 Packham, 'The Gothic Coast', p. 205. Packham's analysis here is in reference to *The Many*, but I argue that it also applies to *The Lip*.
123 Carroll, *The Lip*, p. 232.
124 Menmuir, *The Many*, pp. 113–14.
125 Carroll, *The Lip*, pp. 128–32, 129.
126 Ibid., p. 132.
127 Menmuir, *The Many*, pp. 117–18.
128 Packham, 'The Gothic Coast', p. 213. Emphasis in the original.
129 Carroll, *The Lip*, p. 231; Menmuir, *The Many*, p. 129.
130 Menmuir, *The Many*, p. 90.
131 Dunmore, *The Lie*, p. 1.

132 Ibid., pp. 158, 78, 157.
133 Ibid., pp. 157, 56–57.
134 Ibid., pp. 58–62.
135 Stansfield, *The Visitor*, p. 146.
136 Ibid., p. 107.
137 Ibid., pp. 65–66.
138 Dunmore, *The Lie*, p. 273.
139 Dodman, *Shell Shock, Memory and the Novel*, p. 5; Bonikowski, *Shell Shock and the Modernist Imagination*, p. 3.
140 Bonikowski, *Shell Shock and the Modernist Imagination*, p. 2.
141 Ibid., p. 3.
142 Dunmore, *The Lie*, p. 260.
143 Ibid., pp. 287–92.
144 Stansfield, *The Visitor*, pp. 17–18.
145 Ibid., p. 13.
146 Ibid., pp. 62–63.
147 Ibid., p. 335.
148 Ibid., p. 292.
149 Bitenc, 'Dementia Narratives', pp. 3, 11.
150 Stansfield, *The Visitor*, p. 342.

Chapter Four: Urban Cornwall

1   Phillipps, ed., *The Cornish Journal of Charles Lee*, p. 2.
2   Marsden, *The Levelling Sea*, p. 5.
3   Charlestown doubles as Truro throughout all five series. For series one, some of the Truro street scenes were filmed in Corsham, Wiltshire and from series two onwards in Frome, Somerset (see Ruminski, 'Corsham Goes Back in Time' and Radio Times Staff, 'Poldark').
4   Kent, *Dan Daddow's Cornish Comicalities*, p. 282.
5   Mudd, *About the City*, p. 42.
6   Although safer than places like London, Truro was also bombed in 1942.
7   Beckett and Windsor, 'Truro: Diocese and City', pp. 222–25.
8   Qtd in Mudd, *About the City*, p. 73.
9   Stockdale, *Excursions Through Cornwall*, p. 57.
10 Qtd in Acton and Acton, *A History of Truro*, II, p. 34.
11 Graham, *Ross Poldark*, p. 21. Emphasis in the original.
12 For more on the history of Falmouth, see Philip Marsden's *The Levelling Sea*.
13 Kent, *Dan Daddow's Cornish Comicalities*, p. 68.
14 Acton, *A History of Truro*, I, p. 130.
15 Mais, *The Cornish Riviera*, p. 55; Mudd, *About the City*, p. 39; Acton, *A History of Truro*, I, p. 91.

Notes

16 Acton, *A History of Truro*, I, pp. 27, 57–58.
17 Qtd in ibid., p. 91.
18 Ibid., p. 118
19 Acton and Acton, *A History of Truro*, II, pp. 13, 15.
20. This whole area is commonly referred to as Lemon Quay now but the quay directly outside the rear entrance of the Town Hall (now the Hall for Cornwall) is Back Quay and directly opposite is Lemon Quay.
21 Ibid., p. 58.
22 Ibid., p. 24; Acton, *A History of Truro*, I, pp. 118, 205.
23 Ibid., p. 188.
24 There is no complete consensus on exactly when Middle Row was demolished. It is likely it was gone by the beginning of the nineteenth century. Truro Buildings Research Group found that rent books contain an entry for properties in Middle Row in 1790 but not in 1791, suggesting it was demolished within this year (*Truro: Boscawen Street Area*, p. 21). Christine Parnell, however, finds reference to Middle Row during the town's celebrations for the end of the Napoleonic Wars and suggests that it was not all demolished in one go (*Truro: History and Guide*, pp. 63–64).
25 Graham, *The Four Swans*, p. 157.
26 Truro Buildings Research Group, *Truro: Boscawen Street Area*, p. 43. Boscawen Street is named after Admiral Edward Boscawen, the third son of Lord Falmouth.
27 Mais, *The Cornish Riviera*, p. 55.
28 Guthrie, *Cornwall in the Age of Steam*, p. 159; Miller, 'Bishop Benson's Vision', p. 213. In 2016–17 luxury townhouses were built on the outskirts of Truro. While not built using Bath stone, Trevethow Riel (Royal Crescent) replicates the Georgian style found elsewhere in the city.
29 Charles Barry is best known for his redesign of the Houses of Parliament in the mid-nineteenth century. Viewers of ITV's *Downton Abbey* will be very familiar with his Jacobean-style exterior of Highclere Castle.
30 Information about the architectural history of the Hall for Cornwall building comes from a talk given by Richard Hill of Richard Griffith Architects, as part of their research for their refurbishment of that building, that I was allowed to attend in February 2017. Thanks to Richard, and to Helen Tiplady at the Hall for Cornwall for allowing me to sit in.
31 Kent, *Dan Daddow's Cornish Comicalities*, p. 27.
32 Ibid., p. 11.
33 Ibid., pp. 19–20.
34 For example: Graham, *Ross Poldark*, p. 293.
35 Urry, 'City Life and the Senses', p. 354.
36 Kent, *Dan Daddow's Cornish Comicalities*, p. 20.
37 Urry, 'City Life and the Senses', pp. 352–54.
38 Qtd in ibid., p. 352.

39 Classen, Howes, and Synnott, *Aroma*, pp. 8, 81.
40 In reality, the asylum was located at Bodmin and has been transferred to Truro within this fictional narrative.
41 Moss, *Signs for Lost Children*, p. 34. Mizzle is misty drizzle.
42 Kent, *Dan Daddow's Cornish Comicalities*, p. 20.
43 Acton, *A History of Truro*, I, p. 28.
44 Graham, *The Loving Cup*, pp. 425–26. While his mines mainly raised copper and while he is grateful not to have to go through the laborious process of coinage (it was only carried out on tin, never copper), the ingots represent for George pure wealth, and wealth to his bank as a by-product of the process of the loans that mines necessarily have to undertake to keep them afloat between coinages.
45 Graham, *Ross Poldark*, p. 393; Graham, *The Four Swans*, p. 156; Kent, *Dan Daddow's Cornish Comicalities*, p. 19.
46 Graham, *The Four Swans*, p. 156.
47. Payton, *Cornwall*, p. 209.
48 Graham, *Ross Poldark*, p. 294.
49 Kent, *Dan Daddow's Cornish Comicalities*, p. 477.
50 Engels, *The Condition of the Working Class in England in 1844*, pp. 45–46.
51 Kent, *Dan Daddow's Cornish Comicalities*, p. 104.
52 Payton, *Cornwall*, p. 187.
53 Graham, *Demelza*, pp. 142–50.
54 Williams, *The Country and the City*, p. 210.
55 Graham, *Demelza*, p. 149.
56 Ibid., pp. 143, 145.
57 Ibid., pp. 143–45.
58. Acton, *A History of Truro*, I, pp. 30–31. In the Victorian era, the leats were extended within Truro's streets to help with sanitation (Acton, *A History of Truro*, I, pp. 180–83).
59 Graham, *Demelza*, pp. 143–46.
60 Gaskell, *North and South*, p. 94.
61 Graham, *Demelza*, pp. 144–45.
62 Kent, *Dan Daddow's Cornish Comicalities*, pp. 39–40. Mumming is the act of dressing up and acting in a traditional play known as a mummers' play.
63 Ibid.
64 Williams, *The Country and the City*, p. 211; Engels, *The Condition of the Working Class in England in 1844*, p. 26.
65 Graham, *Bella Poldark*, pp. 47–48.
66 Kent, *Dan Daddow's Cornish Comicalities*, p. 64.
67 Graham, *The Four Swans*, pp. 120, 509, 140.
68 Graham, *The Angry Tide*, pp. 117–18, 219.
69 Ibid., pp. 226–30.
70 Graham, *Ross Poldark*, p. 84.
71 Hamilton Jenkin, *Cornwall and the Cornish*, p. 172.

Notes

72 Qtd in Ibid., pp. 172–73.
73 Graham, *Demelza*, p. 62.
74 Graham, *Warleggan*, pp. 274, 446.
75 Graham, *Jeremy Poldark*, p. 309.
76 Graham, *The Black Moon*, p. 151.
77 Graham, *The Four Swans*, p. 6.
78 Bridge and Watson, 'Reflections on Publics and Cultures', p. 383.
79 Graham, *Demelza*, p. 450.
80 Graham, *Ross Poldark*, p. 100.
81 Graham, *Jeremy Poldark*, pp. 309–12.
82 Graham, *Ross Poldark*, pp. 287–95.
83 Graham, *The Four Swans*, pp. 152–53.
84 Parnell, *Truro*, p. 19.
85 Acton and Acton, *A History of Truro*, II, p. 65.
86 For more on the gendering of public space and women in public spaces, see: McDowell, *Gender, Identity and Place*; Massey, *Space, Place and Gender*; Nord, *Walking the Victorian Streets*; Parsons, *Streetwalking the Metropolis*; and Ingham, *The Language of Gender and Class*.
87 For more on women and walking, including in rural environments, see: Mathieson, *Mobility in the Victorian Novel*; Solnit, *Wanderlust*; and Parkins, *Mobility and Modernity*.
88 Graham, *Ross Poldark*, p. 392.
89 Ibid., pp. 395–97.
90 Graham, *Demelza*, pp. 250–52.
91 Ibid., p. 277.
92 For more on the consequences for women in urban spaces, see the discussion of Margaret Hale in *North and South* in Ingham, *The Language of Gender and Class*, pp. 55–77.
93 Ingham, *The Language of Gender and Class*, p. 67.
94 Clemo, *Wilding Graft*, p. 145.
95 Ibid., p. 140.
96 Ibid., p. 163.
97 Ibid., p. 41.
98 Ibid., pp. 37–41.
99 Ibid., p. 39.
100 Ibid., p. 219.
101 Ibid., pp. 233–34.

Chapter Five: Moor and Clay

1 Causley, 'The Seasons in North Cornwall', p. 100.
2 Hamilton Jenkin, *The Story of Cornwall*, p. 113.

3   Those novels are: *Wilding Graft* (1948), *The Shadowed Bed* (1986), and *The Clay Kiln* (2000).
4   Charlotte Dymond was murdered on Bodmin Moor in 1844. Her boyfriend Matthew Weeks was hanged for her murder but always claimed to be innocent.
5   There is a Probus situated on the edge of the clay area between St Austell and Truro. Its church is dedicated to Saint Probus.
6   Godden, *China Court*, pp. 27–28. This is now understood to be a pejorative term.
7   Ibid., pp. 68–70.
8   Goodman, 'Seeing the Clay Country', p. 40.
9   Godden, *China Court*, p. 70.
10 Ibid., p. 37.
11 For example, there are now some installations at the back of the harbour referencing the show and a stall at the harbour front selling items related to the programme.
12 *The Clay Kiln* was published posthumously with editing by Donald Rawe to make it ready for publication.
13 While it is not stated, it is possible that these paintings are of china clay pits in West Cornwall rather than mid-Cornwall, but the pits and the extractive processes will have been the same.
14 Marsden, *Rising Ground*, p. 34.
15 Stansfield, *Falling Creatures*, p. 63.
16 du Maurier, *Jamaica Inn*, p. 13.
17 Marsden, *Rising Ground*, pp. 34, 37.
18 Moseley, *Picturing Cornwall*, p. 194.
19 Ibid., p. 195.
20 Stansfield, *Falling Creatures*, pp. 7, 58.
21 du Maurier, *Jamaica Inn*, pp. 25, 91.
22 Stansfield, *Falling Creatures*, pp. 88, 39.
23 du Maurier, *Jamaica Inn*, p. 10.
24 Stansfield, *Falling Creatures*, p. 194.
25 See Goodman, 'Seeing the Clay Country'.
26 Clemo, *The Clay Kiln*, pp. 246–47.
27 Goodman, 'Seeing the Clay Country', p. 40.
28 Clemo, *The Clay Kiln*, p. 55.
29 Thomas, 'See Your Own Country First', p. 120.
30 Goodman, 'Seeing the Clay Country', p. 45.
31 Clemo, *The Clay* Kiln, p. 55. This is an environment that can break people, but it is also 'only within this landscape that their spiritual journey can be played out' (Ibid., p. 49). The characters' choice to reject the other available places on the horizon, therefore, has something to do with the grace that they can access in what might initially seem to be the least likely of environments for communion with God. For Clemo, though, the paradoxical clay world is an appropriate

environment for the fulfilment of God's will. It is because of this world's triumph over nature that Joel, Lorraine, Gwen, and Euan ultimately access what is divinely predestined by God rather than the natural fate that could also have been their lot (see Rawe, 'Introduction', pp. 5–6; and for discussion of this in more detail, Goodman, 'Seeing the Clay Country', pp. 45–49.)

32   Horner and Zlosnik, *Daphne du Maurier*, p. 76.
33   du Maurier, *Jamaica Inn*, pp. 3, 12, 13, 14, 31.
34   Goodman, 'Seeing the Clay Country', p. 41.
35   Ibid., p. 302.
36   Ibid., p. 110.
37   'Summer Season: Daphne du Maurier'.
38   Goodman, 'Women at Sea', p. 171.
39   Only Par docks and Fowey are still used today for the export of clay.
40   Rowse, *A Cornish Childhood*, pp. 15, 124, 14–15.
41   Stevenson, *Across the Plains*, pp. 58–59.
42   Those same routes are used today by clay lorries transporting clay to the ports or by road to many global destinations. You can still see white clay powder along the sides of the roads in the clay area.
43   Rowse, *A Cornish Childhood*, pp. 12, 14, 228.
44   Bawden, 'Castle Dor', p. v.
45   Clemo, *Wilding Graft*, p. 8.
46   du Maurier and Quiller-Couch, *Castle Dor*, p. 226.
47   Ibid., p. 226.
48   Ibid., pp. 225–26.
49   Qtd in Baker, *A View from Land's End*, p. 136.
50   Qtd in ibid., pp. 113–14.
51   Qtd in ibid., p. 124.
52   Horner and Zlosnik, *Daphne du Maurier*, p. 68.
53   du Maurier, *Jamaica Inn*, pp. 38–39.
54   Ibid., p. 280.
55   Ibid., p. 287.
56   Ibid., pp. 286–87.
57   Clemo, *The Clay Kiln*, p. 14.
58   du Maurier, *Jamaica Inn*, pp. 38–39.
59   Clemo, *The Clay Kiln*, p. 29.
60   Ibid., p. 71. Roche is located in what Rowse above calls the 'Higher Quarter' (Rowse, *A Cornish Childhood*, p. 14).
61   Clemo, *The Clay Kiln*, p. 72.
62   Ibid., p. 29. Micas are a series of channels which form part of the refining process of china clay whereby the heavier mica particles settle to the bottom of the china clay slurry and are removed.
63   Ibid., pp. 13–14.

64 Ibid., p. 72.
65 Ibid., p. 37.
66 Ibid., p. 153.
67 Ibid., p. 122.
68 Ibid., pp. 36, 106–07.
69 Ibid., p. 62.
70 Ibid., pp. 121–22.
71 Ibid., pp. 126–27.
72 Ibid., p. 107.
73 Ibid., pp. 104–5.
74 Ibid., p. 25; Goodman, 'Seeing the Clay Country', p. 41.
75 Thomas, 'See Your Own Country First', p. 107.
76 Ibid., p. 27.
77 Ibid., pp. 25–26.
78 Ibid., p. 55.
79 Ibid., p. 66.
80 Ibid., p. 122.
81 Ibid., pp. 66–67.
82 Ibid., p. 67.
83 For further discussion of the revival and the Gorsedh see Payton, 'Paralysis and Revival'.
84 See also, Goodman, 'Seeing the Clay Country', p. 41.

Conclusion: Looking and Seeing

1 Qtd in Baker, *A View from the Land's End*, p. 154.
2 Dickinson, 'Changing Landscapes of Difference', p. 170.
3 Rowse, 'Home-Coming to Cornwall: December 1942', pp. 134–36 (p. 136).
4 Ibid., pp. 134–36 (p. 135).
5 See Seamus Carey's podcast *The Reason Why*, where he discusses how social media has altered our relationship to landscape.
6 Moseley, *Picturing Cornwall*, p. 79.
7 Winn, *Landlines*, pp. 296, 244.
8 Cohen, 'The Sociology of Tourism', p. 378.
9 I first heard the term 'swinging the lens' used by Adjoa Andoh (it's also the name of her production company) on the following podcast episode: 'Adjoa Andoh', *Bookshelfie: Women's Prize for Fiction Podcast*, 02:52.
10 *Cornwall's Red River*, 09:11.

Bibliography

Primary Texts

'Adjoa Andoh', *Bookshelfie: Women's Prize for Fiction Podcast*, 26 May 2022, https://podcasts.apple.com/gb/podcast/bookshelfie-womens-prize-for-fiction-podcast/id1462403729?i=1000564028068 [accessed 15 January 2023]

Anon., 'On the Way to the Lizard', *All the Year Round*, 17.415 (1876), pp. 208–12

Ashley, Phillipa, *A Perfect Cornish Escape* (London: Avon, 2020)

Atwood, Margaret, *The Handmaid's Tale* (London: Vintage, 1996)

Austen, Jane, *Northanger Abbey* (1818; repr. London: Penguin Books, 1994)

Bait, dir. by Mark Jenkin (UK: British Film Institute, 2019)

Ballantyne, R.M., *Deep Down: A Tale of the Cornish Mines* (1868; repr. Liskeard: Diggory Press, 2006)

Behind the Postcard, dir. by Mydd Pharo (UK: Screen Cornwall, 2021)

Bosanketh, Edward, *Tin* (1888; repr. Marazion: Justin Brooke, 1988)

Braddon, Mary Elizabeth, *Wyllard's Weird: A Novel*, in *The Complete Works of Mary Elizabeth Braddon* (1885; repr. [n.p]: e-artnow, 2019), pp. 8250–684, https://amzn.eu/d/eEUNnbe [accessed 9 September 2021]

Brown Willy, dir. by Brett Harvey (UK: o-region, 2016)

Bude, John, *The Cornish Coast Murder* (1935; repr. London: The British Library, 2014)

Burley, W.J., *Wycliffe and the Dune Mystery* (1993; repr. London: Orion Books, 2016)

Carey, Seamus, 'Overexposure', *The Reason Why*, 10 February 2022, https://podcasts.apple.com/gb/podcast/the-reason-why/id1607064518?i=1000550726454 [accessed 15 January 2023]

Carroll, Charlie, *The Lip* (London: Two Roads, 2021)

Causley, Charles, 'The Seasons in North Cornwall', in *The Dreamt Sea: An Anthology of Anglo-Cornish Poetry 1928–2004*, ed. by Alan M. Kent (1951; repr. London: Francis Boutle, 2004), p. 100

Christie, Agatha, *Peril at End House* (1932; repr. London: HarperCollins, 2015)
Clemo, Jack, *Wilding Graft* (1948; repr. London: Anthony Mott, 1983)
——, *Confession of a Rebel* (London: Chatto & Windus, 1949)
——, *The Shadowed Bed: A Novel* (Tring: Lion Publishing, 1986)
——, *The Clay Kiln*, ed. by Donald R. Rawe (Cornish Hillside Publications, 2000)
Collins, Wilkie, *Rambles Beyond Railways: Notes in Cornwall Taken A-Foot* (1851; repr. Launceston: Westcountry Books, 2004)
——, *The Dead Secret* ([1856]; repr. Oxford: Oxford University Press, 1997)
Conan Doyle, Arthur, 'The Adventure of the Devil's Foot', in *Cornish Horrors: Tales from the Land's End*, ed. by Joan Passey (1910; repr. London: The British Library, 2021), pp. 329–62
Cornwall's Red River, Simon Willis Films (UK: BBC, 2023)
Daldorph, Brian, 'King Tin', in *The Dreamt Sea: An Anthology of Anglo-Cornish Poetry 1928–2004*, ed. by Alan M. Kent (1973; repr. London: Francis Boutle, 2004), pp. 189–90
Dalla, 'Bal Maidens' Chant' from *Rooz* (UK: CD Baby, 2007)
Danckerts, Hendrick, 'A View of Falmouth Harbour', c.1678, oil on canvas, 66.5 × 133.5 cm, National Maritime Museum
Darke, Nick, *Ting Tang Mine & Other Plays* (London: Metheun, 1987)
Dawson Scott, C.A., 'Foreword', in *Wheal Darkness* (London: Hutchinson, [1927])
du Maurier, Daphne, *The Loving Spirit* (1931; repr. London: Virago Press, 2003)
——, *Jamaica Inn* (1936; repr. London: Virago Press, 2003)
——, *Rebecca* (1938; repr. London: Arrow, 1992)
——, *Frenchman's Creek* (1941; repr. London: Virago Press, 2003)
——, *The King's General* (1946; repr. London: Virago Press, 2004)
——, *The House on the Strand* (1969; repr. London: Virago Press, 2003)
——, *Rule Britannia* (1972; repr. London: Virago Press, 2004)
du Maurier, Daphne, and Arthur Quiller-Couch, *Castle Dor* (1962; repr. London: Virago Press, 2004)
Dunmore, Helen, *Zennor in Darkness* (London: Penguin Books, 1994)
——, *Talking to the Dead* (London: Penguin Books, 1997)
——, *Mourning Ruby* (London: Penguin Books, 2004)
——, *The Lie* (London: Windmill Books, 2014)
Engraving of Boscawen Street, c.1830, photograph, Kresen Kernow
Enys Men, dir. by Mark Jenkin (UK: British Film Institute, 2023)
Gaskell, Elizabeth, *North and South* (1854–55; repr. London: Penguin Books, 1995)
George, Rena, *The Loveday Mysteries* ([York]: Rosmorna Publishing, 2013–22)
Goddard, Robert, *Beyond Recall* (1997; repr. London: Corgi, 2011)
Godden, Rumer, *China Court: The Hours of a Country House* (1993; repr. London: Virago Press, 2013)
Graham, Winston, *Ross Poldark*, Poldark Series, I (1945; repr. London: Pan Books, 2008)

——, *Demelza*, Poldark Series, II (1946; repr. London: Pan Books, 2008)
——, *Jeremy Poldark*, Poldark Series, III (1950; repr. London: Pan Books, 2008)
——, *Warleggan*, Poldark Series, IV (1953; repr. London: Pan Books, 2008)
——, *The Black Moon*, Poldark Series, V (1973; repr. London: Pan Books, 2008)
——, *The Four Swans*, Poldark Series, VI (1976; repr. London: Pan Books, 2008)
——, *The Angry Tide*, Poldark Series, VII (1977; repr. London: Pan Books, 2008)
——, *The Stranger from the Sea*, Poldark Series, VIII (1981; repr. London: Pan Books, 2008)
——, *The Miller's Dance*, Poldark Series, IX (1982; repr. London: Pan Books, 2008)
——, *The Loving Cup*, Poldark Series, X (1984; repr. London: Pan Books, 2008)
——, *The Twisted Sword*, Poldark Series, XI (1990; repr. London: Pan Books, 2008)
——, *Bella Poldark*, Poldark Series, XII (2002; repr. London: Pan Books, 2008)
Green, Cass, *In a Cottage in a Wood* (London: HarperCollins, 2017)
Harding Davis, Rebecca, *Life in the Iron Mills*, ed. by Cecelia Tichi (1861; repr. London: Macmillan, 1998)
Hardy, Thomas, *A Pair of Blue Eyes* (1872–73; repr. London: Penguin Books, 1998)
——, '1899 Preface', 'The Persons', 'The Scene', in *A Pair of Blue Eyes* (1872–73; repr. [n.p.]: Floating Press, 2005), pp. 6–9, https://www.floatingpress.com
——, *A Mere Interlude* (1885; repr. London: Penguin Classics, 2007)
——, *Tess of the D'Urbervilles* (1891; repr. London: Penguin Books, 1978)
Harris, John, 'Christian Heroism', in *Lays from the Mine, the Moor, and the Mountain*, 2nd edn (London: Alexander Heylin, 1856), pp. 33–45
——, 'The Mine', in *Wayside Pictures, Hymns, and Poems* (London: Hamilton, Adams, 1874), pp. 52–57
Heath-Stubbs, John, 'To the Mermaid at Zennor', in *Selected Poems*, ed. by John Clegg (Manchester: Carcanet Press, 2018), p. 46
Hocking, Salome, *Norah Lang: The Mine Girl* (London: Andrew Crombie, [1886])
Hocking, Silas K., *Tales of a Tin Mine* (1898; repr. Liskeard: Diggory Press, 2006)
Innes, Hammond, *Killer Mine* (1947; repr. London: Vintage, 2013)
Jackson, Kurt, *Washing in the Sunshine*, 2018, mixed media on paper, 57 x 61 cm, Worcester City Art Gallery and Museum
Johnson, Debbie, *Pippa's Cornish Dream* (London: HarperImpulse, 2015)
Kane, Jenny, *A Cornish Escape* (Cardiff: Accent Press, 2020)
Kent, Alan M., *Dan Daddow's Cornish Comicalities* (Wellington: Ryelands, 2016)
Kneehigh Theatre, *Tristan and Yseult, The Bacchae, The Wooden Frock, The Red Shoes* (London: Oberon Books, 2005)
Knight, Laura, *Men Working in a China Clay Pit*, 1912, watercolour on paper, 62 × 87 cm, Penlee House Gallery & Museum
——, *The China Clay Pit*, 1914, watercolour on paper, 45.5 × 69 cm, Penlee House Gallery & Museum
Lakeman, Seth, 'Bal Maiden', from *Word of Mouth* (UK: Cooking Vinyl, 2014)

Lawrence, D.H., letter to Bertrand Russell, 13 January 1916, in *The Letters of D.H. Lawrence*, ed. by George J. Zytaruk and James T. Boulton, 7 vols (Cambridge: Cambridge University Press, 1981), II, pp. 505–06

——, letter to Dollie Radford, 15 February 1916, in *The Letters of D.H. Lawrence*, ed. by George J. Zytaruk and James T. Boulton, 7 vols (Cambridge: Cambridge University Press, 1981), II, pp. 540–41

le Carré, John, *The Night Manager* (1993; repr. London: Penguin Books, 2013)

Lee, Charles, *Cynthia in the West* (London: Grant Richards, 1900)

Lower Lemon Street, c.1911, photograph, Royal Cornwall Museum

Lowry, H.D., and C.A. Dawson Scott, *Wheal Darkness* (London: Hutchinson, [1927])

Mais, S.P.B., *The Cornish Riviera*, 3rd edn (London: Great Western Railway, 1934)

Martin, Holly, *Ice Creams at Emerald Cove* ([n.p.]: Sunshine, Seaside and Sparkles, 2021)

Menmuir, Wyl, *The Many* (Cromer: Salt Publishing, 2016)

Mitchell, Sally, *Mevagissey: Just Another Overrated Place*, 2022–, graphic art print, https://www.jettystreetpress.co.uk/category/overrated-cornwall [accessed 17 January 2023]

——, *Overrated Cornwall*, 2022–, graphic art prints, https://www.jettystreetpress.co.uk/category/overrated-cornwall [accessed 17 January 2023]

Moss, Sarah, *Signs for Lost Children* (London: Granta Books, 2016)

Murray, John Middleton, ed., *Journal of Katherine Mansfield* (1927; repr. London: Persephone Books, 2006)

New, Edmund Hort, 'The Wessex of the Novels and Poems', map, in Bertram Coghill Alan Windle and Edmund Hort New, *The Wessex of Thomas Hardy* (1902; repr. London: Kessinger Publishing, 2010), frontmatter

Orchard, William, 'Wheal Coates', in *The Dreamt Sea: An Anthology of Anglo-Cornish Poetry 1928–2004*, ed. by Alan M. Kent (1973; repr. London: Francis Boutle, 2004), p. 61

O'Reilly, Noel, *Wrecker* (London: HQ, 2019)

Phillipps, K.C., ed., *The Cornish Journal of Charles Lee* (Padstow: Tabb House, 1995)

Pilcher, Rosamunde, *Coming Home* (London: Hodder and Stoughton, 1995)

Poldark, Mammoth Screen (UK: BBC, 2015–2019)

Pollard, Helen, *The Little Shop in Cornwall* (London: Bookouture, 2020)

Purcell, Laura, *Bone China* (London: Raven Books, 2019)

Rowe, Edward (*see also* Kernow King), 'Hireth' (unpublished play text from author, 2018)

Rowse, A.L., *A Cornish Childhood* (1942; repr. Truro: Dyllansow Truran, 1998)

——, 'Passing by the Coast of Cornwall', in *Poems of Cornwall and America* (London: Faber and Faber, 1967), pp. 51–52

——, 'Home-Coming to Cornwall: December 1942', in *A Life: Collected Poems* (1944; repr. Edinburgh: William Blackwood, 1981), pp. 134–36

Smith, Jesse Leroy, *Bal Maiden*, 2016, oil on copper, 50 × 50 cm, artist's own collection

[Stanford of London, possibly from a drawing by Thomas Hardy], 'The Wessex of the Novels', map, in Thomas Hardy, *Tess of the D'Urbervilles*, 17 vols (1891; repr. London: Osgood, McIlvaine, 1895), I, frontmatter

Stansfield, Katherine, *The Visitor* (Cardigan: Parthian Books, 2013)

——, *Falling Creatures* (London: Allison & Busby, 2017)

——, *The Magpie Tree* (London: Allison & Busby, 2018)

——, *The Mermaid's Call* (London: Allison & Busby, 2020)

Stevenson, Robert Louis, *Across the Plains: With Other Memories and Essays* (1892; repr. Cambridge: Cambridge University Press, 2009)

Stockdale, F.W.L., *Excursions Through Cornwall: 1824* (Truro: Bradford Barton, 1972)

Stonex, Emma, *The Lamplighters* (London: Picador Books, 2021)

Tanner, Steve, Balmaidens Appear Behind The Volunteer in *Enys Men*, 2021, photograph

Tremayne, S.K., *The Fire Child* (London: HarperCollins, 2017)

Tremellin, Patty, *Patty Tremellin: The Life of a Cornish Mine Girl* ([Bristol]: Wright and Albright, 1841)

Upson, Nicola, *Angel with Two Faces* (2009; repr. London: Faber and Faber, 2021)

——, *The Dead of Winter* (London: Faber & Faber, 2021)

van Gogh, Vincent, *Head of a Peasant Woman*, 1885, oil on canvas on millboard, 46.4 × 35.3 cm, Scottish National Gallery

Walker, Emery (from a drawing by Thomas Hardy), 'Map of the Wessex of the Novels and Poems', in *The Woodlanders*, 21 vols (1886; repr. London: Macmillan, 1912), VI, backmatter

Wesley, Mary, *The Camomile Lawn* (1984; repr. London: Vintage, 2006)

Winn, Raynor, *The Salt Path* (2018; repr. London: Penguin Books, 2019)

——, *Landlines* (London: Penguin Books, 2022)

Woolf, Virginia, *To the Lighthouse* (1927; repr. London: Penguin Books, 1992)

Zola, Émile, *Germinal*, trans. by Leonard Tancock ([1885]; repr. London: Penguin Books, 1954)

Secondary Texts

Acton, Viv, *A History of Truro: From Coinage Town to Cathedral City*, 2 vols (Truro: Landfall Publications, 1997), I

Action, Viv, and Bob Acton, *A History of Truro: Cathedral City and County Town*, 2 vols (Truro: Landfall Publications, 2002), II

Adams, James Eli, *Dandies and Desert Saints: Styles of Victorian Masculinity* (London: Cornell University Press, 1995), https://doi.org/10.7591/9781501720437

Ameel, Lieven, Jason Finch, and Markku Salmela, 'Introduction: Peripherality and Literary Urban Studies', in *Literature and the Peripheral City*, ed. by Lieven Ameel,

Jason Finch and Markku Salmela (Basingstoke: Palgrave Macmillan, 2015), pp. 1–17, https://doi.org/10.1057/9781137492883_1

'Ant', in *Oxford English Dictionary*, https://doi.org/10.1093/OED/2538147011

Arnold, Matthew, *Celtic Literature* (1891; repr. [n.p.]: Project Gutenberg, 2014), https://www.gutenberg.org/ebooks/5159 [accessed 10 September 2023]

'Bal', in *Gerlyver Kernewek / Cornish Dictionary*, https://www.cornishdictionary.org.uk/?locale=en#bal [accessed 29 May 2024]

Baraniuk, Carol, 'Negotiating Borders: Inspector Devlin and Shadows of the Past', in *The Contemporary Irish Detective Novel*, ed. by Elizabeth Mannion (London: Palgrave Macmillan, 2016), pp. 73–90, https://doi.org/10.1057/978-1-137-53940-3_6

Bawden, Nina, 'Castle Dor', in *The Daphne du Maurier Companion*, ed. by Helen Taylor (London: Virago Press, 2007), pp. 192–95

Beckett, John, and David Windsor, 'Truro: Diocese and City', in *Cornish Studies: 11*, ed. by Philip Payton, 2nd ser. (Exeter: University of Exeter Press, 2003), pp. 220–27

Bender, Michael, 'Why Move the Lighthouse? Virginia Woolf's Relationship with St Ives', in *Cornish Studies: 13*, ed. by Philip Payton, 2nd ser. (Exeter: University of Exeter Press, 2005), pp. 53–69

Berresford Ellis, Peter, *The Celtic Dawn: A History of Pan Celticism* (London: Constable, 1993)

Bitenc, Rebecca Anna, 'Dementia Narratives in Contemporary Literature, Life Writing, and Film'(unpublished doctoral thesis, Durham University, 2017)

Bondi, Liz, Joyce Davidson, and Mick Smith, 'Geography's "Emotional Turn"', in *Emotional Geographies*, ed. by Joyce Davidson, Liz Bondi, and Mick Smith (Aldershot: Ashgate Publishing, 2007), pp. 1–18

Bonikowski, Wyatt, *Shell Shock and the Modernist Imagination: The Death Drive in Post World War I British Fiction* (Abingdon: Routledge, 2016), https://doi.org/10.4324/9781315608921

Brabazon, Tara, *Unique Urbanity?: Rethinking Third Tier Cities, Degeneration, Regeneration and Mobility* (London: Springer, 2015), https://doi.org/10.1007/978-981-287-269-2

Bridge, Gary, and Sophie Watson, 'Reflections on Materialities', in *The New Blackwell Companion to the City*, ed. by Gary Bridge and Sophie Watson (Chichester: Wiley-Blackwell, 2011), pp. 1–14, https://doi.org/10.1002/9781444395105.ch1

—— , 'Reflections on Publics and Cultures', in *The New Blackwell Companion to the City*, ed. by Gary Bridge and Sophie Watson (Chichester: Wiley-Blackwell, 2011), pp. 377–89, https://doi.org/10.1002/9781444395105.ch33

Buckley, Allen, *Cornish Bal Maidens* (Redruth: Tor Mark, 2010)

Burgan, Mary, 'Mapping Contagion in Victorian London: Disease in the East End', in *Victorian Urban Settings: Essays on the Nineteenth-Century City and its Contexts*, ed. by Debra N. Mancoff and D.J. Trela (London: Garland Publishing, 1996), pp. 43–56, https://doi.org/10.4324/9780203054512-ch-2

Bibliography

Burke, Gill, 'The Decline of the Independent Bâl Maiden: The Impact of Change in the Cornish Mining Industry', in *Unequal Opportunities: Women's Employment in England 1800–1918*, ed. by Angela V. John (Oxford: Blackwell, 1986), pp. 179–206

Carter, Simon, 'Disease and Infection in the City', in *The New Blackwell Companion to the City*, ed. by Gary Bridge and Sophie Watson (Chichester: Wiley-Blackwell, 2011), pp. 245–54, https://doi.org/10.1002/9781444395105.ch21

Church, Edward, 'Cornwall Beaches and Their Sand "Twins" on the Other Side of the Planet', *Cornwall Live*, 12 September 2021, https://www.cornwalllive.com/news/cornwall-news/cornwall-beaches-sand-twins-side-5890362 [accessed 21 October 2022]

Clarke, Norma, 'Strenuous Idleness: Thomas Carlyle and the Man of Letters as Hero', in *Manful Assertions: Masculinities in Britain since 1800*, ed. by Michael Roper and John Tosh (London: Routledge, 1991), pp. 25–43, https://doi.org/10.4324/9781003209164-2

Classen, Constance, David Howes, and Anthony Synnott, *Aroma: The Cultural History of Smell* (London: Routledge, 1994)

Cohen, Erik, 'The Sociology of Tourism: Approaches, Issues and Findings', *Annual Review of Sociology*, 10 (1984), pp. 373–92, https://doi.org/10.1146/annurev.so.10.080184.002105

Corbin, Alain, *The Lure of the Sea: The Discovery of the Seaside 1750–1840* (London: Penguin Books, 1995)

Cornwall Council, 'Cornish National Minority', https://www.cornwall.gov.uk/people-and-communities/equality-and-diversity/cornish-national-minority [accessed 2 November 2022]

——, 'Census 2021: Welcomed Increase in the Number of People Identifying as Cornish', https://www.cornwall.gov.uk/council-news/council-budgets-and-economy/census-2021-welcomed-increase-in-the-number-of-people-identifying-as-cornish [accessed 9 January 2023]

Cross, Stephanie, '*The Many* by Wyl Menmuir Review—Fishermen's Blues', *Observer*, 21 August 2016, https://www.theguardian.com/books/2016/aug/21/the-many-wyl-menmuir-review [accessed 21 April 2022]

Cuthbert, Alexander R., *The Form of Cities: Political Economy and Urban Design* (Oxford: Blackwell, 2006), https://doi.org/10.1002/9780470774915

Dalziel, Pamela, 'A Note on the History of the Text', in Thomas Hardy, *A Pair of Blue Eyes* (1872–73; repr. London: Penguin Books, 1998), pp. xxxix–xlii

Danahay, Martin A., *Gender at Work in Victorian Culture: Literature, Art and Masculinity* (London: Routledge, 2016), https://doi.org/10.4324/9781315254654

Davidson, Joyce, and Christine Milligan, 'Embodying Emotion Sensing Space: Introducing Emotional Geographies', *Social and Cultural Geography*, 5.4 (2004), pp. 523–32, https://doi.org/10.1080/1464936042000317677

Deacon, Bernard, '"The Hollow Jarring of the Distant Steam Engines": Images of Cornwall Between West Barbary and Delectable Duchy', in *Cornwall: A Cultural*

Construction of Place, ed. by Ella Westland (Penzance: Patten Press, 1997), pp. 7–24

——, 'In Search of the Missing "Turn": The Spatial Dimension and Cornish Studies', in *Cornish Studies: 8*, ed. by Philip Payton, 2nd ser. (Exeter: University of Exeter Press, 1998), pp. 213–29

——, 'From "Cornish Studies" to "Critical Cornish Studies": Reflections on Methodology', in *Cornish Studies: 12*, ed. by Philip Payton, 2nd ser. (Exeter: University of Exeter Press, 2004), pp. 13–20

——, *Cornwall: A Concise History* (Cardiff: University of Wales Press, 2007)

——, *Industrial Celts: Making the Modern Cornish Identity, 1750–1870* (Redruth: CoSERG, 2018)

DeFazio, Kimberley, *The City of the Senses: Urban Culture and Urban Space* (Basingstoke: Palgrave Macmillan, 2011), https://doi.org/10.1057/9780230370357

Dickinson, Robert, 'Changing Landscapes of Difference: Representations of Cornwall in Travel Writing, 1949–2007', in *Cornish Studies: 16*, ed. by Philip Payton, 2nd ser. (Exeter: University of Exeter Press, 2008), pp. 167–82

Diniejko, Andrezej, 'Thomas Hardy's *A Pair of Blue Eyes* as a Cliffhanger with a Post-Darwinian Message', *The Victorian Web*, 2006, https://victorianweb.org/authors/hardy/diniejko6.html [accessed 5 November 2022]

Dodman, Trevor, *Shell Shock, Memory and the Novel in the Wake of World War I* (New York: Cambridge University Press, 2015), https://doi.org/10.1017/CBO9781316287040

Ellis, Henry Havelock, 'The Men of Cornwall', 2 parts, *New Century Review*, 4 (1897), I, pp. 328–35, http://0-search-proquest-com.pugwash.lib.warwick.ac.uk/historical-periodicals/men-cornwall/docview/3828184/se-2 [accessed 22 October 2022]

——, 'The Men of Cornwall', 2 parts, *New Century Review*, 5 (1897), II, pp. 411–18, http://0-search.proquest.com.pugwash.lib.warwick.ac.uk/historical-periodicals/men-cornwall/docview/3764576/se-2 [accessed 22 October 2022]

Engels, Friedrich, *The Condition of the Working Class in England in 1844*, trans. by Florence Kelley Wischnewetzky (1845; repr. Cambridge: Cambridge University Press, 2010), https://doi.org/10.1017/CBO9780511792700

Everitt, Alan, 'Country, County and Town: Patterns of Regional Evolution in England', *Transactions of the Royal Historical Society*, 5th ser., 29 (1979), pp. 79–108, https://doi.org/10.2307/3679114

Fletcher, Lisa, 'Introduction: Space, Place, and Popular Fiction', in *Popular Fiction and Spatiality: Reading Genre Settings*, ed. by Lisa Fletcher (New York: Palgrave Macmillan, 2016), pp. 1–8, https://doi.org/10.1057/978-1-137-56902-8_1

Forster, Margaret, *Daphne du Maurier* (London: Arrow, 2007)

Foucault, Michel, 'Of Other Spaces: Utopias and Heterotopias', trans. by Jay Miskowiec, *Diacritics*, 16.1 (1986), pp. 22–27, https://doi.org/10.2307/464648

Bibliography

Fox, Pamela, *Class Fictions: Shame and Resistance in the British Working-Class Novel, 1890–1945* (London: Duke University Press, 1994), https://doi.org/10.1215/9780822382935

Gatrell, Simon, *Thomas Hardy's Vision of Wessex* (Basingstoke: Palgrave Macmillan, 2003)

'Glas', in *Gerlyver Kernewek / Cornish Dictionary*, https://www.cornishdictionary.org.uk/#glas [accessed 21 October 2022]

Goodman, Gemma, *Salome Hocking: A Cornish Woman Writer* (Penzance: Hypatia Trust, 2004)

——, 'Seeing the Clay Country: The Novels of Jack Clemo', in *Cornish Studies: 17*, ed. by Philip Payton, 2nd ser. (Exeter: University of Exeter Press, 2009), pp. 34–50

——, 'Rural Geographies: The Figure in the Landscape in Literature of Cornwall', in *Cornish Studies: 20*, ed. by Philip Payton, 2nd ser. (Exeter: University of Exeter Press, 2012), pp. 148–65

——, 'At Work and at Play: Charles Lee's *Cynthia in the West*', in *Gender and Space in Rural Britain: 1840-1920*, ed. by Gemma Goodman and Charlotte Mathieson (London: Pickering and Chatto, 2014), pp. 41–54

——, 'Women at Sea: Locating and Escaping Gender on the Cornish Coast in Daphne du Maurier's *The Loving Spirit* and *Frenchman's Creek*', in *Sea Narratives: Cultural Responses to the Sea, 1600–Present*, ed. by Charlotte Mathieson (London: Palgrave Macmillian, 2016), pp. 171–94, https://doi.org/10.1057/978-1-137-58116-7_7

Goodman, Gemma, and Charlotte Mathieson, 'Introduction: Gender and Space in Rural Britain, 1840–1920', in *Gender and Space in Rural Britain: 1840–1920*, ed. by Gemma Goodman and Charlotte Mathieson (London: Pickering and Chatto, 2014), pp. 1–14

Greenland, R.E., 'Hardy in the Osgood, McIlvaine and Harper (London) Editions', *Thomas Hardy Journal*, 4.3 (1988), pp. 57–60, https://www.jstor.org/stable/45273903

Groom, Nick, '"Let's Discuss Over Country Supper Soon": Rebekah Brooks and David Cameron—Rural Realities and Rustic Representations', *The Clearing*, 22 August 2013, https://www.littletoller.co.uk/the-clearing/lets-discuss-over-country-supper-soon-rebekah-brooks-and-david-cameron-rural-realities-and-rustic-representations-nick-groom/ [accessed 4 January 2023]

Gunne, Sorcha, 'World-Literature, World-Systems, and Irish Chick Lit', in *Globalizing Literary Genres: Literature, History, Modernity*, ed. by Jernej Habjan and Fabienne Imlinger (London: Routledge, 2016), pp. 241–53, https://doi.org/10.4324/9781315708621

Guthrie, A., *Cornwall in the Age of Steam* (Padstow: Tabb House, 1994)

Hale, Amy, 'Genesis of the Celto-Cornish Revival? L.C Duncombe-Jewell and the Kelto-Kernuak', in *Cornish Studies: 5*, ed. by Philip Payton, 2nd Ser. (Exeter: University of Exeter Press, 1997), pp. 100–11

Hall, C.M., et al., 'Vanishing Peripheries: Does Tourism Consume Places?', *Tourism Recreation Research*, 38.1 (2013), pp. 71–92, https://doi.org/10.1080/02508281.2013.11081730

Hamilton Jenkin, A.K., *The Story of Cornwall* (London: Thomas Nelson, 1934)

——, *Cornwall and the Cornish: The Story, Religion, and Folk-lore of 'The Western Land'* (Launceston: Westcountry Books, 2004)

Hechter, Michael, *Internal Colonialism: The Celtic Fringe in British National Development*, rev. edn (London: Routledge, 2017)

'Hireth', in *Gerlyver Kernewek / Cornish Dictionary*, https://www.cornishdictionary.org.uk/?locale=en#hireth [accessed 10 April 2023]

Historic Cornwall, 'How Many Miles Long is Cornwall?', https://www.historic-cornwall.org.uk/how-many-miles-long-is-cornwall/ [accessed 22 October 2022]

Horner, Avril, and Sue Zlosnik, *Daphne du Maurier: Writing, Identity and the Gothic Imagination* (London: Macmillan, 1998), https://doi.org/10.1057/9780230378773

Hurst, John, 'Literature in Cornwall', in *Cornwall Since the War: The Contemporary History of a European Region*, ed. by Philip Payton (Redruth: Institute of Cornish Studies and Dyllansow Truran, 1993), pp. 291–308

Ingham, Patricia, *The Language of Gender and Class: Transformation in the Victorian Novel* (London: Routledge, 1996)

Jakat, Lena, 'The Rosamunde Pilcher Trail: Why German Tourists Flock to Cornwall', *Guardian*, 4 October 2013, https://www.theguardian.com/travel/2013/oct/04/rosamunde-pilcher-german-tourists-cornwall [accessed 3 October 2022]

John, Angela V., *By the Sweat of Their Brow: Women Workers at Victorian Coal Mines* (London: Routledge, 1984)

Kennedy, Neil, and Nigel Kingcome, 'Disneyfication of Cornwall: Developing a Poldark Heritage Complex', *International Journal of Heritage Studies*, 4.1 (1998), pp. 45–59, https://doi.org/10.1080/13527259808722218

Kent, Alan M., 'The Cornish Alps: Resisting Romance in the Clay Country', in *Cornwall: A Cultural Construction of Place*, ed. by Ella Westland (Penzance: Patten Press, 1997), pp. 53–67

——, *Wives, Mothers and Sisters: Feminism, Literature and Women Writers in Cornwall* ([Penzance]: Patten Press, 1998)

——, *The Literature of Cornwall: Continuity, Identity, Difference 1000–2000* (Bristol: Redcliffe Press, 2000)

——, *Pulp Methodism: The Lives and Literature of Silas, Joseph and Salome Hocking, Three Cornish Novelists* (St Austell: Cornish Hillside Publications, 2002)

Kernow King (*see also* Rowe, Edward), 'Proper Job! It's England That's Cut Off from Cornwall, Not the Other Way Round', *Guardian*, 6 February 2014, https://www.theguardian.com/commentisfree/2014/feb/06/england-cut-off-from-cornwall [accessed 6 November 2022]

Kilday, Anne-Marie, *Crime in Scotland: 1660–1960: The Violent North?* (Abingdon: Routledge, 2019), https://doi.org/10.4324/9781315767352

Knight, Stephen, 'Regional Crime Squads: Location and Dislocation in the British Mystery', in *Peripheral Visions: Images of Nationhood in Contemporary British Fiction*, ed. by Ian A. Bell (Cardiff: University of Wales Press, 1995), pp. 27–43

———, 'The Postcolonial Crime Novel', in *The Cambridge Companion to the Postcolonial Novel*, ed. by Ato Quayson (Cambridge: Cambridge University Press, 2016), pp. 166–87, https://doi.org/10.1017/CBO9781316459287.011

'Koffiji', in *Gerlyver Kernewek / Cornish Dictionary*, https://www.cornishdictionary.org.uk/?locale=en#koffiji [accessed 16 June 2023]

Leane, Elizabeth, 'Unstable Places and Generic Spaces: Fiction Set in Antarctica', in *Popular Fiction and Spatiality: Reading Genre Settings*, ed. by Lisa Fletcher (New York: Palgrave Macmillan, 2016), pp. 25–44, https://doi.org/10.1057/978-1-137-56902-8_3

Light, Alison, *Forever England: Femininity, Literature and Conservatism Between the Wars* (London: Routledge, 1991)

Louttit, Chris, 'Working-Class Masculinity and the Victorian Novel', in *The Victorian Novel and Masculinity*, ed. by Phillip Mallett (Basingstoke: Palgrave Macmillan, 2015), pp. 31–50, https://doi.org/10.1057/9781137491541_2

Low, Setha, 'Spatializing Culture: Embodied Space in the City', in *The New Blackwell Companion to the City*, ed. by Gary Bridge and Sophie Watson (Chichester: Wiley-Blackwell, 2011), pp. 463–75, https://doi.org/10.1002/9781444395105.ch41

Low, Setha M., and Denise Lawrence-Zúñiga, 'Locating Culture', in *The Anthropology of Space and Place: Locating Culture*, ed. by Setha M. Low and Denise Lawrence-Zúñiga (Oxford: Blackwell, 2003), pp. 1–47

Lowerson, John, 'Celtic Tourism—Some Recent Magnets', in *Cornish Studies: 2*, ed. by Philip Payton, 2nd ser. (Exeter: University of Exeter Press, 1994), pp. 128–37

Lyne, Arthur, *Around Truro in Old Photographs: From the Archives of the Royal Cornwall Museum* (Stroud: Alan Sutton, 1992)

Mallett, Phillip, 'Masculinity, Imperialism and the Novel', in *The Victorian Novel and Masculinity*, ed. by Phillip Mallett (Basingstoke: Palgrave Macmillan, 2015), pp. 151–71, https://doi.org/10.1057/9781137491541_7

Manford, Alan L., 'The "Texts" of Thomas Hardy's Map of Wessex', *Library*, 6th ser., 4.3 (1982), pp. 297–306

Marcus, Laura, 'Detection and Literary Fiction', in *The Cambridge Companion to Crime Fiction*, ed. by Martin Priestman (Cambridge: Cambridge University Press, 2003), pp. 245–67, https://doi.org/10.1017/CCOL0521803993.015

Marsden, Philip, *The Levelling Sea: The Story of a Cornish Haven and the Age of Sail* (London: HarperCollins, 2012)

———, *Rising Ground: A Search for the Spirit of Place* (London: Granta Books, 2015)

Massey, Doreen, *Space, Place and Gender* (Cambridge: Polity Press, 1994)

Mathieson, Charlotte, *Mobility in the Victorian Novel: Placing the Nation* (Basingstoke: Palgrave Macmillan, 2015)

Mayers, Lynne, *Balmaidens*, 2nd rev. edn ([n.p]: Blaize Bailey Books, 2008)

———, 'Bal Maidens and Mining Women', http://www.balmaiden.co.uk [accessed 29 May 2021]

McCormick, Elizabeth Wilde, *Living on the Edge: Breaking up to Break Down to Breakthrough* (London: Sage Publications, 2002), https://doi.org/10.4135/9781446220184

McDowell, Linda, *Gender, Identity and Place: Understanding Feminist Geographies* (Cambridge: Polity Press, 1999)

McNamara, Kevin R., 'Introduction', in *The Cambridge Companion to the City in Literature*, ed. by Kevin R. McNamara (Cambridge: Cambridge University Press, 2014), pp. 1–16, https://doi.org/10.1017/CCO9781139235617.002

Messent, Peter, *The Crime Fiction Handbook* (Chichester: Wiley-Blackwell, 2013)

Miller, David, 'Bishop Benson's Vision for Truro Cathedral and Diocese: The Umbrella and the Duck', in *Cornish Studies: 21*, ed. by Philip Payton, 2nd ser. (Exeter: University of Exeter Press, 2013), pp. 207–23

Mitchell, Don, *Cultural Geography: A Critical Introduction* (Oxford: Blackwell, 2000)

'Moryonen', in *Gerlyver Kernewek /Cornish Dictionary*, https://www.cornishdictionary.org.uk/?locale=en#moryonen [accessed 29 May 2024]

Moseley, Rachel, 'Women at the Edge: Encounters with the Cornish Coast in British Film and Television', *Continuum*, 27.5 (2003), 644–62, https://doi.org/10.1080/10304312.2013.824861

——, *Picturing Cornwall: Landscape, Region and the Moving Image* (Exeter: University of Exeter Press, 2018)

Mudd, David, *About the City: A Portrait of Truro* (Bodmin: Bossiney Books, 1979)

Mukherjee, Upamanyu Pablo, *Crime and Empire: The Colony in Nineteenth-Century Fictions of Crime* (Oxford: Oxford University Press, 2003)

Nesci, Catherine, 'Memory, Desire, Lyric: The Flâneur', in *The Cambridge Companion to the City in Literature*, ed. by Kevin R. McNamara (Cambridge: Cambridge University Press, 2014), pp. 69–84, https://doi.org/10.1017/CCO9781139235617.007

Nord, Deborah Epstein, *Walking the Victorian Streets: Women, Representation, and the City* (London: Cornell University Press, 1995), https://doi.org/10.7591/9781501729232

O'Byrne, Alison, 'The Spectator and the Rise of the Modern Metropole', in *The Cambridge Companion to the City in Literature*, ed. by Kevin R. McNamara (Cambridge: Cambridge University Press, 2014), pp. 57–68, https://doi.org/10.1017/CCO9781139235617.006

Oltermann, Philip, 'Escapist Dreams: Why Germans Love TV Romances Set in Cornwall', *Guardian*, 29 May 2021, https://www.theguardian.com/world/2021/may/29/german-tv-love-cornwall-diplomats-rosamunde-pilcher [accessed 3 October 2022]

Orchard, W.G., ed., *A Glossary of Cornish Mining Terms* (Redruth: Dyllansow Truran, 1990)

Packham, Jimmy, 'The Gothic Coast: Boundaries, Belonging, and Coastal Community in Contemporary British Fiction', *Critique: Studies in Contemporary Fiction*, 60.2 (2019), pp. 205–21, https://doi.org/10.1080/00111619.2018.1524744

Bibliography

Parkins, Wendy, *Mobility and Modernity in Women's Novels, 1850s–1930s: Women Moving Dangerously* (Basingstoke: Palgrave Macmillan, 2009), https://doi.org/10.1057/9780230583115

Parnell, Christine, *Truro* (Stroud: Tempus Publishing, 2001)

——, *Truro: History and Guide* (Stroud: Tempus Publishing, 2002)

——, *Truro Streets* (Stroud: Tempus Publishing, 2007)

Parr, Hester, Chris Philo, and Nicola Burns, '"Not a Display of Emotions": Emotional Geographies in the Scottish Highlands', in *Emotional Geographies*, ed. by Joyce Davison, Liz Bondi, and Mick Smith (Aldershot: Ashgate Publishing, 2007), pp. 87–102

Parsons, Deborah, *Streetwalking the Metropolis: Women, the City, and Modernity* (Oxford: Oxford University Press, 2000)

Passey, Joan, 'Corpses, Coasts and Carriages: Gothic Cornwall, 1840–1913' (unpublished doctoral thesis, University of Exeter, 2019)

——, '"A Delightful Place to be Buried In": Representations of Cornwall in Thomas Hardy's *A Pair of Blue Eyes*', *Victorians: A Journal of Culture and Literature*, 139 (2021), pp. 43–57, https://doi.org/10.1353/vct.2021.0004

——, *Cornish Gothic, 1830–1913* (Cardiff: University of Wales Press, 2023)

Payton, Philip, 'Introduction', in *Cornish Studies: 1*, ed. by Philip Payton, 2nd ser. (Exeter: University of Exeter Press, 1993), pp. 1–3

——, 'Paralysis and Revival: The Reconstruction of Celtic-Catholic Cornwall 1890–1945', in *Cornwall: A Cultural Construction of Place*, ed. by Ella Westland (Penzance: Patten Press, 1997), pp. 25–39

——, *Cornwall: A History*, rev. edn (Exeter: University of Exeter Press, 2017)

——, *The Cornish Overseas* (Fowey: Cornwall Editions, 2005)

——, *A.L. Rowse and Cornwall: A Paradoxical Patriot* (Exeter: University of Exeter Press, 2005)

——, *John Betjeman and Cornwall: 'The Celebrated Cornish Nationalist'* (Exeter: University of Exeter Press, 2010)

Payton, Philip, and Paul Thornton, 'The Great Western Railway and the Cornish-Celtic Revival', in *Cornish Studies: 3*, ed. by Philip Payton, 2nd ser. (Exeter: University of Exeter Press, 1995), pp. 83–103

Pearce, Cathryn J., *Cornish Wrecking, 1700–1860: Reality and Popular Myth* (Woodbridge: The Boydell Press, 2010)

Phillipps, K.C., *A Glossary of the Cornish Dialect* (Padstow: Tabb House, 1993)

Pite, Ralph, *Hardy's Geography: Wessex and the Regional Novel* (Basingstoke: Palgrave Macmillan, 2002), https://doi.org/10.1057/9780230512665_7

Priestman, Martin, 'Post-war British Crime Fiction', in *The Cambridge Companion to Crime Fiction*, ed. by Martin Priestman (Cambridge: Cambridge University Press, 2003), pp. 173–90, https://doi.org/10.1017/CCOL0521803993.011

Radio Times Staff, 'Poldark: Our Guide to the Upcountry Locations from Frome to Berkeley Castle', *Radio Times*, 11 June 2017, https://www.radiotimes.com/travel/

poldark-our-guide-to-the-upcountry-locations-from-frome-to-berkeley-castle [accessed 17 October 2022]

Rawe, Donald, 'Introduction', in *The Clay Kiln* (St Austell: Cornish Hillside Publications, 2000), pp. 3–7

Robbins, Keith, *Nineteenth Century Britain: Integration and Diversity* (Oxford: Clarendon Press, 1988)

Roberts, Ed, '10 of the Best Beaches You Wouldn't Believe Are in Cornwall', *Holidaycottages.co.uk*, 17 May 2022, https://www.holidaycottages.co.uk/blog/10-beaches-you-wouldnt-believe-are-in-cornwall?utm_source=pocket_mylist [accessed 21 October 2022]

Rodman, Margaret C., 'Empowering Place: Multilocality and Multivocality', in *Anthropology of Space and Place: Locating Culture*, ed. by Setha M. Low and Denise Lawrence-Zúñiga (Oxford: Wiley-Blackwell, 2003), pp. 204–23

Roper, Michael, and John Tosh, 'Introduction: Historians and the Politics of Masculinity', in *Manful Assertions: Masculinities in Britain since 1800*, ed. by Michael Roper and John Tosh (London: Routledge, 1991), pp. 1–24, https://doi.org/10.4324/9781003209164-1

Rose, Sonya, *Limited Livelihoods* (London: Routledge, 1992)

Ruminski, Michelle, 'Corsham Goes Back in Time for Poldark Location Filming', *BBC News*, 7 May 2014, https://www.bbc.co.uk/news/av/uk-england-wiltshire-27304893 [accessed 17 October 2022]

Schwartz, Sharron P., 'In Defence of Customary Rights: Labouring Women's Experience of Industrialization in Cornwall, c1750–1870', in *Cornish Studies: 7*, ed. by Philip Payton, 2nd ser. (Exeter: University of Exeter Press, 1999), pp. 8–31

——, '"No Place for a Woman": Gender at Work in Cornwall's Metalliferous Mining Industry', in *Cornish Studies: 8*, ed. by Philip Payton (Exeter: University of Exeter Press, 2000), pp. 69–96

Sennett, Richard, 'Reflections on the Public Realm', in *The New Blackwell Companion to the City*, ed. by Gary Bridge and Sophie Watson (Oxford: Wiley-Blackwell, 2011), pp. 390–97, https://doi.org/10.1002/9781444395105.ch34

Sewell, Jessica Ellen, 'Gendering Urban Space', in *The New Blackwell Companion to the City*, ed. by Gary Bridge and Sophie Watson (Oxford: Wiley-Blackwell, 2011), pp. 596–605, https://doi.org/10.1002/9781444395105.ch52

Shields, Rob, *Places on the Margin: Alternative Geographies of Modernity* (London: Routledge, 1991)

Showalter, Elaine, 'Victorian Women and Insanity', *Victorian Studies*, 23.2 (1980), pp. 157–81, https://www.jstor.org/stable/3827084

——, *A Literature of Their Own: From Charlotte Brontë to Doris Lessing*, rev. edn (London: Virago Press, 1999)

Smith, Kate, 'In Her Hands: Materializing Distinction in Georgian Britain', *Cultural and Social History*, 11.4 (2015), pp. 489–586, https://doi.org/10.2752/147800414X14056862571989

Solnit, Rebecca, *Wanderlust: A History of Walking* (London: Granta Publications, 2014)

Stanley, Liz, 'Introduction', in *The Diairies of Hannah Cullwick, Victorian Maidservant*, ed. by Liz Stanley (London: Virago Press, 1984), pp. 1–28

'Daphne du Maurier', *Summer Season* (BBC, 1971)

Talivee, Elle-Mari, and Jason Finch, 'Eduard Vilde and Tallinn's Dynamic Peripheries, 1858–1903', in *Literature and the Peripheral City*, ed. by Lieven Ameel, Jason Finch, and Markku Salmela (Basingstoke: Palgrave Macmillan, 2015), pp. 164–83, https://doi.org/10.1057/9781137492883_10

Tambling, Jeremy, 'Detroit and Paris, Paris as Detroit', in *Literature and the Peripheral City*, ed. by Lieven Ameel, Jason Finch, and Markku Salmela (Basingstoke: Palgrave Macmillan, 2015), pp. 21–39, https://doi.org/10.1057/9781137492883_2

Taylor, Catherine, '*The Many* by Wyl Menmuir Review—a Disturbing Debut', *Guardian*, 4 August 2016, https://www.theguardian.com/books/2016/aug/04/the-many-wyl-menmuir-review [accessed 21 April 2022]

Thacker, Andrew, *Moving Through Modernity: Space and Geography in Modernism* (Manchester: Manchester University Press, 2003)

Thompson, Luke, *Clay Phoenix: A Biography of Jack Clemo* ([n.p.]: Ally, 2016)

Tomalin, Claire, *Thomas Hardy: The Time-Torn Man* (London: Penguin Books, 2007)

Tosh, John, *Manliness and Masculinities in Nineteenth Century Britain: Essays on Gender, Family and Empire* (London: Routledge, 2016), https://doi.org/10.4324/9781315838533

Trip Fiction, 'Talking Location with Emma Stonex, Author of *The Lamplighters*—Cornwall', 2021, https://www.tripfiction.com/talking-location-with-emma-stonex-author-of-the-lamplighters-cornwall/ [accessed 16 November 2022]

Trower, Shelley, 'On the Cliff Edge of England: Tourism and Imperial Gothic in Cornwall', *Victorian Literature and Culture*, 40.1 (2012), pp. 199–214, https://doi.org/10.1017/S1060150311000313

——, *Rocks of Nation: The Imagination of Celtic Cornwall* (Manchester: Manchester University Press, 2015)

Truro Buildings Research Group, *Truro: Boscawen Street Area* (Truro: Truro Buildings Research Group and Truro Civic Society in Association with University of Exeter Extra-mural Department, 1981)

Tuan, Yi-Fu, *Space and Place: The Perspective of Experience* (London: University of Minnesota Press, 1977)

Urry, John, 'The Place of Emotions Within Place', in *Emotional Geographies*, ed. by Joyce Davison, Liz Bondi, and Mick Smith (Aldershot: Ashgate Publishing, 2007), pp. 77–86

——, 'City Life and the Senses', in *The New Blackwell Companion to the City*, ed. by Gary Bridge and Sophie Watson (Oxford: Wiley-Blackwell, 2011), pp. 347–56, https://doi.org/10.1002/9781444395105.ch30

Val Baker, Denys, *The Timeless Land: The Creative Spirit in Cornwall* (Somerset: Adams and Dart, 1973)

——, *A View from Land's End: Writers Against a Cornish Background* (London: Kimber, 1982)

Vernon, James, 'Border Crossing: Cornwall and the English (Imagi)nation', in *Imagining Nations*, ed. by Geoffrey Cubitt (Manchester: Manchester University Press, 1998), pp. 153–72

Waters, Rebecca, 'Cornwall Local Turns One Star TripAdvisor Reviews About Mevagissey into Art', *Cornwall Live*, 16 August 2022, https://www.cornwalllive.com/news/cornwall-news/cornwall-local-turns-one-star-7471151 [accessed 3 January 2023]

Westland, Ella, 'The Passionate Periphery: Cornwall and Romantic Fiction', in *Peripheral Visions: Images of Nationhood in Contemporary British Fiction*, ed. by Ian A. Bell (Cardiff: University of Wales Press, 1995), pp. 153–72

——, ed., *Cornwall: A Cultural Construction of Place* (Penzance: Patten Press, 1997)

——, 'Introduction', in Daphne du Maurier, *Rule Britannia* (1972; repr. London: Virago Press, 2004)

——, *Reading Daphne: A Guide to the Writing of Daphne du Maurier for Readers and Book Groups* (Truro: Truran Books, 2007)

Williams, Colin H., 'On Ideology, Identity and Integrity', in *Cornish Studies: 10*, ed. by Philip Payton, 2nd ser. (Exeter: University of Exeter Press, 2002), pp. 67–79

Williams, Raymond, *The Country and the City* (1973; repr. London: Vintage Books, 2016)

Woodbridge, Beth, 'Why Are There So Many Mentally Ill Drug Addicts in Cornwall?', *Vice*, 29 July 2013, https://www.vice.com/en/article/vdy5am/penzance-is-the-end-of-the-line?utm_source=pocket_mylist [accessed 21 October 2022]

'Zawn', in *Oxford English Dictionary*, https://doi.org/10.1093/OED/4631435340

Index

A30 (road) 165, 166
aesthetics 14, 18, 19, 20, 22–23, 59, 64, 65, 96, 97–99, 103, 112, 114–16, 120–21, 122, 131, 132, 134, 138, 140–41, 142, 162, 165–66, 168–69, 171, 186
America 86, 91–92, 94, 136, 172
American 91–92, 94, 135, 136
Arnold, Matthew 61
Arthurian 3, 55, 174, 175
Austen, Jane 189n3
   Northanger Abbey 153

Ballantyne, R.M.
   Deep Down 17, 24, 31–35, 37, 41–42, 46, 47–48, 192n56
balmaidens (*see also* mining and miners) 17, 23–28, 35, 36, 39–48, 84, 141, 185, 191n11, 191n18, 193n70, 193n87
Barry, Charles 139, 205n29
Bath 49, 138–40, 153, 205n28
BBC 132, 165, 170–71
beaches (*see also* coast, cliffs, edge, littoral and sea) 70, 83, 85, 87–88, 90, 97–99, 102–04, 111, 116, 117–18, 121–22, 125

bodies
   alive 8, 23, 29–30, 31, 33–35, 47–48, 59, 64–65, 66, 67, 80, 111, 117, 119, 129, 141, 147, 148, 154, 157–58
   dead 73, 75, 76, 78, 83–84, 85, 87–88, 102, 109–10, 129, 167–68
Bodmin 51, 134, 137, 206n40
Bodmin Moor (*see also* moorland) 19, 79, 80, 132, 142, 162, 163, 164, 166–67, 169, 175–77, 187, 208n4
Bonikowski, Wyatt 129
Bosanketh, Edward
   Tin 17, 24, 31, 37–38, 41
Boscastle 81, 104
Botallack (Crowns) mine 10, 31–33, 34, 37, 97
Braddon, Mary Elizabeth
   Wyllard's Weird 49
Brexit 52, 186
Britain / British Isles 7, 11, 14, 19, 37, 49, 55, 79, 91–92, 100, 133, 137, 149, 158, 186
   nineteenth century / Victorian Britain 15, 24, 30, 37, 40, 61, 102, 193n71
British / Britishness 5, 7, 15, 23, 28, 51, 59, 76–79, 91, 102

Brittany 61, 100
Brunel, Isambard Kingdom 50, 54

Camborne 92, 133
capitalism 92, 93–94, 146
Carlyle, Thomas 29, 35
Carroll, Charlie
   The Lip 119–26, 203n102
Castle-an-Dinas 173, 174
Causley, Charles 4
   'The Seasons in North Cornwall' 162
Celtic / Celticity 53, 56, 61
   Celtic Cornish / Cornwall 3, 4, 17, 18, 23, 30, 53, 54, 55, 60–61, 79, 84, 86, 87, 104, 123, 175, 177–82
   Celtic other (*see also* otherness) 7, 16, 17, 54, 76, 77
   Celtic territories 5, 7, 52, 53, 61, 91–94
   Celts 15, 61, 74, 86, 89, 172
Charlestown 12, 132, 163, 165, 171, 172, 204n3
china clay area and clay mining (*see also* the texts covered in Chapter Five and mining and miners) 2, 19, 23, 132, 142, 159, 162–66, 171–74, 177–78, 187, 208n5, 208n13, 209n39, 209n42, 209n62
   inhabitants 92, 158, 159–61, 163, 165, 168–69, 172, 179–83, 208–09n31
Christie, Agatha 59
   Peril at End House, 18, 62, 68, 69–71
city (*see also* urban) 57, 58, 59–60, 76, 112, 124, 133, 134, 137, 140, 141, 142, 145, 153, 154, 155, 156, 158, 159, 161, 187, 205n28
class 5, 17, 18, 19, 42, 44, 81, 84, 90, 104, 141–42, 143, 145–46, 147, 148, 149, 155, 158, 183
   aristocracy 135, 139, 152, 153
   bourgeoisie 141, 182–83
   middle class 15, 40, 141, 145

working class 10, 16, 18, 23–24, 26, 28–31, 33–35, 45–48, 80, 84, 85–87, 89, 90, 104, 141, 145–47, 148–50, 154, 157, 159, 165, 182, 183
underclass 145, 150
upper class 15, 41, 46, 69, 84, 85, 134, 141, 145, 150–55, 157, 158
Clemo, Jack 4, 19–20, 163–64, 170, 171, 187
   The Clay Kiln 165, 168–69, 177–83, 208n3, 208n12, 208–09n31
   The Shadowed Bed 165, 208n3
   Wilding Graft 19, 134, 156, 158–61, 165, 168, 173, 208n3
cliffs (*see also* beaches, coast, edge, littoral and sea) 1, 5, 15, 32, 56, 63, 67, 71, 73, 95, 97–98, 101, 102–03, 107–11, 114, 119, 123, 125, 126, 127, 129, 166, 186, 189n3, 203n101
coast (*see also* beaches, cliffs, edge, littoral and sea) 1–2, 14, 18, 19, 56, 75, 84, 85, 89, 92, 95–97, 99, 100, 102, 103, 104, 107, 108, 111–13, 114–15, 116–17, 119–27, 131, 132, 136, 142, 156, 161, 162–63, 165, 166–67, 169, 171, 172–73, 179, 186, 187, 199–200n9, 200n12, 200n34, 200n36, 201n39, 201n47, 202n98
Collins, Wilkie 59, 101
   Rambles Beyond Railways 10, 133
   The Dead Secret 18, 64–65
colonization (*see also* imperialism) 7, 37, 69, 72, 76–79, 91, 92, 94
Conan Doyle, Arthur 59, 101
   'The Adventure of the Devil's Foot' 18, 68, 76–79
Corbin, Alain 97–99, 122
Cornish / Cornishness
   culture 6, 16, 17, 22–24, 48, 53, 55, 85, 89, 175, 182–83, 186

Index

dialect 4, 39, 145, 193n67, 203n103
identity 5, 10–11, 22, 23, 30–31, 37, 51–53, 57, 77, 82, 86, 94, 101, 142, 192n51
language 4, 11, 39, 49, 51, 53, 96, 182, 191n8, 191n12, 203n101, 203n102
people 11–12, 16, 23, 30, 37, 50, 51, 61, 66, 73, 76, 77, 82–83, 84, 86, 89, 91, 94, 101, 102, 123, 146, 165, 171, 186
Cornish Gorsedh 182–83, 210n83
Cornish Revival 17, 53, 55, 175, 182–83, 210n83
Cornish Riviera 54–55, 72
Cornish Studies 4–5, 59, 163, 168
Cornwall (Kernow)
  areas within Cornwall:
    East Cornwall 10
    mid-Cornwall 2, 10, 19, 158, 159, 162, 163, 171, 187, 192n67, 208n13
    North Cornwall 95, 119, 120, 156, 201n47
    north-east Cornwall 162, 187
    South Cornwall 95
    West Cornwall 10, 95, 179, 208n13
  Cornwalls 1, 2–3, 5–6, 8, 16, 17, 18, 50, 55, 164, 183, 184–85, 186, 187, 189–90n19
  relationship with England 7, 8, 9, 14, 15, 17, 18, 49–54, 55–56, 58, 59, 60–61, 66, 68, 70, 72–73, 76–79, 91–92, 93–95, 98–99, 100, 101–02, 103, 104, 142, 175, 185–86, 194n3, 195n24
country (*see also* nation) 10, 49, 50, 55, 58, 59, 68, 70, 82, 86, 91, 92, 93, 94, 139, 184
country (*see also* rural) 14, 57, 59, 60, 73, 84, 111, 152, 163, 164, 169, 175

crime 60–61, 69
crime fiction 18, 56, 58–61, 64, 67, 68–83, 85, 126

Daldorph, Brian
  'King Tin' 21–23
Dalla
  'Bal Maidens' Chant' 25
Danahay, Martin A. 29–30, 34–35, 40
Darke, Nick
  Ting Tang Mine 27
Deacon, Bernard 5–7, 11–12, 16, 17, 30–31, 189n19
De'Ath, Wilfred 170–71
Defoe, Daniel 15, 137
Devon 28, 113
'domestic exotic' 55, 97, 98, 169, 181, 195n20
Duchy of Cornwall 50–51, 136, 138
du Maurier, Daphne 4, 20, 57, 108, 163–64, 170–71, 194n3, 195n29
  Castle Dor (with Arthur Quiller-Couch) 19, 170, 172–74, 183, 187
  Frenchman's Creek 103–04, 170, 171, 195n24
  Jamaica Inn 19, 83, 84, 163, 166–68, 169, 175–78, 179, 183
  Rebecca 171
  Rule Britannia 56, 91–94, 185–86
  The House on the Strand 170
  The King's General 170
  The Loving Spirit 103–04, 195n24
Dunmore, Helen
  Mourning Ruby 19, 116–19
  Talking to the Dead 19, 116–19
  The Lie 19, 126–30
Dymond, Charlotte 79–80, 82, 163, 166, 167–68, 198n129, 208n4
economy 3, 10, 11, 15, 16, 17, 35, 36, 38, 55, 91, 95, 97, 124, 136, 137, 153, 156, 162, 165, 184, 187

edge (*see also* beaches, cliffs, coast, littoral and sea)
  location 18–19, 21, 63, 73, 96–98, 99–100, 101, 102–04, 105, 108–11, 111–12, 114–15, 119, 127, 129–30, 131, 164, 166, 167, 171, 175, 183, 186–87, 201n47, 208n5
  psychic / psychological edge (*see also* emotion) 18–19, 96, 111–12, 127, 129–31, 186
Ellis, Henry Havelock 61, 172
emigration (*see also* mining and miners) 11, 16, 30, 36–38, 186
emotion (*see also* edge) 19, 56, 98, 111–12, 118, 126, 131, 180
Engels, Friedrich 145–46, 150
England 11, 40, 84, 133
  relationship with Cornwall (*see* Cornwall)
English Channel 95, 173
English / Englishness (*see also* Cornwall) 4, 7, 18, 50, 52, 55, 57–58, 79, 189n3, 203n103
Europe 149, 186, 193n71
European 79, 91, 100
Exeter 49, 93

Falmouth 92, 98, 99–100, 135–37, 149, 168, 173, 181, 183, 204n12, 205n26
Fiennes, Celia 15, 137
First World War 26, 39, 126–29, 192n51
fishing 10, 14, 23, 94, 95, 118, 119–20, 121, 122, 124, 127, 128, 130–31, 134, 140–41, 142
foreignness 1, 15, 38, 50, 54, 55, 59, 66, 70, 77, 78, 100, 101, 164, 182
Fowey 163, 171, 173–74, 209n39
Framework Convention for the Protection of National Minorities (FCPNM) 52
France 92, 149

Gaskell, Elizabeth
  North and South 146, 148, 207n92
gender (*see also* mining and miners) 5, 17, 104, 105, 109, 141, 143, 155, 164
  and work 23, 24, 28–31, 34, 35, 40, 42, 46, 48, 80, 185
  construction / performance of 18, 23, 40, 42, 46, 81, 104, 110–11, 156, 158, 207n86
Godden, Rumer
  China Court 19, 163, 164–65, 208n9
Gothic literature 4, 59, 102, 108, 117, 163, 175–76, 201n58
Graham, Winston 132
  Poldark book series (*see also Poldark* television series) 19, 134, 135, 137, 138, 141, 143–44, 146–48, 150–58, 159, 195n29
granite 58, 66, 92, 138–39, 140, 162, 164, 166, 176–77, 187–88
Great Western Railway 12, 15, 16–17, 54–55

Hamilton Jenkin, A.K. 162
Harding Davis, Rebecca 45
Hardy, Thomas 4, 16, 54, 101
  A Changed Man 106
  'A Mere Interlude' 133
  A Pair of Blue Eyes 19, 104–05, 107–11, 201n53
  Tess of the D'Urbervilles 105, 201n48
  Wessex 105–08, 109, 201n47, 201n48
Harris, John
  'Christian Heroism' 9–10
  'The Mine' 21–22
Heath-Stubbs, John
  'To the Mermaid at Zennor' 58–59
Helford 169–70
Henwood, George 28, 40, 42, 48
Hocking, Salome 4, 191n18
  Norah Lang 17, 24, 43–48, 193n87
Horner, Avril and Sue Zlosnik 169, 175

Index

imperialism (*see also* colonization) 37, 69, 76–79, 92
inland / interior 19–20, 63, 96, 97, 100, 108, 132–33, 136, 140, 142–43, 162–63, 164, 171, 172–73, 183, 187
Ireland 5, 7, 52, 53, 60, 61, 62, 100, 101
Irish 37, 52, 59, 72
Isles of Scilly 72, 168
Italy 15, 55, 96, 99

Jenkin, Mark 199n9
  Enys Men 24–25
John, Angela V. 41, 46

Kent, Alan M. 4, 9, 31, 32, 53
  Dan Daddow's Cornish Comicalities 19, 133, 134, 136, 140–41, 142–46, 148–49, 150–51, 154, 206n62
King Mark 100–01, 174
Kneehigh Theatre 100–01
Knight, Laura 103, 168, 200n36
  Men Working in a China Clay Pit 166
  The China Clay Pit 166
Kynance Cove 12, 49

Lakeman, Seth
  'Bal Maiden' 24–25
landscape 1, 2, 6, 12, 19, 20, 51, 82, 95, 103, 111, 112, 116, 118, 125, 126, 127, 131, 143, 163, 169, 171, 185, 188, 210n5
  industrial (*see also* mining and miners and china clay) 10, 19, 22–23, 159, 163, 164, 169, 172, 174, 177, 178, 179, 183, 208n31
  palimpsestic and / or threatening 20, 24, 59, 64–65, 66–67, 76, 83, 84, 117, 120, 126, 175–79, 183
  romanticized / exoticized 16, 22, 54, 56, 171
Land's End 4, 49, 50, 62–63, 66, 72, 105
Lawrence, D.H. 4, 16, 54, 172, 175

le Carré, John 59
  The Night Manager 18, 64, 65–67
Lee, Charles 132
  Cynthia in the West 103–04
lighthouses 7, 19, 62–64, 112–13
liminality 99, 102–04, 200n34, 200n36
littoral (*see also* beaches, coast, cliffs, edge and sea) 96, 97, 99, 102, 103, 111, 120, 121, 122, 125, 131, 199–200n9
Lizard, the 49–50
London 50, 57, 64, 72, 73, 74, 76, 81, 93, 99, 108, 110, 111, 116, 139, 152, 154, 157, 158, 159, 204n6
Lowry, H.D. and Dawson Scott, C.A.
  Wheel Darkness 17, 24, 37, 38–39, 41

Mais, S.P.B. 54, 138
Manchester 145, 150
Manford, Alan L. 106, 201n48
Mansfield, Katherine 95
Marsden, Philip 99–100, 132, 166
masculinity (*see also* mining and miners) 17, 18, 23, 28–31, 32–37, 40, 41, 46, 48, 104
Mayers, Lynne 28, 43, 191n11, 193n70, 193n71
McDowell, Linda 8–9, 207n86
Mediterranean 15, 100
Menmuir, Wyl
  The Many 19, 119–26, 202n98
Messent, Peter 68
Methodism 16, 31, 34, 43, 84, 85, 88–90
Mevagissey 12–14
Minack Theatre 71, 73, 75
mining and miners (*see also* balmaidens, china clay mining and class) 58, 148, 172, 191n8, 193n71, 200n12
  engine houses 10–11, 21–22, 97, 121, 129, 165, 187–88
  gendered reading of (*see also* gender and masculinity) 17–18, 23–24, 28, 41–42, 44–48, 185

231

male miner and work (see also *bodies*) 23, 26–28, 30, 32–35, 41, 43, 46–48, 104, 144–48, 149, 157–58, 184, 191n13, 200n12

success and decline (see also emigration) 3, 9–11, 15–17, 22–23, 24, 26, 28, 30–31, 35–39, 40, 54, 95, 97, 121, 129, 137, 187, 192n56

industrial prowess' 11, 12, 18, 30–32, 35–37, 40, 42, 47–48, 144, 190n38

tin and copper 17, 21–22, 23, 24, 31, 35, 37–38, 41, 42, 47, 77, 137, 143–44, 146, 153, 154, 192n56, 206n44

Mitchell, Sally 12–14

moorland (see also Bodmin Moor) 162, 163, 166, 169, 170, 174, 176

Moseley, Rachel 9, 51, 52, 95–96, 99, 103, 167, 186, 194n3

Moss, Sarah
Signs for Lost Children 142, 206n41

Mukherjee, Upamanyu Pablo 69, 79

myth 12, 56, 83–85, 87, 95–96, 111, 173, 175, 192n51

Napoleonic Wars 15, 83, 112, 205n24

nation (see also country) 4, 27, 30, 50, 51–52, 53, 61, 69, 71, 76, 78, 85, 91, 100, 101, 102, 103, 104, 105, 158, 186

Newquay 98, 114

'On the Way to the Lizard' 49

Orchard, William
'Wheal Coates' 21–22

O'Reilly, Noel
Wrecker 18, 56, 83–90, 185–86

otherness (see also Celtic) 7, 12, 16–17, 53–54, 86, 175, 186

Par 163, 171, 173, 209n39

Passey, Joan 4, 59, 76, 99, 102

Payton, Philip 4, 11, 16, 23, 30–31, 36, 50–51, 54–55, 61, 190n38, 192n51, 192n56, 210n83

Pearce, Cathryn 84–85, 99, 100

Penryn 100, 135

Penzance 54, 71–72, 88, 106

performance 19, 70, 90, 92, 134, 135, 137, 138, 140, 141, 142, 143, 145, 149, 152, 153–54, 157–58, 161

peripherality (see also remoteness) 7, 9, 18, 46, 60, 69, 70, 73, 83, 99, 100–01, 103, 112, 113, 114, 149, 158, 175

picturesqueness 96, 97, 121, 165, 171, 174, 186

Pilcher, Rosamunde 58, 103

Plymouth 54, 78, 159

Poldark television series (2015) (see also Graham, Winston) 23, 57, 132, 165, 200n12, 204n3

poverty 38, 42, 80, 85, 86–87, 89, 96, 141, 145, 147, 148, 150, 186, 199n9

primitiveness (see also Celtic) 12, 60, 61, 66, 77, 102, 179–82

prospect view 97, 108, 117, 142–43

Redruth 77, 106, 133

remoteness (see also peripherality) 18, 54, 56, 60, 62, 64, 65–66, 67, 69, 70, 77–78, 84, 99, 100, 104, 108, 111, 133, 136, 171

rioting 11–12, 30, 61, 146–48, 149, 150, 157–58

rivers 49, 83, 101, 106, 135, 138, 147–48, 151, 159, 187
River Allen 145
River Fal 132, 135–36, 173
River Kenwyn 137, 139
River Par 173
River Tamar 49–50

Roche 178, 209n60

Roche Rock 177–82

romantic 55, 66, 73, 76, 104, 112, 171
romantic fiction 7, 16, 18, 22, 56–58,

Index

59, 66, 91, 95, 170–71, 195n25, 195n29
romanticization 2, 7, 16, 15, 22, 23, 29, 55, 56, 62, 67, 73, 99, 118, 120, 121, 140, 171
Roper, Michael and John Tosh 29, 36, 37
Roughtor 166, 176
Rowe, Edward 53
  'Hireth' 26
Rowse, A.L. 4, 19
  A Cornish Childhood 19, 171–72, 209n60
  'Homecoming to Cornwall: December 1942' 186
  'Passing by the Coast of Cornwall' 1–2
rural (*see also* country) 8–9, 14, 15, 18, 56, 57, 58, 59, 60, 64, 73, 96, 112, 133, 136, 153, 158, 159, 161, 187, 207n87
Ruskin, John 29–30

St Austell 159, 163, 171–72, 173, 208n5
St Ives 7, 112, 115–19, 127
sea (*see also* beaches, cliffs, coast, edge and littoral) 8, 19, 21, 22, 32, 33, 49, 56, 62–63, 65, 70, 73, 78, 81, 87, 95–102, 104, 107–09, 112, 114, 115, 116–19, 120–23, 125–28, 130–31, 132, 136, 142, 162, 163, 166–67, 184, 186–87
seaside (*see* beaches)
Second World War 92, 103, 134, 158, 186, 192n51
Scotland 5, 7, 52, 60–61, 72, 80, 91, 92, 93, 94, 99
Scottish 7, 59, 60–61, 94
Shields, Rob 102–03, 104, 200n34
shipwrecks 15, 83–87, 90, 101, 102, 119
Smith, Jesse Leroy
  Bal Maiden 26–27
smuggling 11, 30, 61, 85, 169

Stansfield, Katherine
  Falling Creatures 18, 19, 68, 79–83, 163, 166, 167–68, 176, 198n129
  The Magpie Tree 18, 68, 79–83
  The Mermaid's Call 18, 68, 79–83
  The Visitor 19, 126–28, 130–31
stereotypes 30, 42, 44, 52, 60, 69, 85, 112, 123, 184, 186, 187
Stevenson, Robert Louis
  Across the Plains 172
Stonex, Emma
  The Lamplighters 18, 62–64
sublime, the 98–99, 122

Thomas, Chris 54–55, 195n20
Thornton, Paul 54, 55
tourism
  emergence and dominance 3, 15–16, 21–22, 24, 35, 37, 95, 97, 108, 121, 140
  touristic versons of place and responses / counter-narratives 2, 3, 9, 12–15, 16–17, 18, 19, 20, 22–23, 53–59, 61, 64, 72–73, 92–94, 96–98, 112, 114, 115–18, 121–23, 124, 130–31, 132–33, 161, 162, 163, 165, 166, 169, 170, 175, 183, 184, 187, 199–200n9
tourists 10, 14, 16, 21–22, 49–50, 54, 57, 58, 71, 76, 77, 92, 93, 94, 98, 108, 114, 117, 120–21, 122–23, 124–25, 165, 168, 203n103
towns 70, 107, 115, 123, 133, 134–35, 136, 137, 138–39, 140, 141, 142, 143, 144, 145, 146–47, 148, 149, 150, 151, 152–53, 155, 157, 159, 161, 171–72, 173, 205n20, 205n24
Trower, Shelley 4, 76–78, 99, 101–102
Truro (*see also* texts covered in Chapter Four) 19, 106, 162, 204n3, 204n6, 205n28, 206n40, 206n58, 208n5

233

how experienced by different classes (*see also* class, rioting and visibility) 145–55, 158–60
how experienced by women 155–58, 160–61
location and status (*see also* city, Falmouth, performativity, urban, and wealth) 132–39, 142–45, 152–53, 187
coinage 135, 143–45, 206n44
locations within:
Assembly Rooms 138, 146, 149, 152–53, 157, 161
Boscawen Street 138–40, 143–44, 146–47, 149–50, 153, 154, 155–56, 160–61, 205n26
cathedral 134, 137, 138, 150, 160, 161
Lemon Street 138, 140, 155–56, 159
Lemon Quay and Back Quay 137, 139, 159, 205n20
Middle Row 138, 143, 205n24
Royal Cornwall Museum 156, 160
Squeeze Guts Alley 150
smell 140–42, 187
Tuan, Yi-Fu 7–8

United Kingdom (UK) 4, 5, 52, 91–93
Upson, Nicola
Angel with Two Faces 18, 68, 71–76
urban (*see also* city) 8, 14, 19, 59–60, 63, 64, 133, 134, 141–42, 143, 144–47, 148–49, 151–52, 153, 157–61, 162, 187, 207n92
Urry, John 112, 141

Vernon, James 50, 194n3
villages 43, 60, 66, 84, 86, 87, 88, 89, 90, 103, 119, 120, 126, 127, 130–31, 132, 159, 163, 164, 165, 169, 171–72, 174, 175, 177, 178, 180, 181, 193n67
visibility 19, 22–23, 24, 26, 28, 35, 39, 40, 44, 55, 93, 116, 129, 134, 142, 143, 144–46, 149–52, 158, 160, 164–65, 166, 180, 185, 187, 193n70, 193n87
Vyvyan, C.C. 184

Wales (*see also* Welsh) 5, 7, 37, 51, 53, 59, 60, 91, 92, 93, 100, 113
wealth 19, 34, 37, 70, 80, 141, 142, 143–45, 147, 152, 153–54, 165, 184, 187, 206n44
weather 65, 125, 144, 163
fog and mist 65–67, 78, 87, 117, 118, 167
hail and sleet 144, 152
rain and flooding 109–10, 125–26, 142, 145, 147–48, 200n12, 206n41
wind 66–67, 98, 101, 108, 116, 118, 176, 178
Wedgwood Clarke, John 188
Welsh (*see also* Wales) 52, 59, 94
'West Barbary' 11–12, 15, 30, 61, 146
Westland, Ella 4, 15, 56, 91
Williams, Raymond 97, 147, 150
Winn, Raynor
Landlines 186–87
The Salt Path 19, 113–15, 117
Woolf, Virginia 19, 54, 116, 175, 189n3
Mrs Dalloway 129
To the Lighthouse 7, 19, 112–13
wrecking 11, 30, 56, 61, 83–90

Zola Émile
Germinal 34–35, 44–45, 47, 146

Milton Keynes UK
Ingram Content Group UK Ltd.
UKHW041255121124
2786UKWH00003B/8